# REA's Interactive
# Flashcards®

# PCAT™

## Pharmacy College Admission Test™

Staff of
Research & Education Association

*Research & Education Association*
*Visit our website at*
**www.rea.com**

*Research & Education Association*
61 Ethel Road West
Piscataway, New Jersey 08854
E-mail: info@rea.com

# REA's Interactive Flashcards® PCAT (Pharmacy College Admission Test)

Printed in the United States of America

Library of Congress Control Number 2006922739

International Standard Book Number 0-7386-0140-3

PCAT™ and Pharmacy College Admission Test™ are
trademarks of Harcourt Assessment, Inc.

# REA's Interactive Flashcards® PCAT

## What they're for and how to use them

The Pharmacy College Admission Test (PCAT) is a specialized test for students seeking admission to a pharmacy college and for schools to identify qualified candidates. The exam tests general and scientific knowledge needed for an education in pharmaceuticals. To help you study, REA has put together this book of flashcards, which you can take with you to study anywhere, even on the go. You'll find this flashcard book to be perfect for self-study, for reference, or just for a quick review.

REA's *PCAT Flashcards* contains questions based on the actual test. Studying for the PCAT with the unique features of flashcards in a book format makes your test preparation easier. There are no loose cards to misplace. The cards are always in order for easier, more organized study. Study smarter, using the unique interactive feature not found in other flashcards. Write your answer to a card's question on the front, and then compare it with the answer on the back.

The material presented on the following pages is separated into sections like those found on the PCAT itself, including Verbal Ability, Quantitative Ability, Biology, and Chemistry. On the PCAT, you will also find a Reading Comprehension section and a Writing subtest. The Writing subtest allows you 30 minutes to write an essay in response to a statement that either expresses an opinion or presents a problem needing a solution. To improve your essay-writing skills, consult *www. rea.com* for a host of additional study guides.

Bonus material throughout this book offers fast facts on a career in pharmacy and other helpful sidelights.

Much consideration and effort went into making this study aid the best of its kind. It is my hope that you will find this book to be an invaluable reference for your PCAT studies.

Larry B. Kling
Chief Editor

## About Research & Education Association

Founded in 1959, Research & Education Association (REA) is dedicated to publishing the finest and most effective educational materials—including software, study guides, and test preps—for students in middle school, high school, college, graduate school, and beyond.

REA's test preparation series includes books and software for all academic levels in almost all disciplines. REA publishes test preps for students who have not yet entered high school, as well as high school students preparing to enter college. Students at every level, in every field, with every ambition can find what they are looking for among REA's publications.

REA's series presents tests that accurately depict the official exams in both degree of difficulty and types of questions. REA's publications and educational materials are highly regarded and continually receive an unprecedented amount of praise from professionals, instructors, librarians, parents, and students. Our authors are as diverse as the subject matter represented in the books we publish. They are well known in their respective disciplines and serve on the faculties of prestigious colleges and universities throughout the United States and Canada.

Today REA's wide-ranging catalog is a leading resource for teachers, students, and professionals.

We invite you to visit us at *www.rea.com* to find out how "REA is making the world smarter."

## Acknowledgments

We would like to thank Larry B. Kling, Vice President, Editorial, for his overall direction; Pam Weston, Vice President, Publishing, for setting the quality standards for production integrity and managing the publication to completion; Diane Goldschmidt, Senior Editor, for project management and preflight editorial review; Molly Solanki, Associate Editor, for coordinating revisions; Christine Saul, Senior Graphic Designer, for designing our cover; and Rachel DiMatteo, Graphic Designer, for typesetting revisions.

# Table of Contents

# Section I
# Verbal Ability

# Questions

---

**Q-1**

SCULPTOR:BLOWTORCH::

(A)   artist:paint

(B)   writer:word processor

(C)   physician:stethoscope

(D)   conductor:baton

*Your Answer* _B_

---

**Q-2**

LUMBER:ELEPHANT::

(A)   soar:eagle

(B)   scamper:mice

(C)   dive:seal

(D)   waddle:duck

*Your Answer* _D_

# Correct Answers

## A–1

**(B)** How would a SCULPTOR use a BLOW-TORCH? To create his art. This would eliminate (C), but would leave (A), (B), and maybe (D). The sculptor uses the blowtorch as a tool, while the ARTIST uses PAINT as a material, so cross out (A). A WRITER frequently uses a WORD PRO-CESSOR as a tool to create his art; although a CONDUCTOR uses a BATON as a tool, he does not create art in the same sense as a sculptor does, so (B) is the best choice.

## A–2

**(D)** If you wonder what reasonable and in-evitable connection LUMBER could have with ELEPHANTS, then you'll begin to think that maybe lumber doesn't mean wood. When you look at the choices and discover that the first word in each is a verb, then you realize lumber, too, must be a verb and that it must involve motion (since all the other choices do). Lumber means to move clumsily or heavily. This eliminates (A), (B), and (C). This leaves (D).

**Q-3**

AMELIORATE:

(A) decline

(B) pause

(C) aggravate

(D) arrest

*Your Answer* _C_

**Q-4**

CLOYING:

(A) bland

(B) flattering

(C) saccharine

(D) acerbic

*Your Answer* _D_

# Correct Answers

**A–3**

**(C)** AMELIORATE means to improve or make better. We need a word that makes things worse. PAUSE (B) and ARREST (D) are not what we're looking for. This leaves (A) and (C). DECLINE means to deteriorate and could be appropriate, but (C) is a better choice since AGGRAVATE means to make things worse.

**A–4**

**(D)** CLOYING means "too sweet or excessively flattering." (B) and (C) are synonyms for cloying. (A) BLAND is not a good choice either. Choose (D), ACERBIC, meaning "sour or bitter in taste or manner."

# Questions

**Q–5**

BANALITY:TRITE::

- (A)  stereotype:racial
- (B)  genius:intelligent
- (C)  aphorism:apt
- (D)  hackneyed:cutting

*Your Answer* _B_

---

**Q–6**

PLUMP:OBESE::

- (A)  lean:emaciated
- (B)  adipose:turgid
- (C)  narrow:elongated
- (D)  corpulent:swollen

*Your Answer* _A_

# Correct Answers

**A–5**

**(B)** This is a "definition" analogy. A BANAL-ITY is by definition trite and unoriginal so our bridge sentence should state this. Although we often see the words paired, a stereotype need not be racial. This leaves (B), (C), and (D). HACK-NEYED does not mean to hack, so CUTTING is not part of its definition. (It means trite, unoriginal, banal.) An APHORISM is a statement of general truth and should be apt. However, a GENIUS is by definition intelligent, so (B) is the best choice.

**A–6**

**(A)** This is a "degree" analogy. OBESE carries plumpness to an extreme. TURGID (swollen) and ADIPOSE (fatty) do not share this relationship. (D) can be eliminated on similar grounds. ELON-GATED is not excessively NARROW. This leaves (A). EMACIATED is LEAN to the *nth* degree, as in starving.

# Questions

---

**Q–7**

EUPHONY:

(A) eulogy

(B) cacophony

(C) lethargy

(D) verbosity

*Your Answer*

---

**Q–8**

EPHEMERAL:

(A) constant

(B) perennial

(C) eternal

(D) brief

*Your Answer*

# Correct Answers

## A–7

**(B)**     If you had no idea of the meaning of EU-PHONY or CACOPHONY, you still might guess that cacophony was your answer, just by the similar endings of the two words. If you also realized that SYMPHONY and TELEPHONE both have to do with sound, you would guess that "phon" must mean sound. EUPHONY means a pleasing combination of sounds. Its opposite is CACOPHONY, a mixture of harsh and discordant sounds. A EU-LOGY is a speech of praise, normally for the dead. It cannot be an antonym for EUPHONY, nor can any of the other choices.

## A–8

**(C)**     EPHEMERAL means very short-lived or transitory, so we need a word meaning long-lived. PERENNIAL (reappearing each year) meets this criterion. CONSTANT has some appeal, but ETERNAL (C) is more of an opposite to ephemeral than any of these and is the correct choice.

# Questions

**Q-9**

ABSTEMIOUS:ASCETIC::

(A) starving:hungry

(B) gourmand:gourmet

(C) beneficent:donor

(D) unrestrained:libertine

*Your Answer* _B_

**Q-10**

LACONIC:PRATE::

(A) sagacious:think

(B) ascetic:indulge

(C) authoritative:administer

(D) inquisitive:inquire

*Your Answer*

# Correct Answers

## A–9

**(D)** This is a variant of the "degree" analogy. An ASCETIC is one who is ABSTEMIOUS (abstains) to a very high degree. HUNGRY doesn't mean a high degree of STARVING—eliminate (A). Neither is there a difference of degree between a GOURMAND (one who enjoys good food) and GOURMET (a connoisseur of fine food). In (C), a DONOR is one who is BENEFICENT, but we do not know to what extent. The correct choice is (D). A LIBERTINE is one who is highly UNRESTRAINED sexually or morally.

## A–10

**(B)** This is a "lack of" or "not characteristic of" analogy. A LACONIC person is one of few words and therefore does not PRATE (babble). Does a SAGACIOUS (wise) person not THINK? An AUTHORITATIVE person not ADMINISTER? Or an INQUISITIVE person not INQUIRE? Eliminate all but (B). An ASCETIC person does not INDULGE.

# Questions

---

**Q–11**

COGENT:

(A)   lucid

(B)   pedagogical

(C)   abstruse

(D)   inerrant

---

*Your Answer* _____

_____

---

**Q–12**

DEARTH:

(A)   sufficiency

(B)   paucity

(C)   voluminous

(D)   cornucopia

---

*Your Answer* _____

_____

# Correct Answers

## A–11

**(C)** COGENT means clear and to the point as in a "cogent and convincing argument." LUCID is more of a synonym than an antonym; INERRANT (without error) and PEDAGOGICAL (scholarly and boring) are not antonyms either. ABSTRUSE (hard to understand) is best. Choose (C).

## A–12

**(D)** DEARTH is "a lack of something." PAUCITY is a synonym and therefore incorrect. VOLUMINOUS ("large and spacious") is an adjective, and we need a noun. SUFFICIENCY is at the other end of the spectrum from dearth and might seem appropriate, but CORNUCOPIA ("an endless supply") is more nearly opposite in meaning to dearth. Choose (D).

# Questions

**Q–13**

CULPABLE:CENSURE::

(A)   moral:penance

(B)   meritorious:reward

(C)   admirable:judgment

(D)   affable:praise

*Your Answer* _____

_____

**Q–14**

SUNDIAL:SUN::

(A)   electricity:water

(B)   moon:tides

(C)   sun:stars

(D)   light bulb:electricity

*Your Answer* _____

_____

# Correct Answers

**A–13**

**(B)**    A CULPABLE (guilty) person is deserving of CENSURE (condemnation). Is a MORAL person worthy of PENANCE? Is something ADMIRABLE worthy of JUDGMENT? No. This leaves (B) and (D). Is someone AFFABLE (warm and friendly) deserving of PRAISE? Perhaps. But (B) is a better choice. Something MERITORIOUS merits some sort of a REWARD even more than someone affable merits praise.

**A–14**

**(D)**    A SUNDIAL cannot work without the SUN. ELECTRICITY can work without water; there are other means to generate it. (A) is not the right answer. The MOON affects the TIDES, not the other way around. (B) is not correct. SUN and STARS reflects a member:class relationship. (C) is incorrect. A LIGHT BULB cannot work without ELECTRICITY. The correct answer is (D).

# Questions

---

**Q–15**

CONTUMACIOUS:

(A)   obdurate

(B)   sinuous

(C)   facetious

(D)   malleable

*Your Answer* _____

_____

---

**Q–16**

LACONIC:

(A)   terse

(B)   taciturn

(C)   loquacious

(D)   open

*Your Answer* _____

_____

# Correct Answers

## A–15

**(D)** Here is a good opportunity to use the strategy of elimination! If CONTUMACIOUS is unfamiliar to you, you may know SINUOUS and FACETIOUS and have never heard of them in connection with contumacious. That leaves OBDURATE (stubborn, unbending) and MALLEABLE (easy to shape or bend). They are opposites of each other, so probably one is a synonym of contumacious and the other an antonym. This is a time to guess; the odds are 50–50. If you choose malleable, you'd be correct. Contumacious is "stubbornly rebellious or disobedient."

## A–16

**(C)** LACONIC means "sparing of words," so TERSE and TACITURN are basically synonyms. Reject (A) and (B). A laconic person is presumably not very open, so we cannot summarily reject OPEN. However, (C), LOQUACIOUS (talking excessively) is the best choice.

# Questions

**Q–17**

SAGA:TALE::

(A)  book:page

(B)  poetry:prose

(C)  sonnet:verse

(D)  fiction:nonfiction

*Your Answer* _____

_____

**Q–18**

APPLE:PARE::

(A)  cherry:stone

(B)  peach:pit

(C)  grapefruit:peel

(D)  skin:grape

*Your Answer* _____

_____

# Correct Answers

**A-17**

(C)    A SAGA is a kind of TALE. The relationship is member:class. A PAGE is part of a BOOK. The relationship is whole:part, so (A) is incorrect. POETRY and PROSE are two different forms of writing. (B) is not the correct answer. A SONNET is a kind of VERSE. (C) reflects the relationship of member:class and is the correct answer. FICTION and NONFICTION are two different forms of prose writing. (D) is not the correct answer.

**A-18**

(C)    To PARE an APPLE is to take the skin off it. To STONE a CHERRY and to PIT a PEACH both mean to take the stone or pit out of the middle of the fruit. (A) and (B) are not correct answers. To PEEL a GRAPEFRUIT is to take the skin off it. (C) is the correct answer. SKIN:GRAPE reflects the reverse of the analogy sought so (D) is incorrect.

# Questions

**Q–19**

ENCOMIUM:

(A)  aphorism

(B)  epitaph

(C)  euphemism

(D)  diatribe

*Your Answer* _____

_____

**Q–20**

DESICCATE:

(A)  wet

(B)  humidify

(C)  baptize

(D)  dehydrate

*Your Answer* _____

_____

# Correct Answers

## A–19

**(D)**   Probably the best strategy here, if you don't know the word, is elimination. Somehow, ENCOMIUM has a "nice" sound to it, as though it's a compliment (perhaps it makes us think of comrade, compassion, comity). When you are at a loss and no other strategy helps, you must rely on your impressions. If we are right, then "nice" words like EUPHEMISM (a nice way of saying something that's not so nice) and EPITAPH (a statement about a deceased person which epitomizes his or her life) can be eliminated. That leaves APHORISM (a terse statement of a general truth) or DIATRIBE (bitter, harsh criticism). Since the dictionary defines encomium as "expression of high praise," diatribe is the antonym we need. Choose (D).

## A–20

**(A)**   All the choices given seem to involve water in some way (DEHYDRATE, of course, means to remove water) so even if you don't know the meaning of DESICCATE, you assume that it has something to do with dryness. If we guess that desiccate means "to dry out thoroughly" (as it does), then WET is more nearly opposite in meaning than HUMIDIFY. BAPTIZE may involve only a few drops of water or total immersion. The best choice is (A).

# Questions

**Q–21**

ALLUSION:REFERENCE::

(A) brevity:longevity

(B) conglomeration:accumulation

(C) antipathy:apathy

(D) epitome:ennui

*Your Answer* _____

**Q–22**

STUPENDOUS:AMAZE::

(A) monstrous:bewilder

(B) prodigious:perplex

(C) tremendous:distraction

(D) heinous:astound

*Your Answer* _____

# Correct Answers

## A–21

**(B)**  An ALLUSION is a REFERENCE; the relationship is synonymous. BREVITY, meaning shortness, and LONGEVITY, meaning length, are antonyms. (A) is not the correct choice. CONGLOMERATION and ACCUMULATION are synonyms that mean a gathering together. (B) is the correct choice. ANTIPATHY, meaning enmity, and APATHY, meaning indifference, are not synonymous; (C) is not correct. EPITOME means embodiment, and ENNUI means boredom. The words are unrelated and (D) is not the correct answer.

## A–22

**(D)**  STUPENDOUS means astonishingly impressive. AMAZE is to astonish greatly. MONSTROUS means ugly, fabulous, shocking in wrongness. BEWILDER is to perplex or confuse; it does not imply the surprise seen in AMAZE. Therefore, (A) is not the best answer. PRODIGIOUS means a marvelousness beyond belief. PERPLEX is to puzzle, to confuse. PRODIGIOUS behavior does not necessarily result in perplexity; (B) is not the best answer. TREMENDOUS means having the power to terrify or inspire awe. DISTRACTION implies diversion, perplexity. DISTRACTION does not have the intensity of AMAZE. (C) involves using knowledge of the degree of words; it is not the best answer. HEINOUS implies such flagrant conspicuousness that it excites hatred or horror. ASTOUND stresses shock and surprise. Thus, (D) is the best choice.

# Questions

**Q–23**

AVOCATION:

(A)  respite

(B)  profession

(C)  silent

(D)  hobby

*Your Answer* _____

_____

**Q–24**

ADULTERATED:

(A)  ribald

(B)  defiled

(C)  chaste

(D)  infantile

*Your Answer* _____

_____

# Correct Answers

### A-23

**(B)** AVOCATION (not to be confused with VOCATION) means hobby. For (A), a RESPITE is a putting off, a postponement, a delay. It is not the opposite of AVOCATION and (A) should not be selected. A PROFESSION is an occupation, a trade. It is the opposite of AVOCATION and (B) is the correct answer. Since SILENT means quiet, (C) is not the best answer. A HOBBY is an interest to which one gives spare time. It is synonymous with AVOCATION and (D) should not be selected. An AVULSION is a forcible separation.

### A-24

**(C)** ADULTERATED means corrupted or impure. RIBALD means irreverent or vulgar; (A) is not the correct answer. DEFILED means contaminated or corrupted. It is a synonym for ADULTERATED, so (B) is not the correct choice. CHASTE means pure. It is the opposite of ADULTERATED; therefore, (C) is the correct answer. INFANTILE means childish; (D) is incorrect. VICIOUS means spiteful or malicious.

# Questions

**Q–25**

COVEY:QUAIL::

(A)  cub:bear

(B)  pride:lions

(C)  stag:deer

(D)  ewe:sheep

*Your Answer* _____

_____

**Q–26**

CASCADE:CATACLYSM::

(A)  soporific:hypnotic

(B)  defeat:debacle

(C)  scenario:synopsis

(D)  epitaph:epithet

*Your Answer* _____

_____

# Correct Answers

## A–25

**(B)** A COVEY is a group of quail. A CUB is a young BEAR. The analogy in (A) is not the same as for COVEY:QUAIL. A group of LIONS is a PRIDE; (B) is correct. A STAG is a male DEER. The analogy is not that of COVEY:QUAIL. (C) should not be chosen. A EWE is a female SHEEP. Again, the analogy is not that of COVEY:QUAIL. (D) is not the correct answer since the group:individual animal relationship is not there.

## A–26

**(B)** A CASCADE is a waterfall and a CATACLYSM is a deluge or flood. The relationship is one of degree. A DEFEAT is a loss at a game or battle; a DEBACLE is a humiliating rout. The relationship is one of degree. (B) is the correct answer. SOPORIFIC:HYPNOTIC and SCENARIO:SYNOPSIS have synonymous relationships. EPITAPH means a statement in praise, usually after one dies; an EPITHET is an insult.

# Questions

Q–27

AUGMENTATION:

(A) constriction

(B) accession

(C) expansion

(D) perturbation

*Your Answer* _____

Q–28

TACITURN:

(A) reticent

(B) appeased

(C) reserved

(D) effusive

*Your Answer* _____

# Correct Answers

## A–27

(A)    AUGMENTATION means expansion, enlargement, dilation. CONSTRICTION (A) is the antonym and the correct answer. ACCESSION means an increase, an addition. It is synonymous with AUGMENTATION and (B) should not be selected. EXPANSION means the act of increasing in size. It is synonymous with AUGMENTATION and (C) should not be chosen. PERTURBATION is the state of being disturbed. It is not the opposite of AUGMENTATION. (D) is not the correct choice.

## A–28

(D)    TACITURN means silent, uncommunicative. In (A), RETICENT means habitually silent. Since it is a synonym for TACITURN, (A) is incorrect. APPEASED means satisfied, made calm, quiet. (B) is wrong. RESERVED means restrained, in control, silent; (C) is synonymous and not the right answer. EFFUSIVE means overly demonstrative, gushing, unrestrained. It is the antonym and (D) should be selected.

# Questions

**Q–29**

TAUTOLOGOUS:INCONGRUOUS::

(A)   astute:perspicacious

(B)   melange:effluvium

(C)   propinquity:proximity

(D)   ignominious:magnanimous

*Your Answer* _____

_____

**Q–30**

ADVENTITIOUS:INHERENT::

(A)   vitiate:adulterate

(B)   fatuous:asinine

(C)   anathema:anastrophe

(D)   facile:onerous

*Your Answer* _____

_____

# Correct Answers

## A–29

**(D)** TAUTOLOGOUS, meaning redundant, and INCONGRUOUS, meaning contradictory, are antonyms. ASTUTE and PERSPICACIOUS are synonyms; (A) is not the correct answer. MELANGE, meaning a mixture of elements, and EFFLUVIUM, meaning an offensive odor, are unrelated. (B) is not the correct answer. PROPINQUITY and PROXIMITY are synonyms; (C) is not the correct answer. IGNOMINIOUS, meaning dishonorable, and MAGNANIMOUS, meaning having nobility of spirit, are antonyms. The correct answer is (D).

## A–30

**(D)** ADVENTITIOUS means not innate; INHERENT means innate, or inborn. The terms are antonyms. VITIATE:ADULTERATE and FATUOUS:ASININE exhibit synonymous relationships; (A) and (B) are incorrect choices. ANATHEMA, which means something accursed, and ANASTROPHE, which means inverting the usual syntactical order for rhetorical effect, are unrelated terms. (C) is not the correct choice. FACILE, meaning easy, and ONEROUS, meaning difficult, are antonyms. (D) is the correct answer.

# Questions

**Q–31**

HELICAL:

(A) spiral

(B) coiled

(C) curved

(D) straight

*Your Answer* _____

_____

**Q–32**

ASININE:

(A) fatuous

(B) cunning

(C) idiosyncratic

(D) eccentric

*Your Answer* _____

_____

# Correct Answers

## A–31

**(D)** A helix is composed of round curves that form a spiral; something that is HELICAL, then, is COILED, SPIRAL, CURVED, and ROUND. (A), (B) and (C) are all incorrect choices. The one choice that is the opposite of HELICAL is STRAIGHT; the correct answer is (D).

## A–32

**(B)** ASININE means stupid. FATUOUS means foolish. (A) is synonymous with ASININE and should not be chosen. CUNNING is the antonym and (B) is the correct answer. IDIOSYNCRATIC means the following of one's own peculiar temperament. (C) should not be chosen as the best answer. ECCENTRIC means diverges from the usual. (D) is not the best answer.

# Questions

---

**Q–33**

SOLID:LIQUID::

(A) oxygen:air

(B) water:steam

(C) grass:wood

(D) fire:air

*Your Answer* _____

_____

---

**Q–34**

LEAVE:RETURN::

(A) dry:wet

(B) black:white

(C) open:close

(D) down:up

*Your Answer* _____

_____

# Correct Answers

## A–33

**(B)**    A SOLID becomes a LIQUID if exposed to a high enough temperature. OXYGEN is one of the components of AIR. It will not become air, no matter how much it is heated. (A) is not the correct choice. WATER will become STEAM when heated enough; (B) is the correct answer. GRASS cannot become WOOD and FIRE cannot become AIR, no matter how they are manipulated. (C) and (D) are incorrect choices.

## A–34

**(C)**    LEAVE:RETURN are opposites, as are all of the answer choices. However, to LEAVE implies that one will RETURN. If something is DRY, there is no implied concept that it will later become WET. If something is BLACK, there is no implication that it will become WHITE. (A) and (B) are incorrect. If something is OPEN, there is an implication that, sooner or later, it may CLOSE. (C) is the correct answer. If something is DOWN, there is no implication that later it will be UP (the South is thought of as "down"—there is no implication that at any time it will be "up"). (D) is incorrect.

# Questions

**Q–35**

SAGACIOUS:

(A)  shrewd

(B)  astute

(C)  procumbent

(D)  incapable

*Your Answer* _____

_____

**Q–36**

NADIR:

(A)  zephyr

(B)  knave

(C)  epitome

(D)  zenith

*Your Answer* _____

_____

# Correct Answers

## A–35

**(D)**  SAGACIOUS means shrewd. SHREWD is synonymous with SAGACIOUS and (A) should not be selected as the correct answer. ASTUTE means sagacious, shrewd. Since it is a synonym and not an antonym, (B) should not be selected as the correct answer. PROCUMBENT means lying down. (C) is not the antonym sought for SAGACIOUS. INCAPABLE means not efficient, not capable, not able. It is the antonym for SAGACIOUS and (D) is the correct answer.

## A–36

**(D)**  The NADIR is the lowest point on a celestial sphere. Its opposite, the highest point, is the ZENITH. (D) is the correct answer. A ZEPHYR (A) is a breeze. A KNAVE (B) is a rascal or rogue. EPITOME (C) means an ideal example.

# Questions

---

Q–37

FEALTY:LORD::

(A)  patriotism:country

(B)  tax:government

(C)  fidelity:spouse

(D)  money:creditor

---

*Your Answer* _____

_____

---

Q–38

LINEN:FLAX::

(A)  chintz:silk

(B)  madras:linen

(C)  coal:nylon

(D)  chamois:leather

---

*Your Answer* _____

_____

# Correct Answers

**A–37**

(C)     FEALTY is the loyalty one pledges to a LORD through a vow or oath. One feels PATRIOTISM to one's COUNTRY, but one does not take a vow of patriotism. (A) is not the correct answer. One pays TAX to the GOVERNMENT, but the obligation is a legal, not a voluntary, one. (B) is not correct. FIDELITY is the faithfulness one pledges to one's SPOUSE through a marriage vow. (C) is the correct answer. One might owe MONEY to a CREDITOR, but one can incur the debt without taking an oath or vow. (D) is incorrect.

**A–38**

(D)     CHINTZ is made from cotton, not SILK, so (A) is incorrect. MADRAS is made from cotton, not LINEN. (B) is wrong. NYLON is made from COAL, but the order does not duplicate LINEN: FLAX. (C) is incorrect. CHAMOIS is a soft cloth made from LEATHER. (D) is correct.

# Questions

**Q–39**

BEATIFIC:

(A) animalistic

(B) melancholy

(C) urbane

(D) civilized

*Your Answer* _____

_____

**Q–40**

TURGID:

(A) aggressive

(B) tumid

(C) bilious

(D) deflated

*Your Answer* _____

_____

# Correct Answers

## A–39

**(B)**    BEATIFIC means manifesting bliss, joy. ANIMALISTIC means like an animal. (A) is incorrect. MELANCHOLY means sad. It is the opposite of BEATIFIC and (B) is the correct answer. URBANE means civilized. (C) is an incorrect choice. CIVILIZED means educated, refined. It is not the opposite of BEATIFIC and (D) should not be selected.

## A–40

**(D)**    TURGID implies distension, as with air. AGGRESSIVE means having the disposition to dominate. It is not the opposite of TURGID and (A) should not be selected as the correct answer. TUMID, like TURGID, implies having a fullness. It is a synonym for TURGID and (B) is not the antonym sought. BILIOUS means ill-tempered, suffering—as from too much bile. (C) is not the opposite of TURGID. DEFLATED is the antonym, or opposite, of TURGID. DEFLATED means reduce the amount of, to let the air out, reduced. (D) is correct.

# Questions

---

**Q–41**

PUGILISM:FISTS::

(A) lexicographer:animals

(B) gynecology:genes

(C) nepotism:relatives

(D) archeology:fossils

---

*Your Answer* _____

_____

---

**Q–42**

DOOR:KEY::

(A) gem:ring

(B) perfume:aroma

(C) enigma:clue

(D) effort:achievement

---

*Your Answer* _____

_____

# Correct Answers

## A–41

**(C)** PUGILISM means fighting with the FISTS. FISTS are necessary to PUGILISM. In (A), a LEXICOGRAPHER is one who works with words, one who writes a dictionary. There is no direct relationship between a LEXICOGRAPHER and ANIMALS. (A) is an inappropriate choice. GYNECOLOGY is a branch of medical science that deals with the functions and diseases peculiar to women; it is not directly related to GENES. (B) is inappropriate. NEPOTISM is a term relating to RELATIVES; for instance, hiring family to fill positions in a business is called NEPOTISM. (C) is the correct choice. ARCHEOLOGY is a study of the people, customs, and life of ancient times; archeologists may excavate, classify, and study the remains of ancient cities, tools, monuments, or other records that remain. It is paleontology (not archeology) that is a study of FOSSILS. (D) is an incorrect choice.

## A–42

**(A)** A KEY can be used to unlock a DOOR. This relationship is also evidenced in alternative (C) ENIGMA:CLUE. A CLUE may unlock a riddle. The relationship in (A) GEM:RING is that of use. A GEM may be used in a RING. The relationship in (B) PERFUME:AROMA is that of entity and characteristic. AROMA is characteristic of PERFUME. Alternative (D) EFFORT:ACHIEVEMENT presents the relationship of prerequisite:event. EFFORT is a prerequisite to ACHIEVEMENT.

# Questions

Q–43

CANAILLE:

(A) aggregate

(B) fulgurant

(C) fulminant

(D) aristocracy

*Your Answer* _____

_____

Q–44

PAUCITY:

(A) dearth

(B) loquacious

(C) sanative

(D) plethora

*Your Answer* _____

_____

# Correct Answers

**A–43**

**(D)** CANAILLE is a mob, a pack, the lowest class of people, the rabble. An AGGREGATE is a mass, a body, a sum total. (A) is not the opposite of CANAILLE. FULGURANT means resembling lightning. (B) is obviously not the opposite of CANAILLE. FULMINANT means attacking suddenly. (C) is not the correct choice. ARISTOCRACY (the upper class) is the opposite of CANAILLE. (D) is correct.

**A–44**

**(D)** PAUCITY means a lack. DEARTH (A) is a scarcity. It is not an antonym for PAUCITY; it is more like a synonym. (A) should not be selected as the correct answer. (B) LOQUACIOUS means talkative. It is an incorrect choice. (C) SANATIVE (an adjective) means curative, healing. It is not a correct answer choice. PLETHORA (D) is a vast amount, a great excess. It is the opposite of PAUCITY and thus the correct choice.

# Questions

---

**Q–45**

EDIFICE:FACADE::

(A)   dorsal:ventral

(B)   turtle:shell

(C)   anachronism:chronologic

(D)   body:skeleton

*Your Answer* _____

---

**Q–46**

DEFICIT:PECULATION::

(A)   attire:dress

(B)   hunger:abstinence

(C)   appear:manifest

(D)   drought:famine

*Your Answer* _____

# Correct Answers

## A–45

**(B)** An EDIFICE is a building; a FACADE is the front part of a building or any part that faces a street or other open area. A FACADE, then, is the outer part of an EDIFICE. For (A), DORSAL is on, of, or near the back; VENTRAL is of or having to do with the belly—the opposite of DORSAL. Since this opposite relationship is not the same as that between EDIFICE:FACADE, (A) should not be chosen. Since the SHELL is the outer covering of a TURTLE (just as a FACADE is the outer part of an EDIFICE), (B) is the correct answer. ANACHRONISM is the act of putting some thing, person, or event where it does not belong. CHRONOLOGIC, like chronological, means arranged in the order in which the events happened. The two are opposite in meaning; they do not fit the pattern of EDIFICE: FACADE. (C) is incorrect. A SKELETON is the inner (not the outer) part of the BODY. (D) should not be selected since the two words do not have the same relationship as do EDIFICE:FACADE.

## A–46

**(B)** A DEFICIT is the result of PECULATION (the act of embezzling). For (A), ATTIRE is synonymous for DRESS, so (A) is not the correct answer. HUNGER is the result of ABSTINENCE. (B) is the correct answer. APPEAR and MANIFEST are synonymous verbs. The analogy is not that sought. (C) is incorrect. FAMINE is the result of DROUGHT; the order is inverted, however. (D) is incorrect.

**Q–47**

CONSONANCE:

(A) conscience

(B) conscious

(C) coalesce

(D) contention

*Your Answer* _____

_____

**Q–48**

TILT:

(A) incline

(B) align

(C) list

(D) pitch

*Your Answer* _____

_____

# Correct Answers

**A–47**

**(D)** CONSONANCE means agreement. In (A), CONSCIENCE is the sense of the moral goodness of one's own conduct. It is not related to CONSONANCE. (B) CONSCIOUS means aware, sensible. It is unrelated to CONSONANCE. (C) COALESCE is synonymous with blend (which suggests a mixing). (D) CONTENTION suggests argument. CONSONANCE suggests harmony, agreement, accordance. CONTENTION is the opposite of CONSONANCE. (D) is the opposite and thus the correct answer.

**A–48**

**(B)** ALIGN, which means to straighten, to line up, is the antonym of TILT, which means to place at an angle. INCLINE (A), LIST (C), and PITCH (D), are all synonymous with TILT, and are incorrect choices.

# Questions

Q–49

UNCTUOUS:BRUSQUE::

(A) gauche:suave

(B) abstruse:recondite

(C) bumptious:deleterious

(D) lustrous:luminous

*Your Answer* _____

Q–50

VENIAL:

(A) hedonic

(B) ineffable

(C) peccadillo

(D) heinous

*Your Answer* _____

# Correct Answers

## A–49

**(A)** UNCTUOUS, meaning fawning or ingratiating, and BRUSQUE, meaning rude or abrupt, are antonyms. GAUCHE, which means lacking social grace or awkward, and SUAVE, which means well-mannered or smooth, are also antonyms. (A) is the correct answer. ABSTRUSE and RECONDITE are synonyms for difficult to comprehend. (B) is not the correct choice. BUMPTIOUS, meaning impertinent, and DELETERIOUS, meaning harmful, are unrelated. (C) is not the correct answer. LUSTROUS and LUMINOUS are synonyms for bright; (D) is not the correct choice.

## A–50

**(D)** VENIAL means forgivable. (A) HEDONIC means pertaining to pleasure. It is not antonymous with VENIAL. (B) INEFFABLE means indescribable, difficult to put in words. It should not be selected as the opposite of VENIAL. (B) is incorrect. PECCADILLO (C) means small offense. (C) should not be selected. HEINOUS means abominable, outrageous. Since it suggests unforgivable behavior, (D) is the correct answer.

# Questions

**Q–51**

CATAPULT:PROJECTILE::

(A)   glacier:ice

(B)   precipice:cliff

(C)   transmit:message

(D)   perspiration:emit

*Your Answer* _____

_____

*As of May 2004, there were 222,960 pharmacists employed in the U.S. (U.S. Bureau of Labor Statistics)*

# Correct Answers

**A–51**

**(C)** CATAPULT means to throw or to shoot from a weapon. A PROJECTILE is that which has been hurled or shot, as from a sling-shot. (A) is incorrect. A GLACIER is a large mass of ice; ICE is the substance from which the glacier is made. The analogy in (A) is an object:composition relationship—quite different from the analogy existing between CATAPULT and PROJECTILE. (B) is not correct. A PRECIPICE is a CLIFF; the two are synonyms—(B) is not the type of analogy illustrated by the question. (C) is the correct response. TRANSMIT means to send; a MESSAGE is words sent from one person to another. The analogy between TRANSMIT (to send) and MESSAGE (words sent) is the same as that between CATAPULT and PROJECTILE. (D) is incorrect; although the same relationship is present between EMIT (give out) and PERSPIRATION (that which is given out) as between CATAPULT and PROJECTILE, the order is different.

# Questions

Q–52

VITAMIN C:SCURVY::

(A)   sun:skin cancer

(B)   niacin:pellagra

(C)   goiter:iodine

(D)   rickets:calcium

*Your Answer* _____

_____

Q–53

PRODIGAL:

(A)   wandering

(B)   tarrying

(C)   spendthrift

(D)   frugal

*Your Answer* _____

_____

# Correct Answers

## A–52

**(B)** A lack of VITAMIN C causes SCURVY; taking VITAMIN C helps cure SCURVY. (A) is incorrect. The SUN causes SKIN CANCER; care in the SUN can help prevent SKIN CANCER. The analogy is not the same. (B) is the correct answer since NIACIN can prevent PELLAGRA. (C) is incorrect; IODINE in the diet can prevent GOITER. The order is not the same as for VITAMIN C:SCURVY. (D) is incorrect. The order for RICKETS:CALCIUM is different than for VITAMIN C: SCURVY.

## A–53

**(D)** PRODIGAL is an adjective meaning given to extravagant expenditures. WANDERING (A) (roving, roaming) does not relate to PRODIGAL; (A) should not be selected. TARRYING (staying) does not relate to PRODIGAL; (B) is incorrect. SPENDTHRIFT (squanderer) is synonymous with PRODIGAL so (C) is incorrect. FRUGAL (in the habit of saving) is the opposite of PRODIGAL and so (D) is the correct answer.

# Questions

---

**Q–54**

VIABLE:

(A)  remnant

(B)  viands

(C)  subsistence

(D)  moribund

*Your Answer* _____

---

**Q–55**

CONVEY:DUCT::

(A)  transport:transfer

(B)  pollute:filter

(C)  decipher:key

(D)  autograph:biography

*Your Answer* _____

# Correct Answers

## A-54

**(D)** The opposite of VIABLE, which means capable of life, is MORIBUND, which means dying, or in the process of dying. The correct answer is (D). REMNANT (A) means a small trace or remaining piece. VIANDS (B) means food or provisions. SUBSISTENCE (C) is existence or the means of existence.

## A-55

**(C)** CONVEY is a verb which means to carry or transfer; DUCT is a noun that means a tube or canal for carrying. To CONVEY, or carry something, one might use a DUCT. (A) is incorrect. TRANSPORT means to carry across. TRANSFER means to bear across. These two words do not have the same relationship as the verb and noun above. (B) is incorrect. POLLUTE means to make dirty; a FILTER, on the other hand, can be used to remove dirt. (B) is not analogous to CONVEY and DUCT. (C) is correct. To DECIPHER or solve a code, one might use a KEY, which might be an explanation or a book of answers. The relationship between DECIPHER and KEY (C) is the same as that between CONVEY and DUCT. (D) is incorrect. An AUTOGRAPH is a writing written by one's self; a BIOGRAPHY is a writing about someone's life. These terms do not bear the same analogy as CONVEY and DUCT.

# Questions

**Q–56**

BENEVOLENCE:PHILANTHROPY::

(A) lenity:virulence

(B) haunt:sporadic

(C) amiability:complaisant

(D) penurious:hoard

*Your Answer* _____

**Q–57**

RECUMBENT:

(A) prone

(B) obligatory

(C) vertical

(D) supine

*Your Answer* _____

# Correct Answers

**A–56**

**(D)** BENEVOLENCE refers to the *will* to do good, while PHILANTHROPY indicates the act of giving, specifically money, on a large scale, thereby creating a cause-and-effect relationship. LENITY and VIRULENCE (A) are near antonyms in definition, with LENITY referring to indulgence while VIRULENCE describes extreme bitterness. (B) is incorrect; SPORADIC means to occur occasionally, while HAUNT suggests appearing continually. AMIABILITY and COMPLAISANT (C) both refer to being generally agreeable. (D) is correct. PENURIOUS suggests extreme frugality resulting in HOARDING, a cause-and-effect relationship.

**A–57**

**(C)** RECUMBENT means lying down. PRONE (A) and SUPINE (D) are both synonymous with RECUMBENT. OBLIGATORY means mandatory or required, so (B) is not the correct answer. Only VERTICAL (C), or upright, is the opposite of RECUMBENT. The correct answer is (C).

# Questions

---

Q–58

VOLATILE:

(A) explosive

(B) impulsive

(C) mercurial

(D) deliberate

---

*Your Answer* _____

_____

---

Q–59

DESIRE:WANT::

(A) supineness:propensity

(B) disdain:inattention

(C) aspire:seek

(D) avidity:greed

---

*Your Answer* _____

_____

# Correct Answers

## A–58

**(D)** VOLATILE has several meanings, including EXPLOSIVE (A), IMPULSIVE (B), and MERCURIAL (C). The only choice given that means the opposite of VOLATILE is DELIBERATE, meaning to give thorough consideration to; the correct answer is (D).

## A–59

**(D)** (A) is not the correct choice. PROPENSITY is an antonym of SUPINENESS, with PROPENSITY referring to an irresistible attachment to a thing; while SUPINENESS suggests the opposite, "apathetic passivity." (B) is incorrect. DISDAIN suggests looking upon something with scorn. INATTENTION implies a lack of concentration. ASPIRE and SEEK (C) are synonymous, both implying the searching for and laboring to attain. (D) is the correct answer. DESIRE is defined as a longing or craving which is a more intense form of WANT, just as AVIDITY is defined as a consuming GREED. Therefore, DESIRE and AVIDITY denote a maximum degree of WANT and GREED.

# Questions

---

Q–60

PHYLUM:CLASSIFICATION::

(A) cat:feline

(B) commitment:vow

(C) lie:deceit

(D) medal:honor

---

*Your Answer* _____

---

Q–61

FACTIOUS:

(A) bellicose

(B) desultory

(C) fortuitous

(D) consonant

---

*Your Answer* _____

# Correct Answers

### A–60

**(D)** CAT:FELINE (A) presents an animal and its class. COMMITMENT:VOW (B) presents synonyms. LIE:DECEIT (C) presents an example of the second term through the first term. (D) is correct. This is an analogy of purpose. The purpose served by PHYLUM is that of CLASSIFICATION. The purpose of a MEDAL is to HONOR the recipient.

### A–61

**(D)** FACTIOUS means inclined to dispute. BELLICOSE means aggressive. It is not the opposite of FACTIOUS; (A) should not be selected. DESULTORY (B) means without plan. It is not directly related to FACTIOUS and should not be selected as the opposite. FORTUITOUS (C) means accidental. It is not the opposite of FACTIOUS and should not be selected. CONSONANT means harmonious. It is the opposite of FACTIOUS. (D) is the correct answer.

# Questions

---

**Q–62**

PROBITY:

(A) aesthetics

(B) perfidy

(C) abeyance

(D) predilection

*Your Answer* _____

---

**Q–63**

ARACHNIDS:ARTHROPOD::

(A) particle:atom

(B) spear:aperture

(C) rayon:bengaline

(D) theosophy:monastery

*Your Answer* _____

# Correct Answers

## A–62

**(B)** PROBITY is tried and proven honesty. (A) AESTHETICS is a sense of beauty. It is not the opposite of PROBITY and should not be selected. (B) PERFIDY is faithlessness. It is the opposite of PROBITY and should be selected as the right answer. (C) ABEYANCE is the act of suspending. It is not the opposite of PROBITY and, hence, should not be chosen. Since PREDILECTION is the act of having positive feelings toward something, it should not be selected as the opposite of PROBITY.

## A–63

**(C)** PARTICLE and ATOM (A) have a part-to-whole relationship. SPEAR and APERTURE (B) are synonymous. (C) is correct. RAYON and BENGALINE have a member:class relationship. THEOSOPHY and MONASTERY (D) have a relationship of purpose.

# Questions

**Q–64**

SERVICE:CHEVRON::

(A) rank:coronet

(B) decent:libertine

(C) chaste:virtuous

(D) lascivious:licentious

*Your Answer* _____

_____

**Q–65**

FACTITIOUS:

(A) authentic

(B) travesty

(C) pedantic

(D) mordant

*Your Answer* _____

_____

# Correct Answers

## A–64

**(A)**    (A) is correct because RANK:CORONET contains a cause-and-effect relationship, as do the lead words, SERVICE and CHEVRON. DECENT: LIBERTINE (B) refer to attitude and lifestyle, as do the synonymous pairs CHASTE:VIRTUOUS (C) and LASCIVIOUS:LICENTIOUS (D).

## A–65

**(A)**    FACTITIOUS means artificial. AUTHENTIC means genuine, real. It is the opposite of FACTITIOUS and, hence, (A) is the correct answer. TRAVESTY is a caricature. (B) should not be selected as the correct answer. (C) PEDANTIC means in a manner that makes a display of learning. Since it is not the opposite of FACTITIOUS, it should not be selected as the correct answer. (D) MORDANT means biting or stinging. It is not directly related to FACTITIOUS and should not be selected as the correct answer.

# Questions

---

**Q-66**

PROCLIVITY:

(A) penchant

(B) deflection

(C) dilatory

(D) diminish

---

*Your Answer* _____

_____

---

**Q-67**

SPOONERISM:TRANSPOSITION::

(A) Alpha:Omega

(B) spree:carousal

(C) repudiation:sanction

(D) colon:semicolon

---

*Your Answer* _____

_____

# Correct Answers

## A-66

**(B)** PROCLIVITY and PENCHANT (A) are synonyms. (B) is correct. PROCLIVITY means a strong inclination, DEFLECTION is an attempt to avoid. DILATORY (C) means delay-causing. DIMINISH (D) means to lessen.

## A-67

**(B)** (A) is incorrect. ALPHA:OMEGA, (beginning:end), are opposites. (B) is correct. SPREE and CAROUSAL are synonymous, as are SPOONERISM and TRANSPOSITION, in which the initial sounds of two or more words are rearranged. (C) is incorrect. REPUDIATION means rejection and is the opposite of SANCTION, which means condone. (D) is incorrect. COLON and SEMICOLON are two punctuation marks; they don't have a synonymous relationship like the example words.

# Questions

**Q–68**

TWEETER:WOOFER::

(A) grade:slope

(B) high:low

(C) replicate:duplicate

(D) tutelage:protection

*Your Answer* _____

_____

**Q–69**

REMOTE:

(A) foreign

(B) proximate

(C) parallax

(D) inapposite

*Your Answer* _____

_____

# Correct Answers

## A–68

**(B)** (A) is incorrect. GRADE:SLOPE is a synonymous relationship. (B) is correct. HIGH and LOW are opposites, as are TWEETER (a small loudspeaker for reproducing high frequency sounds) and WOOFER (a large loudspeaker for reproducing low frequency sounds). (C) is incorrect. REPLICATE:DUPLICATE is a synonymous relationship. (D) is incorrect. TUTELAGE:PROTECTION is a synonymous relationship.

## A–69

**(B)** FOREIGN suggests being situated outside a place and is synonymous with REMOTE. PROXIMATE (B) means nearness in space and is the correct answer. PARALLAX (C) indicates an apparent difference in the direction of an object as seen from two perspectives. INAPPOSITE (D) refers to being not relevant.

# Questions

**Q–70**

TREPIDATION:

(A) apprehension

(B) sagacity

(C) perturbation

(D) courage

*Your Answer* _____

_____

**Q–71**

ARC:CIRCUMFERENCE::

(A) moon:earth

(B) hour:day

(C) cabin:mansion

(D) exercise:rest

*Your Answer* _____

_____

# Correct Answers

## A–70

**(D)** (A) is incorrect. TREPIDATION and AP-PREHENSION are synonymous, meaning "fear." SAGACITY (B) means the mental capacity to discern character. PERTURBATION (C) refers to the degree of apprehension. (D) is correct. COURAGE is defined as mental and moral strength, as opposed to TREPIDATION.

## A–71

**(B)** (B) is correct. An ARC is a part, or segment, of a circle's CIRCUMFERENCE. An HOUR is a part of a DAY. MOON:EARTH (A), CABIN:MANSION (C), and EXERCISE:REST (D) do not reflect the part-to-whole relationship.

# Questions

**Q–72**

FACADE:BUILDING::

(A)  grill:car

(B)  tongue:shoe

(C)  sheath:knife

(D)  picture:frame

*Your Answer* _____

_____

**Q–73**

ABYSS:

(A)  zenith

(B)  profundity

(C)  interval

(D)  interstice

*Your Answer* _____

_____

# Correct Answers

## A–72

(A)   A FACADE is the front or main face of a BUILDING. The corresponding analogy is (A) GRILL:CAR. A GRILL is the front or main face of a CAR. In relation to the other alternatives, a TONGUE is on the top of a SHOE, a SHEATH is around a KNIFE, and a PICTURE is in a FRAME.

## A–73

(A)   (A) is correct. ZENITH is the highest point, making it opposite to ABYSS, the lowest point. PROFUNDITY (B) means intellectual depth. An INTERVAL (C) is a space of time between two events. An INTERSTICE (D) is an interval of time between two events.

---

**Q–74**

CORPULENT:

(A) portly

(B) vociferate

(C) becoming

(D) anorexic

*Your Answer* _____

---

**Q–75**

GRASS:EROSION::

(A) root:tree

(B) air:tire

(C) clouds:rain

(D) dam:water

*Your Answer* _____

# Correct Answers

## A–74

**(D)**     CORPULENT means solid, dense, fleshy, or fat. PORTLY (A) means stout, obese, or fat. This synonym should not be selected. VOCIFERATE means to cry out loudly. It bears no relationship to CORPULENT; (B) is incorrect. BECOMING can be used as an adjective meaning befitting or suitable. Since it is not the opposite of CORPULENT, (C) should not be selected as the correct answer. ANOREXIC (D) means suppressing appetite for food and, hence, thin; it is the opposite of CORPULENT and the correct choice.

## A–75

**(D)**     The relationship in this analogy is one of effect. GRASS retards or stops EROSION. The corresponding alternative is (D). A DAM retards or stops WATER. Alternatives (A), (B) and (C) are inaccurate because ROOTS do not retard or stop a TREE, AIR does not retard a TIRE, and CLOUDS do not retard RAIN.

# Questions

---

**Q–76**

COMPULSORY:REQUIRED::

(A) committed:avowed

(B) normal:aberrant

(C) free:democratic

(D) voluntary:mandatory

---

*Your Answer* _____

_____

---

**Q–77**

ABJECT:

(A) caring

(B) joyful

(C) empathetic

(D) objective

---

*Your Answer* _____

_____

# Correct Answers

## A–76

**(A)** (A) is correct. COMMITTED and AVOWED are synonyms. (B) is incorrect. NORMAL and ABERRANT are antonyms. (C) is incorrect. FREE and DEMOCRATIC are a cause-and-effect relationship. (D) is incorrect. VOLUNTARY and MANDATORY are antonyms.

## A–77

**(B)** ABJECT means miserable; CARING (A) is not related. (B) is correct. ABJECT is an adjective which means miserable or wretched. Its opposite in the list given is JOYFUL. EMPATHETIC (C) means emotionally sensitive. OBJECTIVE (D) means without bias or prejudice.

# Questions

---

**Q–78**

RESERVED:

(A)  chivalrous

(B)  affable

(C)  ingratiating

(D)  cultivated

---

*Your Answer* _____

_____

---

**Q–79**

NERVOUS:POISE::

(A)  angry:sensibility

(B)  frightened:confidence

(C)  empathetic:rationality

(D)  energetic:enthusiasm

---

*Your Answer* _____

_____

# Correct Answers

## A–78

**(B)** (A) is incorrect. CHIVALROUS means gallant or courteous. RESERVED means undemonstrative, self-restrained, or distant. Its opposite in the list given is AFFABLE (B), which means friendly or sociable. INGRATIATING (C) means bringing oneself into another's favor. CULTIVATED (D) means developed, as in a developed mind.

## A–79

**(B)** (A) ANGRY:SENSIBILITY is not right because SENSIBILITY (the capacity for physical sensation) can be present simultaneously with ANGER. (B) is correct. To be NERVOUS is to lack POISE. This relationship also exists between FRIGHTENED:CONFIDENCE. To be FRIGHTENED is to lack CONFIDENCE. (C) EMPATHETIC:RATIONALITY is incorrect because a person can be RATIONAL and also EMPATHETIC. (D) ENERGETIC:ENTHUSIASM is incorrect because an ENERGETIC person does have ENTHUSIASM.

**Q-80**

LATENCY:EXPOSITION::

(A) pleonasm:verbiage

(B) indigent:poverty

(C) argonaut:astronaut

(D) indigested:structured

*Your Answer* _____

_____

**Q-81**

CALORIC:

(A) fervor

(B) modicum

(C) temperature

(D) frigidity

*Your Answer* _____

_____

# Correct Answers

## A–80

**(D)** (A) is incorrect. LATENCY:EXPOSITION are antonymous; PLEONASM:VERBIAGE are synonyms that refer to redundancy. (B) is incorrect. INDIGENT and POVERTY are synonyms that refer to being without money. ARGONAUTS and ASTRONAUTS (C) are both navigators of sorts. (D) is correct. INDIGESTED and STRUCTURED are antonyms.

## A–81

**(D)** (A) is incorrect. FERVOR is a degree of warmth. MODICUM (B) is a small portion. TEMPERATURE (C) is a measure of hot or cold. (D) is correct. FRIGIDITY refers to coldness; CALORIC refers to heat.

# Questions

**Q–82**

FERAL:

(A) voracious

(B) unconscientious

(C) savage

(D) cultivated

*Your Answer* _____

_____

**Q–83**

AGGRANDIZE:AUGMENT::

(A) declension:ascent

(B) abatement:extenuation

(C) adjunct:detruncate

(D) increment:diminution

*Your Answer* _____

_____

# Correct Answers

## A–82

**(D)** The adjective FERAL means wild or untamed. VORACIOUS means excessively eager, immoderate, gluttonous, ravenous. It certainly is not the opposite of FERAL and (A) should not be chosen. UNCONSCIENTIOUS means not influenced by (a strict regard to) the dictates of conscience. It is seemingly unrelated to FERAL. (B) is wrong. SAVAGE means uncivilized, uncultivated, ferocious. It is not the opposite of FERAL; (C) is an incorrect answer. (D) CULTIVATED means improved, or refined. It is the opposite of FERAL; (D) is the correct answer.

## A–83

**(B)** (A) is incorrect. DECLENSION and ASCENT are antonyms, unlike the example words, which are synonyms. (B) is correct. AGGRANDIZE means to make (appear) greater; AUGMENT means to add to. ABATEMENT and EXTENUATION both mean a forgiveness. ADJUNCT and DETRUNCATE (C) are antonyms. INCREMENT and DIMINUTION (D) are antonyms.

# Questions

---

**Q–84**

INTOXICATION:INEBRIATION::

(A)   gluttony:voracity

(B)   turban:hat

(C)   vim:fatigue

(D)   plover:sandpiper

*Your Answer* _____

_____

---

**Q–85**

UNCTUOUS:

(A)   scrupulous

(B)   morose

(C)   ravenous

(D)   agitated

*Your Answer* _____

_____

# Correct Answers

## A–84

**(A)** (A) is correct. Both the example and GLUTTONY:VORACITY share similar meanings. (B) is incorrect. TURBAN and HAT have a member:class relationship. VIM means energy and is the opposite of FATIGUE. (D) is incorrect. A PLOVER is a type of SANDPIPER.

## A–85

**(D)** UNCTUOUS means smug, characterized by a pretense, especially in trying to persuade or influence others. SCRUPULOUS (A) means careful, exacting. It is not the opposite of UNCTUOUS. MOROSE means gloomy. (B) is not an antonym for UNCTUOUS and should not be selected. RAVENOUS means eager. Since it is not the opposite of UNCTUOUS, (C) is not a suitable choice. AGITATED involves a loss of calmness; there are nervous and emotional signs of emotional excitement. This is quite the opposite of the smug exterior of an unctuous person. (D) is the correct answer.

# Questions

---

**Q–86**

INVIDIOUS:

(A) repugnant

(B) obscure

(C) ransomed

(D) reconcilable

*Your Answer* _____

---

**Q–87**

MANDATORY:OPTIONAL::

(A) pious:indignant

(B) competent:inept

(C) opaque:ornate

(D) chaste:celibate

*Your Answer* _____

# Correct Answers

## A-86

**(D)** INVIDIOUS means likely to give offense, tending to excite ill will. REPUGNANT means distasteful, repellent, hostile; it is more similar than opposite to INVIDIOUS. (A) should not be selected. OBSCURE means not clearly understood. The word does not have the opposite relationship sought; (B) should not be selected. RANSOMED means redeemed, delivered. It is not an antonym for INVIDIOUS. RECONCILABLE means capable of being brought into harmony; it is quite the opposite of INVIDIOUS, which means likely to give offense. (D) is, therefore, the correct answer.

## A-87

**(B)** MANDATORY (required) and OPTIONAL are antonyms. COMPETENT and INEPT are also antonyms; the correct answer is (B). PIOUS: INDIGNANT (A) and OPAQUE:ORNATE (C) are unrelated pairs. CHASTE:CELIBATE (D) is a synonymous pair.

# Questions

**Q–88**

PUNISHMENT:FINE::

(A)   hyacinth:flower

(B)   sandals:shoes

(C)   circulation:heart

(D)   puzzle:jigsaw

*Your Answer* _____

_____

**Q–89**

FORTUITOUS:

(A)   sad

(B)   unfruitful

(C)   unlucky

(D)   disenchanted

*Your Answer* _____

_____

# Correct Answers

## A–88

**(D)** A FINE is a form of PUNISHMENT, and JIGSAW is a form of PUZZLE; therefore, the correct answer is (D). Choices (A), HYACINTH: FLOWER, and (B), SANDALS:SHOES, reflect a specific:general relationship. HEART is the mechanism that provides CIRCULATION, so (C) is not the correct choice.

## A–89

**(C)** SAD (A) is an emotional state of being. UNFRUITFUL (B) means unproductive. (C) is correct. FORTUITOUS means lucky; the opposite is UNLUCKY. DISENCHANTED (D) is an emotional state of being.

# Questions

**Q–90**

ARCHAIC:

(A) exalted

(B) modern

(C) angelic

(D) invisible

*Your Answer* _____

**Q–91**

BANDAGE:WOUND::

(A) stamp:envelope

(B) gloves:hands

(C) diaper:baby

(D) cast:fracture

*Your Answer* _____

# Correct Answers

## A–90

**(B)** EXALTED (A) is an adjective meaning noble or elevated. The adjective ARCHAIC comes from the Greek word for ancient. Its opposite in the list given is MODERN (B). ANGELIC (C) refers to a beautiful, good, angel-like person. (D) INVISIBLE means unable to be seen or imperceptible.

## A–91

**(D)** The key pair and all of the choice pairs give a first term that is something that is put on the second term. However, a BANDAGE is put on a WOUND to promote healing. Only choice (D) reflects this aspect of the key pair. A CAST is put on a FRACTURE to promote healing.

# Questions

Q–92

ESPOUSE:THEORY::

(A) proponent:opponent

(B) advocate:hypothesis

(C) heretic:blasphemy

(D) gourmand:gluttony

*Your Answer* _____

_____

Q–93

INSERT:

(A) exude

(B) extend

(C) extract

(D) explore

*Your Answer* _____

_____

# Correct Answers

## A-92

**(B)** To ESPOUSE a THEORY is to support and promote it. To ADVOCATE a HYPOTHESIS is to support and promote it; the correct answer is (B). PROPONENT and OPPONENT are opposites; (A) is not the correct answer. HERETIC:BLASPHEMY and GOURMAND:GLUTTONY both link a noun with an action associated with that noun. (C) and (D) are not correct answers.

## A-93

**(C)** EXUDE (A) means to ooze or to radiate. (B) EXTEND means to stretch forth. To INSERT means to put or fit into something else. Its opposite is EXTRACT (C), meaning to draw out, as to extract a tooth. (D) EXPLORE means to examine carefully.

# Questions

**Q–94**

LOQUACIOUS:

(A)   daring

(B)   tedious

(C)   silent

(D)   wealthy

*Your Answer* _____

_____

**Q–95**

TRACTABLE:BIDDABLE::

(A)   torpid:lethargic

(B)   viscous:liquid

(C)   truculent:contrite

(D)   colloquial:formal

*Your Answer* _____

_____

# Correct Answers

**A–94**

**(C)** DARING (A) means fearless, bold. TEDIOUS (B) means long and dull, tiresome. LOQUACIOUS means very talkative. Its opposite is SILENT (C). WEALTHY (D) means rich.

**A–95**

**(A)** TRACTABLE and BIDDABLE are synonyms meaning obedient. TORPID and LETHARGIC are synonyms meaning lazy; (A) is the correct answer. VISCOUS:LIQUID and COLLOQUIAL: FORMAL have antonymous relationships; therefore, (B) and (D) are incorrect. TRUCULENT, meaning argumentative, and CONTRITE, or sorry, are unrelated; (C) is not the correct answer.

# Questions

---

**Q–96**

DEIGN:CONDESCEND::

(A) berate:commend

(B) corroborate:repudiate

(C) digress:stray

(D) imbue:desiccate

*Your Answer* _____

---

**Q–97**

MYRIAD:

(A) passel

(B) diverse

(C) legion

(D) individual

*Your Answer* _____

# Correct Answers

**A–96**

(C)     DEIGN:CONDESCEND have a synonymous relationship. BERATE (to belittle) and COMMEND (to praise) are antonyms, as are CORROBORATE (to support) and REPUDIATE (to deny). (A) and (B) are incorrect. DIGRESS and STRAY are synonyms; the correct answer is (C). IMBUE (permeate) and DESICCATE (dry out) are not related; (D) is not correct.

**A–97**

(D)     PASSEL (A) means a group, especially a fairly large group. DIVERSE (B) means different or varied. LEGION (C) means a large number, a multitude. MYRIAD carries the meaning of a great number of persons or things. Its opposite here is INDIVIDUAL (D), meaning existing as a separate thing or being, or relating to a single person or thing.

# Questions

**Q–98**

NEFARIOUS:

(A)  insubordinate

(B)  good

(C)  dangerous

(D)  nervous

*Your Answer* _____

_____

**Q–99**

FRAILTY:VICE::

(A)  felony:misdemeanor

(B)  aggravating:pernicious

(C)  trite:popular

(D)  secreted:veiled

*Your Answer* _____

_____

# Correct Answers

## A–98

**(B)** INSUBORDINATE (A) means disrespectful. (B) is correct. The adjective NEFARIOUS means wicked. Its opposite in the list given is GOOD.

## A–99

**(B)** A FRAILTY is an imperfection. The term VICE is used to denote a serious imperfection. The difference is in the degree, with a FRAILTY being milder. A FELONY is more serious than a MISDEMEANOR. The analogy is, however, inverted. (A) should not be selected. AGGRAVATING is intensifying, making worse. PERNICIOUS is highly injurious. The degree of PERNICIOUS is greater than that of AGGRAVATING. Their relationship is that of FRAILTY:VICE. (B) is the correct answer. TRITE is overworked, overused. POPULAR is common. The degree of the two is different, but the analogy is different from that of FRAILTY:VICE. (C) is not the correct answer. SECRETED is more carefully hidden than VEILED; again the order is inverted. (D) is incorrect.

**Q–100**

AMELIORATE:

(A) clarify

(B) mandate

(C) insist

(D) worsen

*Your Answer* _____

_____

*The situation in which a medication package has both OTC (over the counter) and prescription labeling is commonly referred to as "dual label status." (www.pharmacist.com)*

# Correct Answers

**(D)** CLARIFY (A) means to make clear. MANDATE (B) means to order. INSIST (C) means to take a stand and maintain it. (D) is correct. AMELIORATE conveys the idea to make or become better, to improve. Its opposite in the list given is WORSEN.

*Some of the scales used in pharmacy are so sensitive they can weigh individual grains of salt. (www.hood-meddac.army.mil)*

# Section II

# Quantitative Ability

---

**DIRECTIONS:** Each of the questions or incomplete statements in this section is followed by four suggested answers or completions. Select the one that is best in each case.

# Questions

---

**Q-1**

What part of three-fourths is one-tenth?

(A) $\frac{1}{8}$

(B) $\frac{15}{2}$

(C) $\frac{2}{15}$

(D) $\frac{3}{40}$

---

*Your Answer* _____

_____

---

**Q-2**

Find the value of $x$ in $2x + 12 = 3x + 9$.

(A) 1

(B) 2

(C) 3

(D) 4

---

*Your Answer* _____

_____

# Correct Answers

## A-1

(C)     First, observe that three-fourths is $\frac{3}{4}$ and one tenth is $\frac{1}{10}$. Let $x$ be the unknown part which must be found. Then, one can write from the statement of the problem that the $x$ part of three-fourths is given by

$$\frac{3}{4}x$$

The equation for the problem is given by $\frac{3}{4}x = \frac{1}{10}$. Multiplying both sides of the equation by the reciprocal of $\frac{3}{4}$ one obtains the following:

$$\left(\frac{4}{3}\right)\frac{3}{4}x = \left(\frac{4}{3}\right)\frac{1}{10} \text{ or } x = \frac{4}{30} \text{ or } x = \frac{2}{15}$$

which is choice (C).

Response (D) is obtained by incorrectly finding the product of $\frac{3}{4}$ and $\frac{1}{10}$ to be the unknown part. Response (B) is obtained by dividing $\frac{3}{4}$ by $\frac{1}{10}$.

## A–2

(C)     Simplify $2x + 12 = 3x + 9$.
$$12 - 9 = 3x - 2x$$
$$3 = x$$

# Questions

**Q–3**

Peter has five rulers of 30 cm each and three of 20 cm each. What is the average length of Peter's rulers?

(A)  25

(B)  27

(C)  23

(D)  26.25

*Your Answer* _____

_____

**Q–4**

Two pounds of pears and one pound of peaches cost $1.40. Three pounds of pears and two pounds of peaches cost $2.40. How much is the combined cost of one pound of pears and one pound of peaches?

(A)  $2.00

(B)  $1.50

(C)  $1.60

(D)  $1.00

*Your Answer* _____

_____

# Correct Answers

**A–3**

**(D)**  $\text{Average} = \dfrac{5 \times 30 + 3 \times 20}{8}$

$\text{Average} = \dfrac{150 + 60}{8} = \dfrac{210}{8} = 26.25$

**A–4**

**(D)**  Let $x$ = cost of one pound of pears
Let $y$ = cost of one pound of peaches

$2x + y = 1.4$
$3x + 2y = 2.4$
$4x + 2y = 2.8$
$3x + 2y = 2.4$
$x = .4$
$y = .6$

Therefore, $x + y = 1.00$

# Questions

**Q–5**

One number is 2 more than 3 times another. Their sum is 22. Find the numbers.

(A)  8, 14

(B)  2, 20

(C)  5, 17

(D)  4, 18

*Your Answer* _____

_____

*Most pharmacy graduates can expect to receive multiple job offers at the time of graduation. There is great potential for advancement and competitive salaries within a pharmacy career. (www.aacp.org)*

# Correct Answers

## A–5

**(C)** Based on the information given in the first sentence of the problem one needs to first represent the unknown numbers. So let $x$ be a number. Then, the other number is given by $3x + 2$, which is two more than 3 times the first number. So the two numbers are $x$ and $3x + 2$.

Next, form an equation by adding the two numbers and setting the sum equal to 22 and then solve the equation for the two numbers.

$$x + 3x + 2 = 22$$
$$4x + 2 = 22$$
$$4x = 20$$
$$x = 5, \text{ one of the numbers.}$$

The other number is given by

$$3x + 2 = 3(5) + 2 = 15 + 2 = 17, \text{ the other}$$
number.

Hence, answer choice (C) is correct. The other answer choices fail to satisfy the equation $x + 3x + 2 = 22$.

# Questions

**Q–6**

The length of a rectangle is $6L$ and the width is $4W$. What is the perimeter?

(A)  $12L + 8W$

(B)  $12L^2 + 8W^2$

(C)  $6L + 4W$

(D)  $20LW$

*Your Answer* _____

_____

*Increases in average life span and the increased incidence of chronic diseases as well as the increased complexity, number and sophistication of medications and related products point to a healthy future for a career in pharmacy. (www.aacp.org)*

# Correct Answers

## A–6

(A)      In order to find the perimeter of the rectangle, it is important first to understand the definition, that is, perimeter equals the sum of the dimension of the rectangle. Hence, for the given rectangle,

Perimeter = $6L + 4w + 6L + 4w$ (Add like terms)
Perimeter = $12L + 8w$

Answer choice (C), $6L + 4w$, is incorrect because it represents only one-half of the perimeter of the rectangle. Answer choice (D), $20Lw$, is incorrect because this response is obtained by simply adding the coefficients of $L$ and $w$ which is an incorrect application of algebra. Finally, answer choice (B), $12L^2 + 8w^2$, is incorrect because it is obtained by using the definition of the perimeter of a rectangle incorrectly as follows: perimeter = $2L(6L) + 2w(4w)$.

# Questions

---

**Q–7**

If the length of a rectangle is increased by 30% and the width is decreased by 20%, then the area is increased by

(A)  10%.

(B)  5%.

(C)  4%.

(D)  20%.

*Your Answer* _____

---

**Q–8**

If *n* is the first of three consecutive odd numbers, which of the following represents the sum of the three numbers?

(A)  $n + 2$

(B)  $n + 4$

(C)  $n + 6$

(D)  $3n + 6$

*Your Answer* _____

# Correct Answers

## A–7

**(C)** Let $x$ be the length of the rectangle. Then, a 30% increase in the length of the rectangle is given by $x + .3x$. Let $y$ be the width of the rectangle. Then, a 20% decrease in the width of the rectangle is given by $y - .2y$. The original area is given by $A = xy$ and the new area is given by:

$$A = (x + .3x)(y - .2y)$$
$$= xy - .2xy + .3xy - 0.06xy$$
$$= xy + 0.04xy$$
$$= 1.04xy$$

So, the new area is 104% of the original area which is a $104\% - 100\% = 4\%$ increase, which is answer choice (C). The other answer choices are found by either using the perimeter formula or incorrectly finding the increase and decrease in the length and width, respectively.

## A–8

**(D)** With $n$ being the first odd number, it follows that $n + 2$ and $n + 4$ are the next two odd numbers. This eliminates answer choices (A) and (B) on the basis that each one of them represents only one of the two consecutive odd numbers that follow $n$. Since the sum of the three consecutive odd numbers is $n + (n + 2) + (n + 4) = 3n + 6$, it follows that answer choice (C) is incorrect, which leaves answer choice (D) as correct.

# Questions

**Q–9**

A runner takes nine seconds to run a distance of 132 feet. What is the runner's speed in miles per hour?

(A)  9

(B)  10

(C)  11

(D)  12

*Your Answer* _____

**Q–10**

35 is 7% of what quantity?

(A)  2.45

(B)  5

(C)  245

(D)  500

*Your Answer* _____

# Correct Answers

## A-9

**(B)**    First one must determine the equivalent of 132 ft./9 sec. in terms of miles/hour in order to solve the problem. Recall that 1 hour = 60 min. = 3,600 sec. and 1 mile = 5,280 ft. Thus, one can set up the following proportion:

$$\frac{132 \text{ ft}}{9 \text{ sec}} = \frac{x \text{ ft}}{1 \text{ hr}} = \frac{x \text{ ft}}{3,600 \text{ sec}}$$

and solve for $x$. The result is

$$\frac{9x \text{ ft}}{\text{sec}} = \frac{132(3,600) \text{ ft}}{\text{sec}}$$

$$x = \frac{475,200}{9} = 52,800 \text{ ft or 10 miles.}$$

Hence, the speed is 10 miles per hour.

## A-10

**(D)**     Let $x$ = number

$$.07x = 35$$
$$x = 500$$
$$\frac{.07x}{.07} = \frac{35}{.07}$$

Therefore, the correct choice is (D).

# Questions

---

**Q–11**

After taking four tests, Joan has an average grade of 79 points. What grade must she get on her fifth test to achieve an 83 point average?

(A)  83

(B)  86

(C)  87

(D)  99

*Your Answer* _____

_____

---

**Q–12**

If a triangle of base 6 units has the same area as a circle of radius 6 units, what is the altitude of the triangle?

(A)  $\pi$

(B)  $3\pi$

(C)  $6\pi$

(D)  $12\pi$

*Your Answer* _____

_____

# Correct Answers

## A–11

**(D)**  Let $x$ = the score of Joan's last test

$$83 = \frac{4(79) + x}{5}$$

$$83(5) = 316 + x$$
$$415 - 316 = x$$
$$99 = x$$

## A–12

**(D)**  To find the altitude of the triangle one must recall that the area of a triangle is given by

$$A = \left(\frac{1}{2}\right) bh,$$

where $b$ denotes the base and $h$ denotes the altitude. Also, one must recall that the area of a circle is given by

$$A = \pi r^2,$$

where $r$ denotes the radius of the circle.

Since $b$ = 6 units then $(\frac{1}{2})$ (6)$h$ = 3$h$ = $A$, the area of the triangle. In addition, since $r$ = 6 units, then $A = \pi r^2 = \pi(6)^2 = 36\pi$, the area of the circle. But the area is the same for both figures. Thus,

$$3h = 36\pi$$
$$h = 12\pi$$

is the altitude of the triangle.

# Questions

**Q–13**

A given cube has a surface area of 96 square feet. What is the volume of the cube in cubic feet?

(A)  16

(B)  36

(C)  64

(D)  96

*Your Answer* _____

_____

**Q–14**

Solve the inequality $7 - 3x \leq 19$.

(A)  $x = 4$

(B)  $x = -4$

(C)  $x \geq -4$

(D)  $x \leq -4$

*Your Answer* _____

_____

# Correct Answers

## A–13

**(C)** One needs to first recall that a cube has six equal sized faces. Thus, the area of each face is found by dividing 6 into 96 to obtain 16 square feet. Since each face contains 16 square feet, then one can conclude that each edge of a face is 4 feet long. So, the volume of the cube, given by the formula,

$$V = \text{(length of edge)}^3 \text{ is found to be}$$
$$V = (4 \text{ feet})^3 = 64 \text{ cubic feet.}$$

## A–14

**(C)** Simplify

| | |
|---|---|
| $7 - 3x \leq 19$ | Add –7 to both sides |
| $-3x \leq 19 - 7$ | Divide both sides by (–3). |
| $x \geq 12 \div (-3)$ | The sense of the inequality |
| $x \geq -4$ | changes when multiplied or divided by a negative number. |

# Questions

**Q–15**

A truck contains 150 small packages, some weighing 1 kg each and some weighing 2 kg each. How many packages weighing 2 kg each are in the truck if the total weight of all the packages is 264 kg?

(A)  36

(B)  52

(C)  88

(D)  114

*Your Answer* _____

_____

*Employment of pharmacists is expected to grow 21-35 percent for all occupations through 2012. (U.S. Bureau of Labor Statistics)*

# Correct Answers

## A–15

**(D)**     One way to attack this problem is to solve it algebraically.

Let $x$ represent the number of packages weighing 2 kg each. Then $(150 - x)$ represents the number of packages weighing 1 kg each.

Therefore,

$$2x + 1(150 - x) = 264$$
$$2x + 150 - x = 264$$
$$x = 264 - 150$$
$$x = 114$$

Thus, there are 114 packages weighing 2 kg each on the truck.

Another way to solve this problem is to test each of the answer choices. Note that if, for example, the number of packages weighing 2 kg each is 36 (answer choice [A]), then the number of packages weighing 1 kg each will be $(150 - 36) = 114$. Testing the answer choices yields:

(A)     $(36)(2) + (150 - 36) (1) = 72 + 114 = 186$
        (wrong)

(B)     $(52)(2) + (150 - 52)(1) = 104 + 98 = 202$
        (wrong)

(C)     $(88)(2) + (150-88)(1) = 176 + 62 = 238$
        (wrong)

(E)     $(114)(2) + (150 - 114) (1) = 228 + 36 = 264$
        (correct)

# Questions

---

**Q-16**

A wheel with a diameter of 3 feet makes a revolution every 2 minutes. How many feet will the wheel travel in 30 minutes?

(A)  $3\pi$

(B)  $6\pi$

(C)  $45\pi$

(D)  $30\pi$

*Your Answer* _____

---

**Q-17**

A waitress's income consists of her salary and tips. Her salary is $150 a week. During one week that included a holiday, her tips were ⁵⁄₄ of her salary. What fraction of her income for the week came from tips?

(A)  $\frac{5}{8}$

(B)  $\frac{5}{4}$

(C)  $\frac{4}{9}$

(D)  $\frac{5}{9}$

*Your Answer* _____

# Correct Answers

## A–16

**(C)**    The wheel will travel 1 revolution (2 minutes) $C = \pi d = \pi(3) = 3\pi$ feet. In 30 minutes it will travel $^{30}/_2 = 15$ revolutions. Thus, the wheel will travel $15(3\pi) = 45\pi$ feet in 30 minutes.

## A–17

**(D)**    Note that tips for the week were $\left(\frac{5}{4}\right)(150)$. Thus, the total income was as follows:

$$(1)(150) + \left(\frac{5}{4}\right)(150) = \left(\frac{4}{4}\right)(150) + \left(\frac{5}{4}\right)(150)$$

$$= \left(\frac{9}{4}\right)(150)$$

Therefore, tips made up $\dfrac{\left(\frac{5}{4}\right)(150)}{\left(\frac{9}{4}\right)(150)} = \dfrac{\frac{5}{4}}{\frac{9}{4}} = \frac{5}{9}$ of her income.

Notice that one could figure out the total income in order to arrive at the solution; however, this would be a waste of time.

# Questions

---

**Q–18**

Find the median for the following set of numbers:
16, 22, 18, 21, 17, 21, 19, and 21.

(A)  21.0

(B)  20.0

(C)  22.0

(D)  19.0

*Your Answer* _____

_____

---

**Q–19**

The number missing in the series, 2, 6, 12, 20, $x$,
42, 56,

(A)  36.

(B)  24.

(C)  30.

(D)  38.

*Your Answer* _____

_____

# Correct Answers

## A–18

**(B)** The median is the middle value in a set of an odd number of values or the average of the two middle values of a set of an even number of values. Rearrange the set from smallest to largest values:

16, 17, 18, 19, 21, 21, 21, and 22.

$$\frac{(19 + 21)}{2} = 20.$$

## A–19

**(C)** The difference between the first two numbers is $4(6 - 2)$; the difference between the second and third numbers is $6(12 - 6)$, which is two more than the first difference; the difference between the third and fourth numbers is $8(20 - 12)$, which is two more than the second difference; the difference between the fourth and fifth numbers is $10(x - 20)$. Thus, the value of $x$ is given by $x - 20 = 10$. Solving for $x$ yields 30. So, the correct answer choice is (C).

# Questions

---

**Q–20**

What is the factorization of $x^2 + ax - 2x - 2a$?

(A)  $(x + 2)(x - a)$

(B)  $(x - 2)(x + a)$

(C)  $(x + 2)(x + a)$

(D)  $(x - 2)(x - a)$

---

*Your Answer* _____

_____

*Some pharmacists specialize in specific drug therapy areas, such as intravenous nutrition support, oncology, nuclear pharmacy, geriatric pharmacy and psychopharmacotherapy. (U.S. Bureau of Labor Statistics)*

# Correct Answers

## A–20

**(B)** First, group the expression and then find the monomial factor for each group as follows:

$$(x^2 + ax) + (-2x - 2a) = x(x + a) + (-2)(x + a).$$

Then, the final factorization is formed by using $(x + a)$ and $(x - 2)$. So,

$$x^2 + ax - 2x - 2a = (x - 2)(x + a).$$

Notice that multiplying these two factors together will yield the original algebraic expression. So, (B) is the correct answer choice. The other answer choices are incorrect because when the factors are multiplied together in each case, the results do not yield the original algebraic expression.

# Questions

**Q–21**

Jim is twice as old as Susan. If Jim were 4 years younger and Susan were 3 years older, their ages would differ by 12 years. What is the sum of their ages?

(A)  19

(B)  42

(C)  56

(D)  57

*Your Answer* _____

_____

*About 19% of pharmacists worked part time in 2002. (U.S. Bureau of Labor Statistics)*

# Correct Answers

## A–21

**(D)** The easiest way to determine the result for this problem is to represent the unknown ages, set up an equation, and solve it. Begin by letting $x =$ age of Susan now. Then, $2x =$ the age of Jim now. The next step is to represent Jim's age 4 years ago and Susan's age 3 years from now. Thus, $2x - 4 =$ Jim's age 4 years ago. Then, $x + 3 =$ Susan's age 3 years from now. Finally, an equation can be set up by noting that the age represented by $2x - 4$ differs from the age represented by $x + 2$ by 12 years. So, the equation is given by the following:

$$(2x - 4) - (x + 3) = 12.$$

Solving for $x$ one gets

$$2x - 4 - x - 3 = 12$$
$$x - 7 = 12$$
$$x - 7 + 7 = 12 + 7$$
$$x = 19, \text{ Susan's age now.}$$
$$2x = 38, \text{ Jim's age now.}$$

The sum of their ages (19 + 38) is 57.

# Questions

**Q–22**

Joe and Jim together have 14 marbles. Jim and Tim together have 10 marbles. Joe and Tim together have 12 marbles. What is the maximum number of marbles that Tim may have?

(A)  4

(B)  8

(C)  9

(D)  10

*Your Answer* _____

_____

**Q–23**

Tom received 89, 94, 86, and 96 on the first four algebra tests. What grade must he receive on his last test to have an average of 92?

(A)  92

(B)  94

(C)  91

(D)  95

*Your Answer* _____

_____

# Correct Answers

**A–22**

**(A)** Let $x$ = Joe's marbles, $y$ = Jim's marbles, and $z$ = Tim's marbles. It is given that

$x + y = 14$   (1)
$y + z = 10$   (2)
$x + z = 12$   (3)

Solve equation (2) for $y$ and equation (3) for $x$. Then substitute their values in equation (1) and solve for $z$.

$y + z = 10 \Rightarrow y + z - z = 10 - z \Rightarrow y = 10 - z$

and

$x + z = 12 \Rightarrow x + z - z = 12 - z \Rightarrow x = 12 - z$

Thus,

$$x + y = 14 \Rightarrow (12 - z) + (10 - z) = 14$$
$$-2z + 22 = 14$$
$$-2z + 22 - 22 = 14 - 22$$
$$-2z = -8$$
$$z = 4, \text{ Tim's marbles.}$$

**A–23**

**(D)** Let $x$ = the grade of Tom's last test

$$\frac{89 + 94 + 86 + 96 + x}{5} = 92$$
$$89 + 94 + 86 + 96 + x = 92(5)$$
$$x = 460 - 365$$
$$x = 95$$

# Questions

**Q–24**

$(5x – 3)(4x – 6) =$

(A)  $20x^2 – 42x + 18$

(B)  $20x^2 – 18$

(C)  $20x^2 – 12x – 18$

(D)  $30x^2 – 18$

*Your Answer* _____

**Q–25**

If the measures of the three angles of a triangle are $(3x + 15)°$, $(5x – 15)°$, and $(2x + 30)°$, what is the measure of each angle?

(A)  $75°$

(B)  $60°$

(C)  $45°$

(D)  $25°$

*Your Answer* _____

# Correct Answers

## A–24

**(A)**
$$(5x - 3)(4x - 6) = 5x(4x - 6) - 3(4x - 6)$$
$$= 20x^2 - 30x - 12x + 18$$
$$= 20x^2 - 42x + 18$$

## A–25

**(B)**     This problem can be solved easily by simply using the fact that the sum of the measures of the three interior angles of a triangle is 180°. Thus,

$$(3x + 15) + (5x - 15) + (2x + 30) = 180$$
$$3x + 5x + 2x + 30 = 180$$
$$10x = 180 - 30$$
$$10x = 150$$
$$x = 15$$

This gives us the measure of the

first angle = $(3x + 15)° = (3 \times 15 + 15)° = 60°$

second angle = $(5x - 15)° = (5 \times 15 - 15)° = 60°$

third angle = $(2x + 30)° = (2 \times 15 + 30)° = 60°$

# Questions

Which of the following equations can be used to find a number $x$, if the difference between the square of this number and 21 is the same as the product of 4 times the number?

(A)  $x - 21 = 4x$

(B)  $x^2 - 21 = 4x$

(C)  $x^2 = 21 - 4x$

(D)  $x + 4x^2 = 21$

*Your Answer* _____

_____

*Most full-time salaried pharmacists work about 40 hours a week. (U.S. Bureau of Labor Statistics)*

# Correct Answers

**(B)**     This problem can be easily solved by simply translating the English statements into algebraic expressions. "The difference between the square of this number, $x$, and 21" can be written as $x^2 - 21$. "Is the same as" means equal (=). "The product of 4 times the number" can be written as $4x$. Thus, the information in this problem can be written as follows:

$$x^2 - 21 = 4x.$$

Answer choice (A) is eliminated because the left-hand side of the equation, $x - 21 = 4x$, gives the difference between the number $x$ and 21 and not the difference between the square of the number x and 21. Answer choice (C) is eliminated because it states that the difference between 21 and 4 times the number x is equal to the square of the number $x$. In addition, neither of the equations $x + 4x^2 = 21$ and $x^2 + 21 = 4x$ is equivalent to the equation $x^2 - 21 = 4x$, which was obtained by translating the English statements in this problem into algebraic expressions. Thus, answer choice (D) is also eliminated leaving answer choice (B) as the only correct choice.

# Questions

**Q–27**

Emile receives a flat weekly salary of $240 plus 12% commission of the total volume of all sales he makes. What must his dollar volume be in a week if he is to make a total weekly salary of $540?

(A) $2,880

(B) $3,600

(C) $6,480

(D) $2,500

*Your Answer* _____

*In 2002, about 62% of pharmacists worked in community pharmacies that are either independently owned or part of a drugstore chain, grocery store, department store, or mass merchandiser. (U.S. Bureau of Labor Statistics)*

# Correct Answers

## A–27

**(D)**     Since we do not know Emile's dollar volume during the week in question, we can assign this amount the value of $x$.

Now, Emile's total salary of $540 can be divided into two parts; one part is his flat salary of $240, and the other part is his salary from commissions, which amounts to $540 – $240 = $300. This part of his salary is equal to 12% of his dollar volume, $x$. Thus, 12% of $x$ = $300. This means

$$(0.12)x = 300$$
$$x = 300/0.12 = \$2,500.$$

Another way to attack this problem is to test each answer choice as follows:

(A) $(0.12)(\$2,800) = \$345.60 \neq \$300$     (wrong)
(B) $(0.12)(\$3,600) = \$432 \neq \$300$     (wrong)
(C) $(0.12)(\$6,400) = \$768 \neq \$300$     (wrong)
(D) $(0.12)(\$2,500) = \$300$     (correct)

# Questions

**Q–28**

In the Carco Auto Factory, robots assemble cars. If 3 robots assemble 17 cars in 10 minutes, how many cars can 14 robots assemble in 45 minutes if all robots work at the same rate all the time?

(A) 357

(B) 340

(C) 705

(D) 150

*Your Answer* _____

_____

*In 2002, about 22% of salaried pharmacists worked in hospitals. (U.S. Bureau of Labor Statistics)*

# Correct Answers

## A-28

**(A)**     One method for attacking this problem is to let $x$ be the number of cars that 14 robots can assemble in 45 minutes. Because the robots work at the same rate all the time, we can express this rate by using the information that 3 robots can assemble 17 cars in 10 minutes.

Now, if 3 robots can assemble 17 cars in 10 minutes, then 3 robots can assemble $^{17}/_{10}$ cars in 1 minute. Consequently, 1 robot assembles $^{1}/_{3}(^{17}/_{10})$ or $^{17}/_{30}$ of a car in 1 minute.

Similarly, if 14 robots assemble $x$ cars in 45 minutes, then the 14 robots assemble $^{x}/_{45}$ cars in 1 minute. Thus, 1 robot assembles $^{1}/_{14}(^{x}/_{45})$, or $^{x}/_{45(45)}$ of a car in 1 minute. Because the rates are equal, we have the proportion

$$30x = (630)(17)$$
$$= 10,710$$
$$x = \frac{10,710}{30} = 357.$$

Solving this proportion for $x$ yields

$$\frac{x}{14(45)} = \frac{17}{30}$$

$$\frac{x}{630} = \frac{17}{30}$$

# Questions

**Q–29**

What is the median of the following group of scores?
27, 27, 26, 26, 26, 26, 18, 13, 36, 36, 30, 30, 30, 27, 29

(A)  30

(B)  26

(C)  25.4

(D)  27

*Your Answer* _____

**Q–30**

The solution of the equation $4 - 5(2y + 4) = 4$ is

(A)  $-\frac{2}{5}$.

(B)  8.

(C)  4.

(D)  –2.

*Your Answer* _____

# Correct Answers

## A–29

**(D)** Choices (A), (B), and (C) are incorrect. This is not the median. The median is the middle value in a sequence of numbers when the numbers are arranged in ascending or descending order. (D) is correct. The median is the middle value in a sequence of numbers when the numbers are arranged in ascending or descending order. When this is done 27 is the median value.

## A–30

**(D)** Choices (A), (B), and (C) are incorrect. Try substituting the answer in the original equation. Simplify the equation. Remember that an equation can be multiplied, divided, subtracted, or added by the same number on both sides of the equal sign to help reduce it. (D) is correct.

$4 - 5(2y + 4) = 4$

$4 - 10y - 20 = 4$     On the left-hand side of the equation apply the distributive property.

$4 - 20 - 4 = 10y$     Add $10y$ and $-4$ to both sides of the equation to isolate the terms with $y$.

$-20 = 10y$

$-2 = y$     Divide both sides by 10.

# Questions

**Q–31**

I went to Lucky Duck Casino and in the first game I lost one-third of my money, in the second game I lost half of the rest. If I still have $1,000, how much money did I have when I arrived at the Casino?

(A)  $1,000

(B)  $2,000

(C)  $3,000

(D)  $6,000

*Your Answer* _____

_____

*An aging population means more pharmacy services are required in nursing homes, assisted living facilities, and home care settings, where the most rapid job growth among pharmacists is expected. (U.S. Bureau of Labor Statistics)*

# Correct Answers

## A-31

(C)     (A) is incorrect. This answer is too small since this is the same amount that I had at the end and I had lost some in two games. Let $x$ = the amount of money that I arrived with at the casino. Then set up an equation that follows the given problem. Choices (B) and (D) are also incorrect. Read the problem carefully and make sure that the money lost is subtracted from the equation. Let $x$ = the amount of money that I arrived with at the casino. Then set up an equation that follows the given problem. (C) is correct. Let $x$ = the amount of money that I arrived with at the casino. Then set up an equation that follows the given problem. As follows:

$$x - \frac{1}{3}x = \frac{2}{3}x, \text{ the amount of money left}$$
after the first game.

$$\frac{2}{3}x - \frac{1}{2}\left(\frac{2}{3}x\right) = \frac{1}{3}x, \text{ the amount of money left at}$$
the end.

$$\$1,000 = \frac{1}{3}x, \text{ information given in the}$$
problem.

$$x = \$3,000, \text{ the amount of money}$$
at the start.

# Questions

**Q–32**

Tickets for a particular concert cost $5 each if purchased in advance and $7 each if bought at the box office on the day of the concert. For this particular concert, 1,200 tickets were sold and the receipts were $6,700. How many tickets were bought at the box office on the day of the concert?

(A)  500

(B)  700

(C)  600

(D)  350

*Your Answer* _____

_____

*Median annual wage and salary earnings of pharmacists in 2002 were $77,050. (U.S. Bureau of Labor Statistics)*

# Correct Answers

## A–32

**(D)**  Choices (A), (B), and (C) are incorrect. Create an algebraic formula to find the number of tickets bought at the box office. Recheck the solution with the given information. (D) is correct. Let $x$ be the number of tickets bought at the box office. Then the number of tickets purchased in advance equals $(1,200 - x)$. Set up the formula with the rest of the information as follows:

$$5(1,200 - x) + 7x = 6,700$$
$$6,000 - 5x + 7x = 6,700$$
$$2x = 6,700 - 6,000$$
$$2x = 700$$
$$x = 350$$

# Questions

**Q–33**

If $2a + 2b = 1$, and $6a - 2b = 5$, which of the following statements is true?

(A)   $3a - b = 5$

(B)   $a + b > 3a - b$

(C)   $a + b = -2$

(D)   $a + b < 3a - b$

*Your Answer* _____

_____

*Pharmacists usually work in clean, well-lit, and well-ventilated areas, and spend most of their workday on their feet. (U.S. Bureau of Labor Statistics)*

# Correct Answers

## A–33

**(D)** Choices (A), (B), and (C) are incorrect. Rewrite the equations and compare to the statements given. Be careful when simplifying. (D) is correct. One method to solve this problem is to rewrite the equations and compare the results.

$$2a + 2b = 1 \qquad \text{and} \qquad 6a - 2b = 5$$
$$2(a + b) = 1 \qquad\qquad\qquad 2(3a - b) = 5$$
$$(a + b) = \tfrac{1}{2} \qquad\qquad\qquad (3a - b) = \tfrac{5}{2}$$

Another method to solve this problem is to solve for a and b:

$$2a + 2b = 1$$
$$6a + 2b = 5$$
$$8a + 0b = 6$$
$$8a = 6$$

$$a = \frac{6}{8} = \frac{3}{4}$$

$$2\left(\frac{3}{4}\right) + 2b = 1$$

$$2b = 1 - 1\frac{1}{2}$$

$$2b = -\frac{1}{2}$$

$$b = -\frac{1}{4}$$

These numbers can then be substituted into the equation given.

# Questions

**Q–34**

If $6x + 12 = 5$, then the value of $(x + 2)$ is

(A) $-19/6$

(B) $-1\,1/6$

(C) $5/6$

(D) $3\,1/6$

*Your Answer* _____

**Q–35**

The most economical price among the following prices is

(A) 10 oz. for 16¢.

(B) 2 oz. for 3¢.

(C) 4 oz. for 7¢.

(D) 20 oz. for 34¢.

*Your Answer* _____

# Correct Answers

## A–34

**(C)**  (C) is correct. One way to solve the problem is to find the value of $x$, then substitute it into $(x + 2)$. Another way is to factor the equation as

$$6x + 12 = 5$$
$$6(x + 2) = 5$$
$$(x + 2) = \tfrac{5}{6}.$$

This gives the answer directly.

Choices (A), (B), and (D) are incorrect. Solve for $x$ and find the value of $(x + 2)$.

## A–35

**(B)**  Choices (A), (C), and (D) are incorrect. Find the price per ounce for the given prices. Compare the prices. (B) is correct. Divide each price by the number of ounces in each price to obtain the following prices per ounce for the given prices:

$$\frac{16}{10} \quad \frac{3}{2} \quad \frac{7}{4} \quad \frac{34}{20} \quad \frac{13}{8}$$

Then find the least common denominator, 40, to be able to compare the prices.

$$\frac{64}{40} \quad \frac{60}{40} \quad \frac{70}{40} \quad \frac{68}{40} \quad \frac{65}{40}$$

Since the smallest fraction is $^{60}\!/_{40}$, it follows that the most economical price among the given prices is 2 oz. for 3¢.

# Questions

---

**Q–36**

If *n* is an integer, which of the following represents an odd number?

(A)  $2n + 3$

(B)  $2n$

(C)  $2n + 2$

(D)  $3n$

---

*Your Answer* _____

---

*In a November 2003 Gallup Poll, pharmacists' honesty and ethics were rated as "high" or "very high" by 67% of Americans, surpassed in ranking only by nurses. (U.S. Bureau of Labor Statistics)*

# Correct Answers

## A–36

**(A)** (A) is correct. $n$ can be an odd number or an even number. $2n$ is an even number and $2n + 3$ is odd because even + odd = odd. (B) is incorrect. $n$ can be an odd number or an even number. $2n$ is always an even number. (C) is incorrect. $n$ can be an odd number or an even number. $2n$ is an even number and $2n + 2$ is even because even + even = even. (D) is incorrect. n can be an odd number or an even number. When $n$ is odd, $3n$ is odd (odd $\times$ odd = odd). But this is not true if $n$ is an even number, since $3n$ is even (odd $\times$ even = even).

# Questions

### Q–37

A postal truck leaves its station and heads for Chicago, averaging 40 mph. An error in the mailing schedule is spotted and 24 minutes after the truck leaves, a car is sent to overtake the truck. If the car averages 50 mph, how long will it take to catch the postal truck?

(A)  2.6 hours

(B)  3 hours

(C)  2 hours

(D)  1.6 hours

*Your Answer* _____

_____

*In 1546, the first pharmacopoeia (list of drugs and their preparation) appeared in Germany. (Encyclopedia Britannica, 2005.)*

# Correct Answers

**(D)** Choices (A), (B), and (C) are incorrect. Use Distance = Rate × Time and set up an algebraic equation to solve for the time. Let $t$ be the time, in hours, it takes the car to catch up with the postal truck. Then the time of travel of the truck should be $(t + {}^{24}/_{60})$ hours. (D) is correct. Use Distance = Rate × Time and set up an algebraic equation to solve for the time. Let $t$ be the time, in hours, it takes the car to catch up with the postal truck. Then the time of travel of the truck should be $(t + {}^{24}/_{60})$ hours.

Using the distance formula:

Truck: $\quad d_t = 40(t + 0.4)$
$$= 40t + 16$$

Car: $\quad d_c = 50t$

But the distance traveled by the truck and car will be the same, so

$$d_t = d_c$$
$$40t + 16 = 50t$$
$$16 = 10t$$
$$t = 1.6$$

Thus, it takes the car 1.6 hours to catch up with the postal truck.

# Questions

---

**Q–38**

If $a \times b = 6a - 2bx$ and $9 \times 6 = 6$, then $x =$

(A) 2.

(B) 0.

(C) 1.

(D) 4.

Your Answer _____

---

**Q–39**

In a class of 40 students, 30 speak French and 20 speak German. What is the lowest possible number of students who speak both languages?

(A) 5

(B) 20

(C) 15

(D) 10

Your Answer _____

# Correct Answers

## A–38

**(D)** Choices (A), (B), and (C) are incorrect. Insert the values of $a$ and $b$ into the expression to solve for $x$. The value of $a = 9$ and the value of $b = 6$. (D) is correct. If $a \times b = 6a - 2bx$ then

$$9 \times 6 = (6 \times 9) - [2 \times 6 \times (x)] = 54 - 12x$$

and $\quad 9 \times 6 = 6$

so $\quad 54 - 12x = 6$

$$12x = 54 - 6 = 48$$

$$x = 4$$

## A–39

**(D)** Choices (A), (B), and (C) are incorrect. Set up an algebraic problem with $x =$ the students who speak both French and German. Total class = students who speak only French + students who speak only German + students who speak both French and German. (D) is correct. Set up an algebraic problem with $x =$ the students who speak both French and German.

Therefore, the number of students who speak only French $= 30 - x$

and the number of students who speak only German $= 20 - x$

Total class = students who speak only French + students who speak only German + students who speak both French and German.

# Questions

**Q–40**

A man who is 40 years old has three sons, ages 6, 3, and 1. In how many years will the combined age of his three sons equal 80% of his age?

(A)  5

(B)  10

(C)  15

(D)  20

*Your Answer* _____

_____

**Q–41**

One wall being made entirely of bricks is 40 percent built. If we need 1,200 more bricks to complete the wall, how many bricks will the wall have?

(A)  1,500

(B)  1,800

(C)  2,000

(D)  2,400

*Your Answer* _____

_____

# Correct Answers

## A–40

**(B)**   Choices (A), (C), and (D) are incorrect. Let $n$ = the number of years until the combined age of the sons equals 80% of the father's age. Remember to add $n$ to each age. (B) is correct. Let $n$ = the number of years until the combined age of the sons equals 80% of the father's age.

Their ages will be

$$\text{father} = 40 + n$$
$$\text{son \#1} = 6 + n$$
$$\text{son \#2} = 3 + n$$
$$\text{son \#3} = 1 + n.$$

Therefore,

$$(6 + n) + (3 + n) + (1 + n) = .80(40 + n)$$
$$10 + 3n = 32 + .8n$$
$$2.2n = 22$$
$$n = 10$$

## A–41

**(C)**   If 40% of the bricks is already put in the wall and we need 1,200 more, then 1,200 bricks = 60% of the total bricks. Letting

$$x = \text{total bricks},$$
$$1,200 = \frac{60x}{100}$$
$$x = \frac{12,000}{6}$$
$$x = 2,000$$

# Questions

---

**Q–42**

What percent of 260 is 13?

(A) .05%

(B) 5%

(C) 50%

(D) .5%

---

*Your Answer* _____

---

**Q–43**

Which of the following numbers is the smallest?

(A) –.6

(B) –.66

(C) $\frac{-2}{3}$

(D) $\frac{-666}{1,000}$

---

*Your Answer* _____

---

# Correct Answers

**A–42**

**(B)**   In order to find what percent of 260 is 13, one needs only to form the following equation:

$$x\%(260) = 13$$

$$\frac{x(260)}{100} = 13$$

$$260x = 13(100)$$

$$x = \frac{1,300}{260} = 5\%$$

**A–43**

**(C)**   If we express all the numbers as decimals, we have

(A) $-.6000$

(B) $-.6600$

(C) $-.\overline{6} = -.6666\ldots$

(D) $-.6660$

# Questions

---

**Q–44**

Which of the following has the smallest value?

(A) $\dfrac{1}{0.2}$

(B) $\dfrac{0.1}{2}$

(C) $\dfrac{0.2}{1}$

(D) $\dfrac{0.2}{0.1}$

*Your Answer* _____

_____

---

**Q–45**

What is the smallest positive number that leaves a remainder of 2 when the number is divided by 3, 4, or 5?

(A) 22

(B) 42

(C) 62

(D) 122

*Your Answer* _____

_____

# Correct Answers

**(B)**

Note that $\frac{.1}{2} = \frac{.1 \times 10}{2 \times 10} = \frac{1}{20}$ for response (B).

For choice (A), $\frac{1}{.2} = \frac{1 \times 10}{.2 \times 10} = \frac{10}{2} = 5$

which is larger than $\frac{1}{20}$.

For choice (C), $\frac{.2}{1} = \frac{.2 \times 10}{1 \times 10} = \frac{2}{10} = \frac{1}{5}$

which is larger than $\frac{1}{20}$.

For choice (D), $\frac{.2}{.1} = \frac{.2 \times 10}{.1 \times 10} = \frac{2}{1} = 2$

which is larger than $\frac{1}{20}$.

---

**A–45**

**(C)**   First find the least common multiple (LCM) of 3, 4, and 5, which is simply $3 \times 4 \times 5 = 60$. Since 3 divides into 60, 4 divides into 60, and 5 divides into 60, then one needs only to add 2 to 60 in order to guarantee that the remainder in each case will be 2 when 3, 4, and 5, respectively, are divided into 62.

# Questions

---

**Q–46**

Suppose the average of two numbers is $WX$. If the first number is $X$, what is the other number?

(A) $WX - X$

(B) $2WX - W$

(C) $W$

(D) $2WX - X$

---

*Your Answer* _____

_____

---

**Q–47**

Three times the first of three consecutive odd integers is three more than twice the third. What is the second of the three consecutive odd integers?

(A) 7

(B) 9

(C) 11

(D) 13

---

*Your Answer* _____

_____

# Correct Answers

## A–46

**(D)**  Since $X$ is the first number, then let $y$ represent the second number in the average of two numbers. Thus, from what is given in the problem, one can write:

$$\frac{X+y}{2} = WX,$$

the average. Solving for $y$ gives the other number. Hence,

$$X + y = 2WX$$
$$y = 2WX - X,$$

the second number.

## A–47

**(D)**  Let $x$ = the first odd integer, $x + 2$ = the second consecutive odd integer, and $x + 4$ = the third consecutive odd integer. Then, the following equation can be written based on what is given in the problem. Solve the equation.

$$3x = 2(x + 4) + 3$$
$$3x = 2x + 8 + 3$$
$$3x - 2x = 11$$
$$x = 11,$$

the first odd integer.

So, the second consecutive odd integer is $x + 2 = 11 + 2 = 13$.

# Questions

**Q–48**

Jay and his brother Ray own a janitorial service. Jay can do a cleaning job alone in 5 hours and Ray can do the same job in 4 hours. How long will it take them to do the cleaning job together?

(A)   5 hours

(B)   1 hour

(C)   4 hours

(D)   $2\frac{2}{9}$ hours

*Your Answer* _____

_____

*Among the earliest modern pharmaceuticals were anesthetics such as morphine (1804); ether (1842); chloroform (1847); and cocaine (1860). (Encyclopedia Britannica, 2005.)*

# Correct Answers

**(D)**     The traditional way to solve this problem is to set up and solve an equation. Consider what part of the job could be done in 1 hour by each person. Thus, Jay could do $\frac{1}{5}$ of the job in 1 hour and Ray could do $\frac{1}{4}$ of the job in the same amount of time. What is unknown is the part of the job they could do together in 1 hour, which can be represented by $\frac{1}{x}$. The $x$ represents the amount of time the brothers can do the job together.

The sum of the amount of the job each brother can do in 1 hour equals the amount of the job they can do together in 1 hour. Hence, the equation is given by:

$$\frac{1}{5} + \frac{1}{4} = \frac{1}{x}$$

Solving for $x$ you calculate as follows:

$$\frac{1}{5} \times \frac{4}{4} + \frac{1}{4} \times \frac{5}{5} = \frac{1}{x}$$

Side Notes

$$\frac{4}{20} + \frac{5}{20} = \frac{1}{x}$$   1) Find the LCD.
2) Add like fractions on left side of the equation.

$$\frac{9}{20} = \frac{1}{x}$$   3) Cross multiply.

$$9x = 20$$

$$\frac{9x}{9} = \frac{20}{9}$$   4) Divide by 9 on both sides of the equation.

$$x = \frac{20}{9} \text{ or } 2\frac{2}{9} \text{ hours.}$$

To understand why answer choices (A) and (C) are incorrect one should consider another approach to the solution of the problem. The approach is referred to as a "logical" or "reasonable" method.

**(Continued)**

# Correct Answers

## A–48 (Continued)

It is logical to believe that since Ray can complete the job in 4 hours by himself, he should finish the job in less than 4 hours with the help of his brother. Hence, answer choice (A) cannot be correct. Finally, answer choice (B), 1 hour, is also incorrect. To see this one needs to assume for a moment that Jay could also do the cleaning job in 4 hours rather than the required 5 hours. Then together the brothers should be able to complete the job in one-half of the time or just 2 hours. Thus, it is logical that answer choice (B) does not represent enough time for both to do the job using the assumption.

# Questions

**Q–49**

A box contains 6 red marbles and 4 blue marbles. What is the probability that if 2 marbles are simultaneously drawn from the box, both will be red?

(A)  $\frac{2}{3}$

(B)  $\frac{1}{3}$

(C)  $\frac{1}{2}$

(D)  $\frac{1}{5}$

*Your Answer* _____

**Q–50**

If $x - (4x - 8) + 9 + (6x - 8) = 9 - x + 24$, then $x =$

(A)  4.

(B)  2.

(C)  8.

(D)  6.

*Your Answer* _____

171

# Correct Answers

## A–49

**(B)** First find the number of different ways of drawing two marbles from the box. Use the permutation formula as follows:

$$P(10,2) = \frac{10!}{(10-2)!} = \frac{10!}{8!} = \frac{10(9)(8!)}{8!}$$

$$= 10(9) = 90 \text{ ways.}$$

Then find the number of different ways of drawing two red marbles from the box. Use the permutation formula as follows:

$$P(6, 2) = \frac{6!}{(6-2)!} = \frac{6!}{4!} = \frac{6(5)\,(4!)}{4!}$$

$$= 6(5) = 30 \text{ ways.}$$

Finally, to get the probability, form a ratio of P(6, 2) to P(10, 2). One gets the following:

The probability of drawing two red marbles from the box = $^{30}\!/_{90} = \frac{1}{3}$.

## A–50

**(D)** The most direct way to solve this problem is to perform the indicated operations in the given equation and solve it for $x$. Thus,

$$x - (4x - 8) + 9 + (6x - 8) = 9 - x + 24$$
$$x - 4x + 8 + 9 + 6x - 8 = 9 - x + 24$$
$$(x + 6x - 4x) + (8 - 8 + 9) = (9 + 24) - x$$
$$(7x - 4x) + 9 = 33 - x$$
$$3x + x = 33 - 9$$
$$4x = 24$$
$$x = 6$$

# Questions

---

**Q–51**

If $x$ and $y$ are two different real numbers and $xz = yz$, then what is the value of $z$?

(A) $x - y$

(B) 1

(C) $\frac{x}{y}$

(D) 0

*Your Answer* _____

---

**Q–52**

If it takes $s$ sacks of grain to feed $c$ chickens, how many sacks of grain are needed to feed $k$ chickens?

(A) $\frac{ck}{s}$

(B) $\frac{k}{cs}$

(C) $\frac{cs}{k}$

(D) $\frac{sk}{c}$

*Your Answer* _____

# Correct Answers

## A–51

**(D)** Observe that $xz = yz$ implies that $x = y$ if $z$ is not 0. But $x$ and $y$ are two different real numbers according to the original assumption in the problem. So, the only possible way for the equality to hold is for $z$ to have a value of 0.

## A–52

**(D)** Obviously, the more (less) chickens we have, the more (less) sacks of grain needed. Thus, this problem can be solved by using a direct proportion as follows:

$$\frac{\text{Number of sacks of feed } x}{\text{Number of chickens } x}$$

$$\frac{\text{Number of sacks of feed } y}{\text{Number of chickens } y}$$

Since it takes s sacks of grain to feed c chickens it follows that the correct proportion to use is

$$\frac{s}{c} = \frac{y}{k}$$

where $y$ is the required number of sacks of grain needed to feed $k$ chickens. Solving this proportion for $y$ in terms of $s$, $c$, and $k$ yields

$$\frac{s}{c} = \frac{y}{k}$$

$$cy = sk$$

$$y = \frac{sk}{c}$$

# Questions

**Q-53**

Tilda's car gets 34 miles per gallon of gasoline and Naomi's car gets 8 miles per gallon. When traveling from Washington, D.C. to Philadelphia, they both used a whole number of gallons of gasoline. How far is it from Washington, D.C. to Philadelphia?

(A)   21 miles

(B)   32 miles

(C)   68 miles

(D)   136 miles

*Your Answer* _____

_____

*Pharmacology is the study of the interaction of drugs with living systems.*
*It is an essential component in the study of pharmacy. (www.aacp.org)*

# Correct Answers

**(D)**    Tilda's car gets 34 miles per gallon of gasoline, and Naomi's car gets eight miles per gallon. Since each of them used a whole number of gallons of gasoline while traveling from Washington, D.C. to Philadelphia, it follows that the distance between the two cities must be a multiple of the two numbers 34 and 8.

The least common multiple of two (or more) whole numbers is the smallest non-zero whole number that is a multiple of both (all) of the numbers.

The least common multiple of 34 and 8 can be found by factoring each of 34 and 8 into their prime factors expressed in exponential form as follows:

$$8 = 2 \times 2 \times 2 = 2^3$$
$$34 = 2 \times 17$$

Then the least common common multiple of 34 and 8 is equal to $2^3 \times 17 = 136$.

Another procedure for finding the least common multiple of two whole numbers is called the intersection-of-sets method. First, find the set of all positive multiples of both numbers, then find the set of all common multiples of both numbers, and, finally, pick the least element in the set.

In this problem, multiples of 8 are

8, 16, 24, 32, 40, 48, 56, 64, 72, 80, 88, 96, 104, 112, 120, 128, 136, 144, 152, 160, 168, …

Multiples of 34 are

34, 68, 102, 136, 170, …

The intersection of the multiples of 8 and 34 is the set

{ 136, 272, 408, … }

Because 136 is the least common multiple of 34 and 8, the distance from Washington, D.C., to Philadelphia is 136 miles.

*(Continued)*

# Correct Answers

**A–53 (Continued)**

Yet another way to attack this problem is to check if any of the answer choices is a common multiple of both 34 and 8. Checking the answer choices given yields

(A)  21 is not a multiple of 34 or 8.
(B)  32 is a multiple of 8, but not of 34.
(C)  68 is a multiple of 34, but not of 8.
(D)  136 is a multiple of both 34 and 8.

# Questions

**Q–54**

If $m$ and $n$ are consecutive integers, and $m < n$, which one of the following statements is always true?

(A)  $n - m$ is even.

(B)  $m$ must be odd.

(C)  $m^2 + n^2$ is even.

(D)  $n^2 - m^2$ is odd.

*Your Answer* _____

_____

*Pharmoeconomics is a branch of economics that applies cost-benefit, cost-effectiveness, cost-minimization, and cost-utility analyses to compare the economics of different pharmaceutical products or to compare drug therapy to other treatments. (www.aacp.org)*

# Correct Answers

**(D)**    If $m$ and $n$ are consecutive integers, and $m < n$, it follows that

$$n = m + 1$$

Now, we can check each of the answer choices (A) through (D) as follows:

(A) $n - m = (m + 1) - m = m + 1 - m = 1$, which is odd. Thus, the statement in answer choice (A) is false.

(B) Since no specific information is given about the integer m, m can be an odd integer or an even integer. So, the statement in answer choice (B) is false.

(C) $m^2 + n^2 = m^2 + (m + 1)^2 = m^2 + m^2 + 2m + 1$
$$= 2m^2 + 2m + 1$$
$$= 2(m^2 + m) + 1$$

Since 2 times any integer (even or odd) yields an even integer, it follows that $2(m^2 + m)$ is an even integer, and hence, $2(m^2 + m) + 1$ is an odd integer. Hence, the statement in answer choice (C) is false.

(D) $n^2 - m^2 = (m + 1)^2 - m^2 = m^2 + 2m + 1 - m^2$
$$= 2m + 1$$

Again, since 2 times any integer (even or odd) yields an even integer, it follows that $2m$ is an even integer and $2m + 1$ is always an odd integer. Hence, the statement in answer choice (D) is correct.

# Questions

**Q–55**

Pete and Lynn travel on bicycles from the same place, in opposite directions, Pete traveling 4 mph faster than Lynn. After 5 hours, they are 120 miles apart. What is Lynn's rate of travel?

(A)   20 mph

(B)   9 mph

(C)   10 mph

(D)   12 mph

*Your Answer* _____

_____

*Pharmacogenomics is the science of understanding the correlation between an individual patient's genetic make-up (genotype) and their response to drug treatment. (www. aacp.org)*

# Correct Answers

**A–55**

**(D)** Certainly, the easiest and the most direct way to answer this question is to translate the given information into an algebraic equation in one unknown variable, then solve it for that variable.

In this problem, the distance traveled, the time of travel, and the rate of travel are involved. The relationship between these three quantities is given by

$$\text{Distance} = \text{Rate} \times \text{Time}$$

So, let $r$ be Lynn's rate of travel in miles per hour. Then Pete's rate of travel will be $(r + 4)$ miles per hour. After 5 hours of travel, the distance traveled by

Pete is $d_1 = \text{Rate} \times \text{Time}$
$$= (r + 4)\,5 = (5r + 20) \text{ miles}$$
Lynn is $d_2 = \text{Rate} \times \text{Time}$
$$= r(5) = 5r \text{ miles}$$

Since they are traveling in opposite directions, the total distance, $d$, traveled by both is equal to the sum of the distances traveled by both. A diagram, such as illustrated below, is helpful.

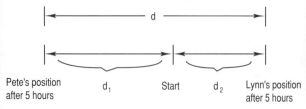

| Pete's position after 5 hours | $d_1$ | Start | $d_2$ | Lynn's position after 5 hours |

Now, total distance after 5 hours of travel is
$$d = d_1 + d_2$$
$$= (5r + 20) + 5r$$
$$= 5r + 20 + 5r$$
$$= 10r + 20$$
$$\frac{y}{x} = 10r + 20$$

# Questions

---

**Q–56**

$\frac{x+y}{y} = a; \frac{y}{x} =$

(A)  1

(B)  $a$

(C)  $\frac{1}{a}$

(D)  $\frac{1}{(a-1)}$

---

*Your Answer* _____

---

**Q–57**

I filled $^2/_3$ of my swimming pool with 1,800 ft$^3$ of water. What is the total capacity of my swimming pool?

(A)  2,400 ft$^3$

(B)  2,700 ft$^3$

(C)  3,000 ft$^3$

(D)  3,600 ft$^3$

---

*Your Answer* _____

# Correct Answers

## A–56

**(D)** What is an expression for $y$ as a function of $a$ if $\frac{x+y}{y} = a$ ?

$$\frac{x+y}{y} = a$$

$$\frac{x}{y} + \frac{y}{y} = a$$

$$\frac{x}{y} + 1 = a$$

$$\frac{x}{y} = a - 1$$

$$\frac{y}{x} = \frac{1}{a-1}$$

## A–57

**(B)** Let $x$ be the total capacity of the swimming pool, then $\frac{2}{3}x$

$$x = \frac{1{,}800 \times 3}{2} = 2{,}700 \text{ ft}^3$$

The correct answer is (B).

**Q-58**

One year ago Pat was three times his sister's age. Next year he will be only twice her age. How old will Pat be in five more years?

(A) 8

(B) 12

(C) 11

(D) 13

*Your Answer* _____

_____

**Q-59**

Which of the following integers is the square of an integer for every integer $x$?

(A) $x^2 + x$

(B) $x^2 + 1$

(C) $x^2 + 2x$

(D) $x^2 + 2x + 1$

*Your Answer* _____

_____

# Correct Answers

**A–58**

**(B)**

|  | Past | Present | Future |
|---|---|---|---|
| Pat | $x-1$ | $x$ | $x+1$ |
| Sister | $y-1$ | $y$ | $y+1$ |

One year ago…
$$x - 1 = 3(y - 1)$$
Next year…
$$x + 1 = 2(y + 1)$$
$$x = 7$$
$$y = 3$$
Pat will be 12 years old in five more years.

**A–59**

**(D)**  If $x = 1$ then response (B) is 2, response (A) is 2, and response (C) is 3. Thus, response (D) is the only response possible. Notice that by factoring the expression one gets
$$x^2 + 2x + 1 = (x + 1)(x + 1) = (x + 1)^2$$
which is the square of an integer for every integer $x$.

# Questions

**Q–60**

What is the value(s) of $x$ in the equation $(4x - 3)^2 = 4$?

(A) $\frac{5}{4}$

(B) $\frac{1}{4}$

(C) $\frac{5}{4}, \frac{1}{4}$

(D) $\frac{1}{2}, \frac{5}{2}$

*Your Answer* _____

_____

*Pharmaceutics is a discipline in the health sciences that is concerned with the design, development and rational use of medications for the treatment and prevention of disease. (www.aacp.org)*

# Correct Answers

**A–60**

**(C)**    Take the square root of both sides of the equation to form two first equations and solve each for $x$ as follows:

$$\sqrt{(4x-3)^2} = \sqrt{4}$$
$$4x - 3 = 2$$
$$4x = 2 + 3$$
$$x = \tfrac{5}{4}$$

and

$$\sqrt{(4x-3)^2} = -\sqrt{4}$$
$$4x - 3 = -2$$
$$4x = -2 + 3$$
$$x = \tfrac{1}{4}$$

Hence, the values of $x$ are $\tfrac{5}{4}$ and $\tfrac{1}{4}$, respectively, which is answer choice (C). Notice also that answer choices (A) and (B) each satisfy the original equation, but two values of $x$ are required since the equation is quadratic.

# Questions

**Q–61**

Simplify the following expression: $6 + 2(x - 4)$.

(A)  $4x - 16$

(B)  $2x - 14$

(C)  $2x - 2$

(D)  $-24x$

*Your Answer* _____

_____

**Q–62**

If six cans of beans cost $1.50, what is the price of eight cans of beans?

(A)  $.90

(B)  $1.00

(C)  $1.60

(D)  $2.00

*Your Answer* _____

_____

# Correct Answers

## A–61

**(C)** When simplifying algebraic expressions, always work from left to right. First perform all multiplications and divisions then once this is done, start again from the left and do all additions and subtractions.

**SUGGESTION:** It can be helpful to translate the algebraic statement to English. For example, $6 + 2(x - 4)$ is "six plus two times the quantity $x$ minus 4." The word "times" indicates multiplication, so we must first perform $2(x - 4)$ by using the distributive property $a(b - c) = ab - ac$:

$$6 + 2(x - 4) = 6 + 2 \times x - 2 \times 4 = 6 + 2x - 8.$$

Then we perform the subtraction to combine the terms 6 and 8:

$$6 + 2x - 8 = 2x + (6 - 8) = 2x - 2.$$

Note that we did not combine the $2x$ term with the other terms. This is because they are not like terms. Like terms are terms that have the same variables (with the same exponents). Since the terms 6 and 8 have no variable $x$, they are not like terms with $2x$.

## A–62

**(D)** Let $x$ be the cost of one can of beans. Then $6x$ is the cost of six cans of beans. So $6x = \$1.50$. Dividing both sides of the equation by 6, we get $x = \$.25$ and, hence, since $8x$ is the cost of eight cans of beans, we have

$$8x = 8 \times \$.25 = \$2.00.$$

# Questions

**Q–63**

Bonnie's average score on three tests is 71. Her first two test scores are 64 and 87. What is her score on test three?

(A)  62

(B)  71

(C)  74

(D)  151

*Your Answer* _____

_____

**Q–64**

A jar contains 20 balls. These balls are labeled 1 through 20. What is the probability that a ball chosen from the jar has a number on it which is divisible by 4?

(A)  $\frac{1}{20}$

(B)  $\frac{1}{5}$

(C)  $\frac{1}{4}$

(D)  4

*Your Answer* _____

_____

# Correct Answers

## A–63

**(A)** Let $t_1$, $t_2$, and $t_3$ represent Bonnie's scores on tests one, two, and three, respectively. Then the equation representing Bonnie's average score is

$$\frac{t_1 + t_2 + t_3}{3} = 71.$$

We know that $t_1 = 64$ and $t_2 = 87$. Substitute this information into the equation above:

$$\frac{64 + 87 + t_3}{3} = 71.$$

Combining 64 and 87 and then multiplying both sides of the equation by 3 gives us

$$3 \times \frac{151 + t_3}{3} = 3 \times 71$$

$$\text{or } 151 + t_3 = 213.$$

Now subtract 151 from both sides of the equation so that

$$t_3 = 213 - 151 = 62.$$

## A–64

**(C)** Note that the numbers 4, 8, 12, 16, and 20 are the only numbers from 1 through 20 that are divisible by 4. The probability that a ball chosen from the jar has a number on it that is divisible by 4 is given by

$$\frac{\textit{total number of balls with numbers that are divisible by 4}}{\textit{total number of possible outcomes}}$$

$$= \frac{5}{20} = \frac{1}{4}$$

# Questions

**Q–65**

If $2x^2 + 5x - 3 = 0$ and $x > 0$, then what is the value of $x$?

(A) $-\frac{1}{2}$

(B) $\frac{1}{2}$

(C) 1

(D) $\frac{3}{2}$

*Your Answer* _____

**Q–66**

How many odd prime numbers are there between 1 and 20?

(A) 7

(B) 8

(C) 9

(D) 10

*Your Answer* _____

# Correct Answers

### A-65

**(B)**    To solve the equation
$$2x^2 + 5x - 3 = 0,$$
we can factor the left side of the equation to get
$$(2x - 1)(x + 3) = 0.$$
Then use the following rule (this rule is sometimes called the Zero Product Property): If $a \times b = 0$, then either $a = 0$ or $b = 0$. Applying this to our problem gives us
$$2x - 1 = 0 \text{ or } x + 3 = 0.$$
Solve these two equations:
$$2x - 1 = 0 \rightarrow 2x = 1 \rightarrow x = \tfrac{1}{2}$$
$$x + 3 = 0 \rightarrow x = -3.$$

But $x > 0$, so $x = \tfrac{1}{2}$.

### A-66

**(A)**    A prime number is an integer that is greater than one and that has no integer divisors other than 1 and itself. So, the prime numbers between 1 and 20 (not including 1 and 20) are: 2, 3, 5, 7, 11, 13, 17, 19. But 2 is not an odd number, so the odd primes between 1 and 20 are: 3, 5, 7, 11, 13, 17, 19. Hence, there are seven odd primes between 1 and 20.

# Questions

---

**Q–67**

Solve the following inequality for $x$: $8 - 2x \leq 10$.

(A) $x \leq 1$

(B) $x \geq -9$

(C) $x \leq -1$

(D) $x \geq -1$

*Your Answer* _____

---

**Q–68**

The ratio of men to women at University X is 3:7. If there are 6,153 women at University X, how many men are at University X?

(A) 879

(B) 1,895

(C) 2,051

(D) 2,637

*Your Answer* _____

# Correct Answers

## A–67

**(D)**   To solve this inequality, we shall use the following rules:

> (i) If $a \leq b$ and $c$ is any number, then $a + c \leq b + c$.
>
> (ii) If $a \leq b$ and $c < 0$, then $ca \geq cb$.

The goal in solving inequalities, as in solving equalities, is to change the inequality so that the variable is isolated (i.e., by itself on one side). So, in the equation $8 - 2x \leq 10$, we want the term $-2x$ by itself. To achieve this, use rule (i) above and add $-8$ to both sides obtaining

$$8 - 2x + (-8) \leq 10 + (-8)$$

or $-2x \leq 2$.

Now we use rule (ii) and multiply both sides of the inequality by $-\frac{1}{2}$ as follows:

$$-\frac{1}{2} \times 2x \geq -\frac{1}{2} \times 2$$

or $x \geq -1$.

## A–68

**(D)**   Let $m$ = the number of men at University X. Then we have the following proportion:

$$\frac{3}{7} = \frac{m}{6,153}$$

To solve this equation, we isolate the variable (i.e., get $m$ by itself) by multiplying both sides of the equation by 6,153 to get

$$\left(\frac{3}{7}\right) 6,153 = \left(\frac{m}{6,153}\right) 6,153 \ or \ m = 2,637.$$

# Questions

---

**Q–69**

Linda bought a jacket on sale at a 25 percent discount. If she paid $54 for the jacket, what was the original price of the jacket?

(A)  $72.00

(B)  $67.50

(C)  $54.00

(D)  $40.50

---

*Your Answer* _____

_____

---

**Q–70**

Mrs. Wall has $300,000. She wishes to give each of her six children an equal amount of her money. Which of the following methods will result in the amount that each child is to receive?

(A)  $6 \times 300{,}000$

(B)  $6 \div 300{,}000$

(C)  $300{,}000 \div 6$

(D)  $6 - 300{,}000$

---

*Your Answer* _____

_____

# Correct Answers

(A)    Let $p$ be the original price of the jacket. Linda received a 25 percent discount so she paid 75 percent of the original price. Thus, 75 percent of p equals 54. Writing this in an equation, we get

$$0.75p = 54 \text{ or } p = 54.$$

To solve this equation, multiply both sides of the equation by the reciprocal of ¾ which is ⁴⁄₃. This will isolate the variable $p$.

$$\frac{4}{3}\left(\frac{3}{4}p\right) = \left(\frac{4}{3}\right)54 \text{ or } p = \frac{216}{3} = 72$$

A–70

(C)    Another way to phrase the second sentence is: She wants to divide her money equally among her six children. Therefore, each child is to receive $300{,}000 \div 6$.

# Questions

**Q–71**

Bob wants to bake some cupcakes. His recipe uses $2\frac{2}{3}$ cups of flour to produce 36 cupcakes. How many cups of flour should Bob use to bake 12 cupcakes?

(A)  $\frac{1}{3}$

(B)  $\frac{8}{9}$

(C)  1

(D)  $1\frac{2}{9}$

*Your Answer* _____

_____

*The islets of Langerhans are the irregularly shaped patches of endocrine tissue located within the pancreas of most vertebrates. (Encyclopedia Britannica, 2005.)*

# Correct Answers

**(B)**   Bob wants to bake 12 cupcakes. The recipe is for 36 cupcakes. Therefore, Bob wants to make $^{12}\!/_{36}$ or $^{1}\!/_{3}$ of the usual amount of cupcakes. Thus, Bob should use $^{1}\!/_{3}$ of the recipe's flour or

$$\left(\frac{1}{3}\right)\left(\frac{8}{3}\right) = \frac{8}{9}.$$

Note we used $^{8}\!/_{3}$ since $^{2}2/_{3} = ^{8}\!/_{3}$.

# Questions

**Q–72**

Ricky drove from Town A to Town B in 3 hours. His return trip from Town B to Town A took 5 hours because he drove 15 miles per hour slower on the return trip. How fast did Ricky drive on the trip from Town A to Town B?

(A)   25.5

(B)   32

(C)   37.5

(D)   45

*Your Answer* _____

*The human growth hormone, or somatotropin, stimulates growth of bone and tissue of the body by stimulating protein synthesis and breaking down fat to provide energy. (Encyclopedia Britannica, 2005.)*

# Correct Answers

**(C)**     Let $s_1$ and $s_2$ be Ricky's speed (rate) on the trip from A to B and the return trip from B to A, respectively. Then, since he drove 15 miles per hour slower on the return trip, $s_2 = s_1 - 15$. Recall that rate times time equals distance. So the distance from A to B is $(s_1)3 = 3s_1$ and the distance from B to A is

$$(s_2)5 = 5s_2 = 5(s_1 - 15) = 5s_1 - 75.$$

But the distance from Town A to Town B is the same as the distance from Town B to Town A, so we have the following equation:

$$3s_1 = 5s_1 - 75.$$

To solve this equation, first add 75 to both sides of the equation:

$$3s_1 + 75 = 5s_1 - 75 + 75 \text{ or } 3s_1 + 75 = 5s_1.$$

Now to isolate the variable, subtract $3s1$ from both sides:

$$3s_1 + 75 - 3s_1 = 5s_1 - 3s_1 \text{ or } 75 = 2s_1.$$

To finish the problem, divide both sides of the equation by 2:

$$s_1 = \frac{75}{2} = 37.5.$$

Thus, Ricky drove 37.5 miles per hour on his trip from Town A to Town B.

# Questions

---

**Q–73**

Simplify the following expression.

$$\frac{x^2 \times x^7}{x}$$

(A) $x^6$

(B) $x^7$

(C) $x^8$

(D) $x^{10}$

---

*Your Answer* _____

_____

---

**Q–74**

If $x = -3$, then find the value of $-x^2 + 2x$.

(A) $-15$

(B) $-3$

(C) $3$

(D) $6$

---

*Your Answer* _____

_____

# Correct Answers

## A–73

**(C)**  Recall the following Laws of Exponents:

$$x^p \times x^q = x^{p+q} \text{ and } \frac{x^p}{x^q} = x^{p-q}$$

So, $x^2 \times x^7 = x^{2+7} = x^9$. Hence,

$$\frac{x^2 \times x^7}{x} = \frac{x^9}{x^1} = x^{9-1} = x^8.$$

## A–74

**(A)**  If $x = -3$ then
$$-x^2 + 2x = -(-3)^2 + 2(-3) = -(9) + (-6) = -15.$$

# Questions

---

**Q–75**

If $a = b^3$ and $a = \frac{1}{8}$, what is the value of $b$?

(A) $\frac{1}{512}$

(B) $\frac{1}{8}$

(C) $\frac{3}{8}$

(D) $\frac{1}{2}$

---

*Your Answer* _____

_____

---

**Q–76**

Solve for $x$ in the following proportion.

$$\frac{12}{x-1} = \frac{5}{6}$$

(A) 14.6

(B) 15.4

(C) 16

(D) 16.6

---

*Your Answer* _____

_____

# Correct Answers

## A–75

**(D)** If $a = b^3$ and $a = \frac{1}{8}$, then substituting into the first equation we have

$$\frac{1}{8} = b^3 \text{ or } \left(\frac{1}{2}\right)^3 = b^3 \text{ so } b = \frac{1}{2}.$$

## A–76

**(B)** To solve the proportion

$$\frac{12}{x-1} = \frac{5}{6}$$

multiply both sides of the equation by 6 and by $(x-1)$ so that we have

$$6(x-1) \times \frac{12}{x-1} = 6(x-1) \times \frac{5}{6} \text{ or } 72 = 5(x-1).$$

Now, use the distributive property:
$$a(b-c) = ab - ac$$
to get $\qquad 72 = 5x - 5$. Add 5 to both sides of the equation: $77 = 5x$
and then divide both sides by 5:

$$x = \frac{77}{5} = 15.4$$

# Questions

In the following figure, line *l* is parallel to line *m*. If the area of $\triangle ABC$ is 40 cm³, what is the area of triangle $\triangle ABD$?

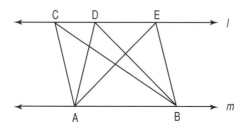

(A)  Less than 40 cm³

(B)  More than 40 cm³

(C)  The length of segment $\overline{AD}$ times 40 cm²

(D)  Exactly 40 cm³

*Your Answer* _____

_____

# Correct Answers

**A–77**

**(D)**     The area of a triangle is equal to the product of the length of its base (any one of its sides) and the length of its altitude (the perpendicular segment drawn from the opposite vertex to the base of the triangle or to the line containing the base of the triangle).

For each of the triangles, the segment $\overline{AB}$ can be used as the base. The altitude of $\triangle ABC$ is the perpendicular distance from $C$ to line $m$. The altitude of $\triangle ABD$ is the perpendicular distance from $D$ to line $m$. Since $C$ and $D$ both lie on line $l$ and lines $l$ and $m$ are parallel, then the altitudes of the triangles must be equal. Thus the area of $\triangle ABD$ is $40 cm^3$.

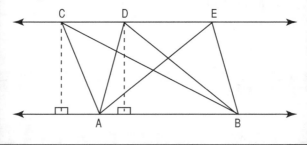

# Questions

If the length of segment *EB* base of triangle *EBC*, is equal to ¼ the length of segment  is the length of rectangle *ABCD*, and the area of triangle *EBC* is 12 square units, find the area of the shaded region.

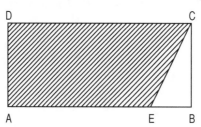

(A)   24 square units

(B)   96 square units

(C)   84 square units

(D)   72 square units

*Your Answer* _____

_____

# Correct Answers

(C)    Let $(AB)$ represent the measure (length) of segment $AB$, then the length of rectangle $ABCD$ is equal to $(AB)$ and the length of its width is $(BC)$.

Obviously, the area of shaded region is equal to the area of rectangle $ABCD$ minus the area of triangle $EBC$.

Recall that the area of a rectangle is equal to the product of the measure of its length and the measure of its width. Thus,

Area of rectangle $ABCD = (AB)(BC)$

The area of any triangle is equal to ½ times the measure of its base (any side of the triangle) times the measure of its altitude (the length of the perpendicular segment drawn from the vertex opposite the base to that base or to the line containing the base). That is, the area of a triangle is equal to ½ $bh$.

Thus,

$$\text{Area of triangle } EBC = \frac{1}{2}(EB)(BC).$$

But $(EB) = \frac{1}{4}(AB)$, hence,

$$\text{Area of triangle } EBC = \frac{1}{2}\left[\frac{1}{4}(AB)\right](BC)$$

$$= \frac{1}{8}(AB)(BC)$$

Since the area of triangle $ABC$ is equal to 12 square units, we have

$$(AB)\,(\mathrm{I}) = 12$$

or

$$(AB)(BC) = 96.$$

But, $(AB)(BC)$ is the area of rectangle $ABCD$. Hence, area of rectangle $ABCD = 96$ square units.

Thus, area of shaded region $= 96 - 12 = 84$ square units.

# Questions

What is the length of side *BC*?

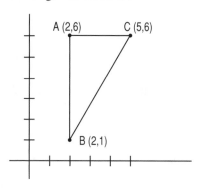

(A)  3

(B)  5

(C)  $\sqrt{34}$

(D)  7

*Your Answer* _____

# Correct Answers

**A–79**

**(C)** (A) This answer is incorrect. The difference between the x-coordinates for points $B$ and $C$ is not the length of I. Use the Pythagorean theorem to find the length of side $BC$. (B) is incorrect. The difference between the y-coordinates for points $B$ and $C$ is not the length of $BC$. Use the Pythagorean theorem to find the length of side $BC$. (C) is correct. Since the triangle $ABC$ is a right triangle, use the Pythagorean theorem to find the length of side $BC$. The length of side $AC$ is $5 - 2 = 3$ and the length of side $AB$ is $6 - 1 = 5$. Find the length of $BC$ as follows:

$$(BC)^2 = (AC)^2 + (AB)^2$$
$$(BC)^2 = 3^2 + 5^2$$
$$(BC)^2 = 9 + 25$$
$$BC = \sqrt{34}$$

Alternatively, use the distance formula: This will give the same answers. (D) is also incorrect. Simply adding the y-coordinates of points $B$ and $C$ will not give the length of $BC$. Use the Pythagorean theorem to find the length of side $BC$.

# Questions

**Q–80**

In the figure shown, all segments meet at right angles. Find the figure's perimeter in terms of $r$ and $s$.

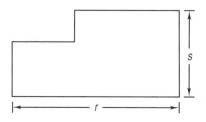

(A)  $r + s$

(B)  $2r + s$

(C)  $2s + r$

(D)  $2r + 2s$

*Your Answer* _____

# Correct Answers

**(D)**      (D) is correct. Label the vertices of the given figure $A, B, C, D, E, F$, and the segment $DE$ to meet $AB$ at $G$, and let $mAB$ denote the length of segment $AB$. Since all the segments in the figure meet at right angles, quadrilaterals $AGEF$ and $GBCD$ are rectangles.

$$m\overline{DE} + m\overline{EG} = m\overline{CB} = r$$

$m\overline{EG} = m\overline{AF}$ since $AGFE$ is a rectangle. Then $m\overline{AF} = m\overline{ED} = r$.

Also, $m\overline{DC} = m\overline{GB}$ since $GBCD$ is a rectangle, and $m\overline{FE} = m\overline{AG}$ since $AGFE$ is a rectangle.

$$m\overline{DC} + m\overline{EF} = m\overline{GB} + m\overline{AG} = m\overline{AB} = s$$

The perimeter of a closed polygon is equal to the sum of the measure of its segments. The perimeter of the given figure is equal to

$$
\begin{aligned}
& m\overline{AB} + m\overline{BC} + m\overline{CD} + m\overline{DE} + m\overline{EF} + m\overline{AF} \\
= \ & m\overline{AB} + m\overline{BC} + m\overline{DC} + m\overline{EF} + \left( m\overline{ED} + m\overline{AF} \right) \\
= \ & s + r + s + r \\
= \ & 2r + 2s
\end{aligned}
$$

# Questions

---

If $\triangle ABC$ has $\angle A = 35°$ and $\angle B = 85°$, then the measure of $\angle x$ in degrees is

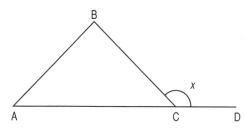

(A)  85.

(B)  90.

(C)  100.

(D)  120.

---

*Your Answer* _____

_____

# Correct Answers

## A–81

**(D)** The measure of the exterior angle $x$ of triangle *ABC* is equal to the sum of the measures of the two remote interior angles, *A* and *B*, respectively. Thus,

$$\text{angle } x = 35° + 85° = 120°.$$

Another approach is to remember that the sum of the angles in triangle *ABC* is 35 + 85 + angle *C* = 180°. Hence, angle *C* = 60°. Then, since angle *C* and angle *x* are supplementary angles, it follows that angle *x* must be 120° since angle *C* is 60°.

# Questions

---

**Q–82**

If 406.725 is rounded off to the nearest tenth, the number is

(A)   406.3

(B)   406.5

(C)   406.7

(D)   406.8

---

*Your Answer* _____

_____

*A Drug Delivery System is a means of getting medicine to the appropriate body part. These range from traditional systems such as tablets, injections, etc. to modern systems such as liposomes, transdermal patches, and those systems which are targeted to particular organs or tissues. (www.aacp.org)*

# Correct Answers

(C)    7 is in the tenths place. Since the next digit (2) is below 5, drop this digit and retain the 7. The answer, therefore, is 406.7

# Questions

**Q–83**

The mean IQ score for 1,500 students is 100, with a standard deviation of 15. Assuming normal curve distribution, how many students have an IQ between 85 and 115? Refer to the figure shown below.

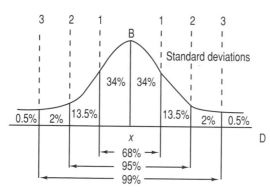

(A)   510

(B)   750

(C)   1,020

(D)   1,275

*Your Answer* _____

_____

# Correct Answers

**A–83**

**(C)**    The mean IQ score of 100 is given. One standard deviation above the mean is 34% of the cases, with an IQ score up to 115. One standard deviation below the mean is another 34% of the cases, with an IQ score till 85. So, a total of 68% of the students have an IQ between 85 and 115. Therefore, $1,500 \times .68 = 1,020$.

# Questions

---

**Q–84**

The sum of 12 and twice a number is 24. Find the number.

(A)  6

(B)  8

(C)  10

(D)  11

*Your Answer* _____

_____

---

**Q–85**

Twice the sum of 10 and a number is 28. Find the number.

(A)  4

(B)  8

(C)  12

(D)  14

*Your Answer* _____

_____

# Correct Answers

**A–84**

(A)
$$12 + 2x = 24$$
$$2x = 24 - 12$$
$$2x = 12$$
$$x = \frac{12}{2}$$
$$x = 6$$

**A–85**

(A)
$$(10 + x)2 = 28$$
$$20 + 2x = 28$$
$$2x = 28 - 20$$
$$2x = 8$$
$$x = \frac{8}{2}$$
$$x = 4$$

# Questions

**Q–86**

Two college roommates spent $2,000 for their total monthly expenses. A pie graph below indicates a record of their expenses.

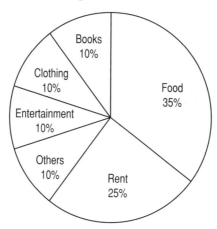

Based on the above information, which of the following statements is accurate?

(A)   The roommates spent $700 on food alone.

(B)   The roommates spent $550 on rent alone.

(C)   The roommates spent $300 on entertainment alone.

(D)   The roommates spent $300 on clothing alone.

*Your Answer* _____

_____

# Correct Answers

**A–86**

**(A)**   $2,000 \times .35 = \$700$.

   The other answer choices have wrong computations.

*The first female pharmacist was Susan Hayhurst, who graduated from the College of Pharmacy in 1883 as both a pharmacist and a doctor. Until that point, women were thought not to be physically strong enough to properly pound the substances used in compounding. (www.hood-meddac.army.mil)*

# Questions

**Q–87**

You can buy a telephone for $24. If you are charged $3 per month for renting a telephone from the telephone company, how long will it take you to recover the cost of the phone if you buy one?

(A)  6 months

(B)  7 months

(C)  8 months

(D)  9 months

*Your Answer* _____

_____

*Antibodies are molecules made by the immune system to identify and destroy specific invaders. (www.pfizerforliving.com)*

# Correct Answers

**A–87**

**(C)** Let $x$ = length of time (# of mos) to recover cost.

$$3x = 24$$
$$x = \frac{24}{3}$$
$$x = 8 \text{ mos.}$$

# Questions

**Q–88**

What would be the measure of the third angle in the following triangle?

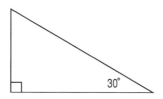

30°

(A)  45°

(B)  50°

(C)  60°

(D)  70°

*Your Answer* _____

_____

# Correct Answers

## A–88

(C)    With one right angle (90°) and a given 30° angle, the missing angle, therefore, is a 60° angle.

$$90° + 30° = 120°$$
$$180° - 120° = 60°$$

# Questions

**Q–89**

What is the perimeter of this figure?

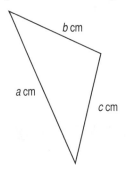

(A)   *abc* cm

(B)   *abc* cm$^2$

(C)   $(a + b + c)$ cm

(D)   $(a + b + c)$ cm$^2$

*Your Answer* _____

_____

# Correct Answers

**A–89**

**(C)**    The perimeter is the distance around the triangle, which is therefore,
$$(a + b + c) \text{ cm.}$$

 *On October 15, 1783, Jean Francois Pilatre de Rozier, a pharmacist from Metz, France, became the first human to experience aerial flight. (www.hood-meddac.army.mil)*

# Questions

**Q–90**

What is the perimeter of the given triangle?

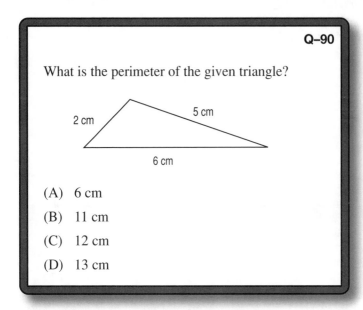

- (A)  6 cm
- (B)  11 cm
- (C)  12 cm
- (D)  13 cm

*Your Answer* _____

_____

*Mast cells are special cells located in your nose, eyes, lungs and gastrointestinal tract. These cells release chemicals such as histamine when an allergen contacts antibodies that are attached to the mast cells. This causes an allergic reaction. (www. pfizerforliving.com)*

# Correct Answers

**A–90**

**(D)**     The perimeter is the distance around the triangle. Therefore,
$$2 \text{ cm} + 6 \text{ cm} + 5 \text{ cm} = 13 \text{ cm}.$$

*In colonial Ste. Genevieve (Missouri) maple syrup was often used a cure for colds and tuberculosis. (www.hood-meddac.army.mil)*

# Questions

Assuming that the quadrilateral in the following figure is a parallelogram, what would be its area?

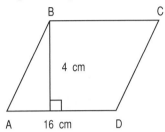

(A)  32 cm

(B)  40 cm

(C)  64 cm

(D)  64 cm$^2$

*Your Answer* _____

_____

# Correct Answers

**(D)**     The area of a parallelogram is base × height. Therefore,

$$A = bh = (16 \text{ cm}) \times (4 \text{ cm}) = 64 \text{ cm}^2.$$

# Questions

Refer to the figure below to determine which of the following statements is correct.

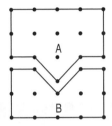

I.   Figures A and B have the same area.

II.  Figures A and B have the same perimeter.

(A)  Only I

(B)  Only II

(C)  Both I and II

(D)  Neither I nor II

*Your Answer* _____

_____

# Correct Answers

**A–92**

**(B)** Figure A has an area of about 9 square units while Figure B has an area of about 7 square units. Both Figures A and B have the same perimeter of about 12 units.

 *More than half of ancient Egypt's home remedies contained honey. That included a contraceptive poultice that also used a bit of camel dung and beeswax. (www.hood-meddac.army.mil)*

# Questions

---

**Q–93**

Which of the following is NOT a proper subset of $\{1, 2, 3, 4\}$?

(A) $\{1, 2\}$

(B) $\{1, 2, 3\}$

(C) $\{1, 3, 4\}$

(D) $\{1, 2, 5\}$

*Your Answer* _____

_____

---

**Q–94**

Which of the following is an example of a rational number?

(A) $\sqrt{17}$

(B) $6\sqrt[3]{7}$

(C) $4\sqrt{11}$

(D) $7 + \sqrt{9}$

*Your Answer* _____

_____

# Correct Answers

**A–93**

**(D)**     Only (D) has an element (which is 5) not present in the given set of $\{1, 2, 3, 4\}$.

**A–94**

**(D)**     Nine is the square of an integer. 17, 11, and 15 are not squares of an integer, therefore, they are irrational numbers. 7 is not the cube of an integer, hence, it is an irrational number as well.

**Q–95**

Which of the following statements includes a cardinal number?

(A) There are 15 volumes in the set of periodicals.

(B) I received my 14th volume recently.

(C) The students meet at Room 304.

(D) My phone number is 213-617-8442.

*Your Answer* _____

*Many studies have shown that Alzheimer's disease rates are higher for women than for men, even after adjusting for differences in life span. (www.pfizerforliving.com)*

# Correct Answers

(A)   15 is used as a cardinal number. The rest are either ordinal (B) or nominal, (C), (D), (E), numbers.

In a group of 30 students, 12 are studying mathematics, 18 are studying English, 8 are studying science, 7 are studying both mathematics and English, 6 are studying English and science, 5 are studying mathematics and science, and 4 are studying all three subjects. How many of these students are taking only English? How many of these students are not taking any of these subjects?

(A)   9 students take only English; 6 students take none of these subjects.

(B)   10 students take only English; 5 students take none of these subjects.

(C)   11 students take only English; 5 students take none of these subjects.

(D)   12 students take only English; 6 students take none of these subjects.

*Your Answer* _____

_____

# Correct Answers

## A–96

(A)     Use the Venn diagram (as shown below) with three circles to represent the set of students in each of the listed subject matter areas. Start with four students taking all three subjects. We write the number 4 in the region that is the intersection of all these circles. Then we work backward: Since seven are taking math and English, and four of these have already been identified as also taking English, math, and science, there must be exactly three taking only math and English. That is, there must be three in the region representing math and English, but not science. Continuing in this manner, we enter the given data in the diagram.

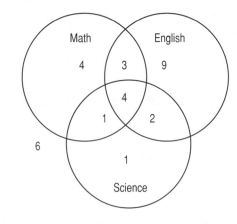

# Questions

**Q–97**

For the given Venn diagram, find n(A « B « C):

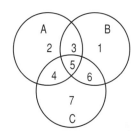

(A)  3

(B)  4

(C)  5

(D)  6

*Your Answer* _____

**Q–98**

Find the next three terms in this sequence: 1, 4, 9, 16, …

(A)  19, 24, 31

(B)  20, 25, 31

(C)  21, 28, 36

(D)  25, 36, 49

*Your Answer* _____

# Correct Answers

**A–97**

**(C)**    There is one element in the intersection of all three sets. Thus,
$$n\,(A \cap B \cap C) = 5.$$

**A–98**

**(D)**    The sequence 1, 4, 9, 16 is the sum of the odd numbers.
1. 1
2. $1 + 3 = 4$
3. $1 + 3 + 5 = 9$
4. $1 + 3 + 5 + 7 = 16$

# Questions

---

**Q–99**

Assume that one pig eats 4 pounds of food each week. There are 52 weeks in a year. How much food do 10 pigs eat in a week?

(A)   40 lb.

(B)   520 lb.

(C)   208 lb.

(D)   20 lb.

*Your Answer* _____

---

**Q–100**

Suppose that a pair of pants and a shirt cost $65 and the pants cost $25 more than the shirt. What did they each cost?

(A)   The pants cost $35 and the shirt costs $30.

(B)   The pants cost $40 and the shirt costs $25.

(C)   The pants cost $43 and the shirt costs $22.

(D)   The pants cost $45 and the shirt costs $20.

*Your Answer* _____

# Correct Answers

## A-99

**(A)**     Here one must use only the needed information. Do not be distracted by superfluous data. Simple multiplication will do. If one pig eats four pounds of food per week, how much will 10 pigs eat in one week? $10 \times 4 = 40$ pounds. The problem intentionally contains superfluous data (52 weeks), which should not distract the reader from its easy solution. Ratio and proportion will also work here

$$\frac{1}{10} = \frac{4}{x}, \; x = 40 \text{ pounds/week.}$$

## A-100

**(D)**     Let the variable S stand for the cost of the shirt. Then the cost of the pair of pants is S + 25 and

$$S + (S + 25) = 65$$
$$2S = 65 - 25$$
$$2S = 40$$
$$S = 20$$
$$\$20 \text{ (cost of shirt)}$$
$$\$20 + \$25 = \$45 \text{ (cost of pants)}$$

# Questions

**Q-101**

There are five members in a basketball team. Suppose each member shakes hands with every other member of the team before the game starts; how many handshakes will there be in all?

(A) 6

(B) 8

(C) 9

(D) 10

*Your Answer* _____

_____

**Q-102**

Tom bought a piece of land for $20,000. If he had to pay 20 percent of the price as a down payment, how much was the down payment?

(A) $2,500

(B) $3,000

(C) $4,000

(D) $4,500

*Your Answer* _____

_____

# Correct Answers

**A–101**

(**D**)    The possible handshakes are illustrated by listing all the possible pairs of letters, thus

| | | | |
|---|---|---|---|
| AB | AC | AD | AE |
| BC | BD | BE | |
| CD | CE | | |
| DE | | | |

(a total of 10 handshakes)

**A–102**

(**C**)    Let

$$D = \text{down payment}$$
$$D = \$20,000 \times .20$$
$$D = \$4,000$$

# Questions

---

**Q–103**

A computer sells for $3,200 to the general public. If you purchase one in the university, the price is reduced by 20 percent. What is the sale price of the computer?

(A)  $640

(B)  $2,000

(C)  $2,410

(D)  $2,560

---

*Your Answer* _____

_____

---

**Q–104**

In order for Sue to receive a final grade of C, she must have an average greater than or equal to 70% but less than 80% on five tests. Suppose her grades on the first four tests were 65%, 85%, 60%, and 90%. What range of grades on the fifth test would give her a C in the course?

(A)  45 up to but excluding 95

(B)  47 up to but excluding 90

(C)  49 up to but excluding 98

(D)  50 up to but excluding 100

---

*Your Answer* _____

_____

# Correct Answers

**A–103**

**(D)**    20% of \$3,200 = \$640 (amount price reduced)

\$3,200 – \$640 = \$2,560 (sale price)

**A–104**

**(D)**    Let $x$ = 5th grade

$$\text{Average} = \frac{65 + 85 + 60 + 90 + x}{5}$$

For Sue to obtain a C, her average must be greater than or equal to 70 but less than 80.

$$70 \leq \frac{65+85+60+90+x}{5}$$

$$70 \leq \frac{300 + x < 80}{5}$$

$$5(70) \leq 5(300 + x \div 5) < 5(80)$$
$$350 \leq 300 + x < 400$$
$$350 - 300 \leq x < 400 - 300$$
$$50 \leq x < 100$$

Thus, a grade of 50 up to but not including a grade of 100 will result in a C.

# Questions

A certain company produces two types of lawn-mowers. Type A is self-propelled while type B is not. The company can produce a maximum of 18 mowers per week. It can make a profit of $15 on mower A and a profit of $20 on mower B. The company wants to make at least 2 mowers of type A but not more than 5. They also plan to make at least 2 mowers of type B. Let $x$ be the number of type A produced, and let $y$ be the number of type B produced.

From the above, which of the following is NOT one of the listed constraints?

(A)  $x \geq 2$

(B)  $x \leq 5$

(C)  $x + y \leq 18$

(D)  $y < 5$

*Your Answer* _____

# Correct Answers

**A–105**

**(D)** The constraint for $y$ is to at least make two mowers.

*The popular drink "7-Up" was originally a version of a "lithiated" patent medicine, containing small amounts of lithium. Ironically, it was introduced to the U.S. markets in the 1930s — during the time of the Great Depression! (www.hood-meddac.army.mil)*

# Questions

**Q–106**

Mr. Smith died and left an estate to be divided among his wife, two children, and a foundation of his choosing in the ratio of 8:6:6:1. How much did his wife receive if the estate was valued at $300,000?

(A) $114,285.71

(B) $120,421.91

(C) $85,714.29

(D) $14,285.71

*Your Answer* _____

_____

**Q–107**

There were 19 hamburgers for nine people on a picnic. How many whole hamburgers were there for each person if they were divided equally?

(A) 1

(B) 2

(C) 3

(D) 4

*Your Answer* _____

_____

# Correct Answers

## A-106

**(A)** The ratio 8:6:6:1 implies that for each $8 the wife received, each child received $6 and the foundation $1. The estate is divided into 8 + 6 + 6 + 1, or 21 equal shares. The wife received $8/21$ of $300,000 or $114,285.71, each child received $6/21$ of $300,000, or $85,714.29, and the foundation received $1/21$ of $300,000 or $14,285.71. As a check,

$114,285.71 + $85,714.29 + $85,714.29 + $14,285.71 = $300,000.

## A-107

**(B)** Simple division: $19/9$ = 2 whole hamburgers with one left over.

# Questions

---

**Q–108**

George has four ways to get from his house to the park. He has seven ways to get from the park to the school. How many ways can George get from his house to school by way of the park?

(A)  4

(B)  7

(C)  28

(D)  3

*Your Answer* _____

_____

---

**Q–109**

If it takes one minute per cut, how long will it take to cut a 15-foot long timber into 15 equal pieces?

(A)  5

(B)  10

(C)  14

(D)  20

*Your Answer* _____

_____

# Correct Answers

**A–108**

(C)     Simple multiplication: 7 × 4 = 28.

**A–109**

(D)     For a 15 ft. log, it will take 14 cuts to make 15 equal pieces. Therefore, 14 minutes for 14 cuts.

# Questions

**Q–110**

Ed has six new shirts and four new pairs of pants. How many combinations of new shirts and pants does he have?

(A)  10

(B)  14

(C)  20

(D)  24

*Your Answer* _____

_____

**Q–111**

The property tax rate of the town of Grandview is $32 per $1,000 of assessed value. What is the tax if the property is assessed at $50,000?

(A)  $32

(B)  $1,000

(C)  $1,562

(D)  $1,600

*Your Answer* _____

_____

# Correct Answers

**A–110**

**(D)**     Simple multiplication.
$$6 \times 4 = 24.$$

**A–111**

**(D)**     First find out how many shares of $1,000 there are in $50,000.
$$\$50,000 \div 1,000 = 50$$
Then multiply the shares by the cost ($50 \times \$32$) and the answer is $1,600.

# Questions

Ralph kept track of his work time in gardening. Refer to the broken-line graph below:

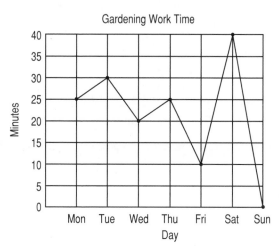

How many minutes did he average per day?

(A)  10 min.

(B)  20 min.

(C)  21.43 min.

(D)  23.05 min.

*Your Answer* _____

_____

# Correct Answers

**A–112**

(C)     Find the sum of the seven days. Thus:

$M = 25$;
$T = 30$;
$W = 20$;
$Th = 25$;
$F = 10$;
$Sat = 40$;
$Sun = 0$,

or a total of 150 minutes. Find the average by dividing 150 by 7 = 21.43 minutes.

# Questions

**Q–113**

Mary had been selling printed shirts in her neighborhood. She made this pictograph to show how much money she made each week.

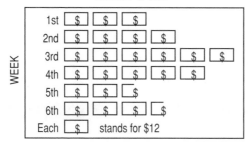

WEEKLY SALES

How many weeks were sales more than $55?

(A)   1 week

(B)   2 weeks

(C)   3 weeks

(D)   4 weeks

*Your Answer* _____

# Correct Answers

**A–113**

**(B)** If each ⬓$⬓ stands for $12, only weeks 3 and 4 had a sale of $72 and $60, respectively. The rest are below $55.

# Questions

**Q–114**

Find the volume of the following figure.

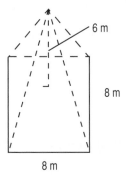

(A)   48 m³

(B)   64 m³

(C)   128 m³

(D)   192 m³

*Your Answer* _____

_____

# Correct Answers

**A–114**

(C)    The volume of a pyramid is

$$V = \tfrac{1}{3}Bh,$$

where $B$ is the area of the base and $h$ is the height of the pyramid. Thus,

$$V = \tfrac{1}{3}(64)(6)$$

$$= \tfrac{1}{3}(384) = 128m^3.$$

# Questions

**Q–115**

The result of Mary's spring semester grades follow. Find her grade point average for the term (A = 4, B = 3, C = 2, D = 1, F = 0).

| Course | Credits | Grades |
|--------|---------|--------|
| Biology | 5 | A |
| English | 3 | C |
| Math | 3 | A |
| French | 3 | D |
| P.E. | 2 | B |

(A)  3.80

(B)  3.50

(C)  2.94

(D)  2.00

*Your Answer* _____

# Correct Answers

**(C)** Total the number of credits earned (in this case = 16 credits). Multiply the credit and the weight for the earned grade per subject (e.g., biology = 5 × 4 = 20). Then add the total of the products of the credits and corresponding weights (in this case = 47). Then divide 47 by 16 to get the grade point average of 2.94. See table below.

$$Biology = 5 \times 4 = 20$$
$$English = 3 \times 2 = 6$$
$$Math = 3 \times 4 = 12$$
$$French = 3 \times 1 = 3$$

$$GPA = \frac{total\ cr \times wt}{total\ cr} = \frac{47}{16} = 2.94$$

$$P.E. = \frac{2}{16\ cr} \times 3 = \frac{6}{47\ cr \times gr\ wt}$$

# Questions

In a biology class at International University, the grades on the final examination were as follows:

| | | | |
|----|----|----|----|
| 91 | 81 | 65 | 81 |
| 50 | 70 | 81 | 93 |
| 36 | 90 | 43 | 87 |
| 96 | 81 | 75 | 81 |

Find the mode.

(A)  36

(B)  70

(C)  81

(D)  87

*Your Answer* _____

*An estimated 11 million American adults have a history of cancer. (www.pfizer.com)*

# Correct Answers

**A–116**

(C)    Mode is the most frequent score. 81 appeared five times and is therefore the mode.

*Benedict Arnold began his pre-military career as a pharmacist in New Haven, Connecticut. From 1761 to 1775 he sold such products as "pectoral Balsam-Honey" and "Frances' Female Elixir." (www.hood-meddac.army.mil)*

# Questions

**Q–117**

One commonly used standard score is a $z$-score. A $z$-score gives the number of standard deviations by which the score differs from the mean, as shown in the following example.

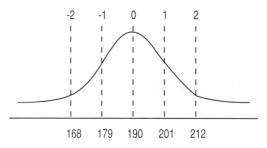

The mean ($x$) is 190 and the standard deviation(s) is 11. The score of 201 has a $z$-score of 1 and the score of 168 has a $z$-score of –2. Consider the mean height of a certain group of people as 190 cm with a standard deviation of 11 cm. Suppose Glenn's height has a $z$-score of 1.6, what is his height? (Note $z = x - x$.)

(A)  207.60 cm

(B)  190 cm

(C)  201 cm

(D)  179 cm

*Your Answer* _____

_____

# Correct Answers

**A–117**

(**A**)    Following the formula

$$z = \frac{x - x}{s.d.}$$

thus,    $1.6 = x - \dfrac{190}{11}$

$$17.60 = x - 190$$
$$x = 190 + 17.60$$
$$x = 207.60 \text{ cm (Glenn's height)}$$

# Questions

---

**Q–118**

What is the least common denominator of $\frac{2}{15}$, $\frac{1}{21}$, and $\frac{4}{35}$

(A)   105

(B)   35

(C)   415

(D)   735

*Your Answer* _____

_____

---

**Q–119**

On July 19, a Friday, Dick received a letter to have a class reunion exactly four years from that day. On what day of the week is his reunion?

(A)   Monday

(B)   Tuesday

(C)   Wednesday

(D)   Thursday

*Your Answer* _____

_____

# Correct Answers

## A–118

**(A)**    The least common denominator of the fractions is the least common multiple of their denominators: 15, 21, and 35. Since

$$15 = 3 \times 5,$$
$$21 = 3 \times 7,$$

and $\quad\quad\quad\quad\quad 35 = 5 \times 7,$

we see that their least common multiple is $3 \times 5 \times 7 = 105$.

## A–119

**(C)**    Since his reunion will be $365 \times 4 + 1 = 1{,}461$ days from a Friday, dividing 1,461 by 7 yields a remainder of 5. Therefore, his reunion is 5 days from a Friday, which makes it on a Wednesday.

# Questions

John and Mary are working on a job together. If John does it alone, it will take him seven days, while Mary can do it alone in five days. How long will it take them to do it together?

(A)   12 days

(B)   2 days

(C)   2 and $\frac{11}{12}$ days

(D)   3 and $\frac{1}{2}$ days

*Your Answer* _____

_____

*It can take up to ten years to develop a new drug. (www.pfizerjournal.com)*

# Correct Answers

**A–120**

**(C)** In one day, John can do ⅐ of the work, and Mary can do ⅕; together, they can do

$$\frac{1}{5} + \frac{1}{7} = \frac{12}{35}$$

of the job. To finish the whole job, it takes

$$\frac{35}{12} = 2 \text{ and } \frac{11}{12} \text{ days.}$$

*Until recently, Florida required all pharmacies to own and display a fancy jar of colored water before they could get their license. (www.hood-meddac.army.mil)*

# Questions

**Q–121**

Which of the following is true about triangle *ABC*?

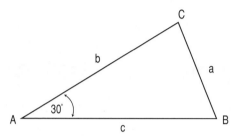

(A)  Sides *b* and *c* are equal in measurement.

(B)  Angle *a* is the smallest angle.

(C)  Side *a* is not the longest side.

(D)  Angle *b* or *c* must be a right angle.

*Your Answer* _____

_____

# Correct Answers

**A–121**

(C)    Since the only information we have concerning the triangle is that angle *A* measures 30°, we know that in a triangle, the largest angle faces the longest side, the sum of the three angles of a triangle is 180°, and a 30° angle is not the largest angle. Therefore, side *A* is not the longest.

*In 1888, Atlanta pharmacist John S. Pemberton developed an "Esteemed Brain Tonic and Intellectual Beverage," which contained: caffeine, "secret" ingredients, and cocaine. Modified for today's taste (and laws), it is now called Coca-Cola. (www. hood-meddac.army.mil)*

# Questions

**Q–122**

If the diameter of circle $A$ is twice that of circle $B$, what is the ratio of the area of circle $A$ to the area of circle $B$?

(A) 2 to 1

(B) 3 to 1

(C) 4 to 1

(D) $\pi$ to 1

*Your Answer* _____

**Q–123**

Jack flies from New York to Los Angeles. His plane leaves New York at 2:15 p.m. The flying time is 5 hours and 45 minutes. Since New York is three hours ahead of Los Angeles, what time does he arrive in Los Angeles?

(A) 11:00 p.m.

(B) 8:00 p.m.

(C) 7:45 p.m.

(D) 5:00 p.m.

*Your Answer* _____

# Correct Answers

## A–122

**(C)** The diameter of circle $A$ is twice that of circle $B$, so if the radius of $B$ is $r$, then the radius of $A$ is $2r$. Since the area of a circle with radius $r$ is $\pi r^2$, the area of $B$ is $\pi r^2$, while the area of $A$ is
$$\pi(2r)^2 = 4\pi r,$$
therefore the ratio is 4:1.

## A–123

**(D)** $2:15 + 5:45 = 8:00$ means he arrives in Los Angeles at 8 p.m. New York time. But New York is 3 hours ahead of Los Angeles, so the Los Angeles time of arrival is 5 p.m.

# Questions

---

**Q–124**

Bob has 50 coins, all nickels and dimes, worth a total of $4.85. How many nickels does he possess?

(A)  30

(B)  15

(C)  37

(D)  3

*Your Answer* _____

---

**Q–125**

A steamboat goes 24 miles upstream and then returns to its original position. The round trip takes six hours. The water flows at three miles per hour. What is the speed of the boat in still water?

(A)  10 miles/hour

(B)  9 miles/hour

(C)  8 miles/hour

(D)  7 miles/hour

*Your Answer* _____

# Correct Answers

**A–124**

**(D)** We set up two equations. Let n be the number of nickels, and let d be the number of dimes. We have

$$n + d = 50.$$

Since each nickel is worth 5 cents and each dime is worth 10 cents, we have

$$5n + 10d = 485.$$

Multiplying the first equation by 10, we obtain

$$10n + 10d = 500.$$

Subtracting the second equation from it, we obtain $5n = 15$, or $n = 3$.

**A–125**

**(B)** Let s be the speed of the boat in still water. Then the speed of the boat upstream is $(s - 3)$ miles per hour, and the speed of the boat downstream is $(s + 3)$ miles per hour. Therefore, the time going upstream,

$$\frac{24}{s - 3}$$

hours plus the time going downstream,

$$\frac{24}{s + 3}$$

hours, equals 6 hours. Solving for s gives s = 9 miles/hour.

$$s^2 - 8s - 9 = 0;$$
$$(s - 9)(s + 1) = 0;$$
$$s = 9 \text{ or } -1,$$

but we require $s > 0$. Thus s = 9 miles per hour.

# Questions

---

**Q–126**

If ten babies drink a total of ten gallons of milk in ten days, how many gallons of milk will 20 babies drink in 20 days?

(A) 20

(B) 25

(C) 35

(D) 40

*Your Answer* _____

---

**Q–127**

A parallelogram *ABCD* has all its sides measure 4, one of the diagonals $\overline{AC}$ also measures 4. What is its area?

(A) Its area is 16.

(B) Its area is 32.

(C) Its area is $4\sqrt{3}$.

(D) Its area is $8\sqrt{3}$

*Your Answer* _____

# Correct Answers

**A–126**

**(D)** Since 10 babies drink 10 gallons of milk in 10 days, each baby drinks $\frac{1}{10}$ gallon of milk per day. Each baby drinks 2 gallons of milk in 20 days, so 20 babies will drink $2 \times 20 = 40$ gallons of milk in 20 days.

**A–127**

**(D)** Draw both diagonals to divide the parallelogram into four equal parts. Each part is a right triangle with hypotenuse measuring 4 and one side measuring 2. Therefore, the other side must measure $2\sqrt{3}$ by the Pythagorean Theorem. The area of one of these triangles is

$$\left(\frac{1}{2}\right) \times \left(2 \times 2\sqrt{3}\right) = 2\sqrt{3}.$$

Since the parallelogram is composed of 4 triangles, the area is

$$\left(2\sqrt{3}\right) \times 4 = 8\sqrt{3}$$

**Q–128**

Jack gave one-third of his money to his daughter and one-quarter of his money to his son. He then had $150,000 left. How much money did he have before he gave away some?

(A) $225,000

(B) $250,000

(C) $300,000

(D) $360,000

*Your Answer* _____

**Q–129**

If Don and Ron can paint a house in five days, and Ron can paint it alone in seven days, how long will it take Don to paint it alone?

(A) 2 days

(B) 7 days

(C) 17.5 days

(D) 9.75 days

*Your Answer* _____

# Correct Answers

## A–128

**(D)** Let the amount of money he had before be $x$.
We have

$$x - \left(\frac{1}{3}\right)x - \left(\frac{1}{4}\right)x = 150,000.$$

Or,

$$\left(\frac{5}{12}\right)x = 150,000.$$

Therefore, $x = 360,000$.

## A–129

**(C)** Since Don and Ron can paint the house in 7 days, they finish $\frac{1}{5}$ of the job in a day. Now Ron's contribution in a day is $\frac{1}{7}$ of the job, so

$$\frac{1}{5} - \frac{1}{7}$$

is Don's contribution in a day, which amounts to $\frac{2}{35}$. Therefore, if Don is to do it alone, it will take him

$$\frac{35}{2} = 17.5 \text{ days.}$$

# Questions

**Q–130**

A steamboat left Hong Kong on May 25, at 6 a.m., New York time. It sailed 400 hours and arrived in New York. When did it arrive?

(A)  10 p.m., June 9

(B)  10 p.m., June 10

(C)  10 p.m., June 11

(D)  4 p.m., June 10

*Your Answer* _____

*Annually, approximately 5% of the global population, or 200 million people use illicit drugs. (New England Journal of Medicine. Volume 353, November 3, 2005.)*

# Correct Answers

## A–130

**(B)** We divide 400 by 24 (number of hours in a day); we obtain a partial quotient of 16 and a remainder of 16. This means that it takes 16 days and 16 hours for the trip. With 31 days in May, the boat must arrive on June 10. And 16 hours from 6 a.m. is 10 p.m.

# Section III

# Biology

---

**DIRECTIONS:** Each of the questions or incomplete statements in this section is followed by four suggested answers or completions. Select the one that is best in each case.

# Questions

**Q–1**

The main abiotic source of carbon in the environment for the carbon cycle comes from:

(A) carbon dioxide in the air

(B) carbon dioxide in water

(C) carbon monoxide in the air

(D) carbon monoxide in water

*Your Answer* _____

_____

**Q–2**

The optimum pH and body site for amylase activity is:

(A) 2, stomach

(B) 5, small intestine

(C) 7, oral cavity

(D) 8, stomach

*Your Answer* _____

_____

# Correct Answers

### A–1

(A)   In the carbon cycle, $CO_2$ circulates between the living and nonliving sectors of an ecosystem. $CO_2$ composes .04 of one percent of the atmosphere. Producers (plants) in food chains fix it into the protoplasm of plants via photosynthesis. The element moves through the other trophic levels by nutrition and eating. Respiration by consumers and decomposers returns it to the abiotic sector, air, from the biotic sector, living organisms.

### A–2

(C)   The interior of the stomach has a pH of 2, which is necessary for the action of pepsin. The surface of the skin has a pH of 5.0 to 5.5. The pH range of the small intestine's lumen includes pH = 8. The pH of the oral cavity is usually about 7, which is necessary for the action of salivary amylase, which begins the digestion of starch.

# Questions

**Q–3**

Hydrolysis of lipid molecules yields:

(A) amino acids and water

(B) amino acids and glucose

(C) fatty acids and glycerol

(D) glucose and glycerol

*Your Answer* _____

_____

**Q–4**

Prokaryotic cells lack:

(A) a cell membrane

(B) cytoplasm

(C) a DNA molecule

(D) a nuclear membrane

*Your Answer* _____

_____

# Correct Answers

### A–3

(C)     Hydrolysis is a type of chemical digestion. Amino acids are the digested building blocks
of proteins. Glucose is a subunit of carbohydrates.
Water molecules are required to split chemical
bonds in hydrolysis but are not produced in the
process.

### A–4

(D)     Prokaryotic cells (bacteria and blue-green
algae) are more primitive, less complex cells than
eukaryotic cells of other species. They do, however, possess all the listed structures except D.
Their genetic material is not encased in a well-
defined nuclear membrane.

# Questions

---

**Q–5**

The useful energy flowing through a food chain is available mostly to the:

(A) herbivores

(B) producers

(C) secondary consumers

(D) tertiary consumers

---

*Your Answer* _____

_____

---

**Q–6**

Enzymes affect biochemical reactions by:

(A) destroying all substances produced in the reactions

(B) raising the temperature of the reaction's environment

(C) reversing their direction

(D) accelerating the reaction rates

---

*Your Answer* _____

_____

# Correct Answers

**A–5**

**(B)** Producers intercept rays of light energy from the sun to conduct photosynthesis. With each succession through the link of a food chain, less energy becomes available for use to run the metabolic processes of the organisms in a particular trophic level. Thus there is less energy available to the herbivores than there is to the plants, the producers. Succeedingly less remains for the secondary and tertiary consumers.

**A–6**

**(D)** Enzymes are organic catalysts, speeding up chemical reactions of living systems by accelerating the attainment of reaction equilibria without shifting their positions. Enzymes are specific with the reaction they catalyze and the substrates they bind to. They do not participate in the reaction itself.

# Questions

**Q–7**

Simple squamous tissue is a type of which of the following kinds of tissue?

(A) connective

(B) epithelial

(C) muscle

(D) nerve

*Your Answer* _____

_____

**Q–8**

The ten-inch human-body tube accepting swallowed food is the:

(A) esophagus

(B) larynx

(C) nasal cavity

(D) pharynx

*Your Answer* _____

_____

# Correct Answers

**A–7**

**(B)**    Epithelial tissue covers the free surfaces of the body. For example, simple (one cell layer) squamous (flat, platelike) epithelial tissue can be found on the surface of the skin, and acts as a protective barrier. Muscle tissue consists of muscle fibers, and contains no simple squamous tissue. Nerve tissue is made almost entirely of neurons and neuroglial cells. Connective tissue, such as bone, blood, and tendons, contain cells that are separated by and suspended in some sort of matrix. Vascular tissue is not a valid tissue category.

**A–8**

**(A)**    The other choices are respiratory tract structures.

**Q–9**

The majority of ATP molecules derived from nutrient metabolism are generated by (the):

(A)   anaerobic fermentation and glycolysis

(B)   fermentation and electron transport chain

(C)   glycolysis and substrate phosphorylation

(D)   Krebs cycle and electron transport chain

*Your Answer* _____

_____

**Q–10**

Mitosis functions in many organism life cycle events EXCEPT:

(A)   body cell replacement

(B)   development

(C)   gametogenesis

(D)   growth

*Your Answer* _____

_____

# Correct Answers

## A–9

**(D)** Only a small fraction of ATP molecules is produced from anaerobic process of fermentation or glycolysis. Once pyruvic acid is formed, its entry into the aerobic Krebs cycle unleashes most of the original glucose molecule's energy. Krebs cycle reactions yield high energy electrons (oxidation) that are then shuttled down a series of transport acceptors located in the inner mitochondrial membrane until they finally combine with oxygen and $H^+$ to form water. During electron transport, a proton gradient is generated across the inner mitochondrial membrane. The collapse of this proton gradient provides energy for the production of ATP molecules from ADP molecules and inorganic phosphates.

## A–10

**(C)** Mitosis produces body cells whereas meiosis is the cell division process yielding gametes or sex cells: gametogenesis.

# Questions

---

**Q–11**

RNA is made by the process of:

(A)   duplication

(B)   fermentation

(C)   replication

(D)   transcription

---

*Your Answer* _____

_____

---

**Q–12**

The scientific name *Escherichia coli* refers to this bacterium's:

(A)   class and family

(B)   family and order

(C)   genus and species

(D)   kingdom and phylum

---

*Your Answer* _____

_____

# Correct Answers

**A–11**

**(D)** This is a rote-memory question. Duplication or replication refers to DNA copying.

**A–12**

**(C)** This is an example of a specific organism's binomial, taxonomical classification. The first name identifies the organism's genus. It is capitalized. The species name begins with a lower-cased letter. Both names, usually derived from Latin or Greek, are underlined or italicized. The genus and species are the two most exact taxonomic categories. Other choices are broader, taxonomic categories from the following hierarchy:

Kingdom (broadest, most general)
   Phylum or Division (in plants)
      Class
         Order
            Family
               Genus
                  Species (most exact, specific)

# Questions

Two parents are heterozygous and display respective blood types A and B. If they mate, the probability of producing an offspring with blood type O is:

(A)  0%

(B)  25%

(C)  50%

(D)  75%

*Your Answer* _____

_____

# Correct Answers

## A–13

**(B)** The blood type A parent is $I^A$ i and the blood type B parent is $I^B$ i. Use of probability shows any one of the four blood types occurring among offspring with equal probability, thus 25% for O, A, B, or AB. Also, using a Punnett square, it is found that the 4 genotypes, $I^A I^B$ (AB), $I^A$ i(A), $I^B$ i (B), ii (O) occur in equal ratio.

|        | $I^A$       | i        |
|--------|-------------|----------|
| $I^B$  | $I^A I^B$   | $I^B$ i  |
| i      | $I^A$ i     | ii       |

it is found that the 4 genotypes, $I^A I^B$ (AB), $I^B$ i(A), $I^B$ i (B), ii (O) occur in equal ratio.

# Questions

---

**Q-14**

The human condition of color blindness is:

(A) caused by a recessive allele

(B) equally common in both sexes

(C) expressed by a heterozygous genotype in females

(D) inherited by males from their fathers

---

*Your Answer* _____

_____

 *Pharmacists can be controversial: Today, some pharmacists across the country are refusing to fill prescriptions for birth control and morning-after pills, saying that dispensing the medications violates their personal moral or religious beliefs. (www. washingtonpost.com)*

# Correct Answers

**A–14**

(A)     Many of the better-known sex-linked human conditions, such as hemophilia and color blindness, are caused by recessive alleles. Sex-linked (X-linked) genes are located on the X-chromosome. Thus males, whose sex chromosomes are X and Y, have only one such gene. Assuming that there are only two alleles for this X-linked gene, males are genotypically either C—(normal) or c—(i.e., color blind). The Y-chromosome does not offer a second gene in this case. Males can thus not be homozygous. For females, whose sex chromosomes are X and X, three genotypes are possible: CC, Cc and cc. A woman of genotype Cc is a carrier of the disease but does not express the recessive effect of color blindness. She can, however, pass on her recessive allele to her offspring. In order to produce a color blind female (cc), a female carrier would have to mate with a color blind male (c—). Each parent offers a C allele on the X chromosome for a c genotype in the offspring. This is unlikely and an infrequent event. An example of a common cross is:

Cc x C—

(female)          (male)

|   | C | c |
|---|---|---|
| C | CC | Cc |
| — | C— | c— |

One-half of the males produced is color blind. One-half of the females produced is a carrier.

# Questions

---

**Q–15**

All are common forms of energy used in metabolism EXCEPT:

(A) chemical

(B) heat

(C) kinetic

(D) nuclear

*Your Answer* _____

_____

---

**Q–16**

Genes control body chemistry by ultimately specifying the structure of:

(A) carbohydrates

(B) lipids

(C) phospholipids

(D) proteins

*Your Answer* _____

_____

# Correct Answers

**A–15**

**(D)**     Chemical energy is stored in the bonds of biomolecules: sugars, lipids, etc. Heat is a by-product of any chemical conversion of metabolism. Light energy drives photosynthesis, and kinetic energy is the energy of motion. Animals move, generating this kinetic energy from conversion of chemical bond energy.

**A–16**

**(D)**     DNA serves as a template for RNA synthesis and RNA serves as a template for protein synthesis. Proteins participate in a wide variety of body chemistry. For instance, as enzymes they catalyze nearly all chemical reactions in biological systems. They serve as transport molecules such as oxygen-carrying molecules, hemoglobins and myoglobins. They protect our bodies against foreign pathogens in the form of antibodies.

# Questions

---

**Q–17**

The gene that turns structural genes off and on in an operon is the:

(A) cistron

(B) operator

(C) promotor

(D) regulator

*Your Answer* _____

---

**Q–18**

The variable portion of a DNA nucleotide is at its:

(A) base

(B) deoxyribose

(C) phosphate group

(D) ribose

*Your Answer* _____

# Correct Answers

## A–17

**(B)** In an operon, the operator gene is adjacent to the first of several consecutive structural genes that code for enzymes that are needed for a particular metabolic pathway. These structural genes are often arranged in the same order that the enzymes which they code for are used in the pathway. The promotor is located next to the operator gene, opposite the side of the linked structural genes and is the location at which the RNA polymerase, which generated the mRNA that is necessary for enzyme synthesis, binds. The regulator gene is at another location on the chromosome. This location can be near or far from the operon that it regulates.

## A–18

**(A)** The base: adenine (A), cytosine (C), guanine (G) or thymine (T) varies from nucleotide to nucleotide building block in a DNA strand. Any DNA nucleotide is occupied by only one of these bases for four possible nucleotide structures. The other choices are constant in the nucleotide. Ribose is a component of an RNA nucleotide.

# Questions

---

**Q–19**

Select the cell type containing the highest concentration of mitochondria.

(A)  erythrocyte

(B)  leukocyte

(C)  muscle

(D)  neuron

---

*Your Answer* _____

_____

---

**Q–20**

The smallest, most specific category of classification is the:

(A)  family

(B)  genus

(C)  phylum

(D)  species

---

*Your Answer* _____

_____

# Correct Answers

**A–19**

**(C)** Muscle cells are the engines of an animal, developing contractile pulling forces to produce work. Mitochondria, cell powerhouses to extract energy from nutrients, are most in demand here.

**A–20**

**(D)** The hierarchy of classification levels is, from most general down to most restrictive:

Kingdom
    Phylum
        Class
            Order
                Family
                    Genus
                        Species

# Questions

**Q–21**

The largest, most general category of classification is the:

(A)  class

(B)  genus

(C)  kingdom

(D)  phylum

*Your Answer* _____

_____

**Q–22**

In the binomial *Quercus alba*, the first term represents the organism's:

(A)  class

(B)  genus

(C)  order

(D)  phylum

*Your Answer* _____

_____

# Correct Answers

**A–21**

**(C)** Refer to the scheme in #20.

**A–22**

**(B)** In the binomial system of organism nomenclature, the first taxonomic name is the genus name and is capitalized. It is followed by the species name, which begins with a lowercase letter. This is the scientific name of the white oak tree.

# Questions

**Q-23**

The largest number of known species is represented by the phylum:

(A)  Arthropoda

(B)  Annelida

(C)  Echinodermata

(D)  Platyhelminthes

*Your Answer* _____

_____

*A qualified pharmacist can also teach in colleges of pharmacy, supervise the manufacture of pharmaceuticals, or get involved with the research and development of new medicines. With more academic work, pharmacists can move into pharmacology, become pharmaceutical chemists, or combine pharmaceutical and legal education to pursue jobs as patent lawyers or consultants on pharmaceutical and drug laws.*

# Correct Answers

**A–23**

**(A)**   There are more arthropod species than species of any other phylum. Arthropods include such well-known groups as arachnids, crustaceans, and insects.

Annelids are segmented worms; echinoderms include sea urchins and sea anemones; phylum Platyhelminthes represents the flatworms.

*The symbol "Rx" is actually a corruption of the ancient symbol for the Roman god Jupiter, whose blessing was invoked upon every prescription to ensure its purity. Others believe that the "R" in the symbol used to be an eye, the "Eye of Horus" — an Egyptian god considered to be the "father of pharmacy." (www.hood-meddac.army.mil)*

# Questions

**Q–24**

A human birth defect produced by a sex-linked recessive allele of a gene is:

(A) albinism

(B) diabetes mellitus

(C) hemophilia

(D) high cholesterol

*Your Answer* _____

_____

SSRIs, or selective serotonin reuptake inhibitors, are a widely used class of antidepressants that came under scrutiny during a recent drug-safety controversy. (Encyclopedia Britannica, 2005.)

# Correct Answers

**A–24**

(C)    Two well-known examples of recessive sex-linked traits in human beings are red-green color blindness and hemophilia. These recessive sex-linked traits occur in a higher frequency in men than in women.

Albinism is an autosomal recessive disease. An individual heterozygous for albinism appears normal because one normal gene can be sufficient for making enough of the functional enzyme that make melanin pigments. Albinism is associated with low melanin levels.

Diabetes mellitus is characterized by an elevated level of glucose in blood and urine and arises from a deficiency of insulin. The causes for the disease are not clear but there is evidence that this defect has molecular basis such as abnormally formed insulin.

High cholesterol level is a genetic disease resulting from a mutation at a single autosomal locus coded for the receptor for LDL (low-density lipoprotein). Whether a trait is dominant or recessive does not apply to this disease because the heterozygotes suffer from a milder problem than the homozygotes. The heterozygotes possess functional LDL receptors though they are present at a deficient level.

# Questions

---

**Q–25**

The skin performs all of the following human body functions EXCEPT:

(A) protection

(B) sensation

(C) storage

(D) temperature regulation

---

*Your Answer* _____

_____

---

**Q–26**

The biceps brachii produce movements by pulling on:

(A) bones

(B) joints

(C) muscles

(D) nerves

---

*Your Answer* _____

_____

# Correct Answers

## A–25

(C)     A study of skin structure reveals skin's ability to perform all but one of the listed capabilities, i.e., blood vessels to vent body heat, receptors to sense stimuli, and layers to protect.

## A–26

(A)     The biceps brachii are the muscles on the ventral portion of the upper arm that pull and bend the forearm. Bones are the rigid bars that yield to skeletal muscles' pulling force. Movable joints allow a source of mobility between articulating bones. Skeletal muscles are stimulated by nerves. Lacking this stimulation they will not respond.

# Questions

---

**Q–27**

Neurons that conduct signals away from the central nervous system are classified as:

(A) afferent

(B) associative

(C) internuncial

(D) motor

*Your Answer* _____

_____

---

**Q–28**

The innermost layer of the eye is the:

(A) choroid coat

(B) cornea

(C) retina

(D) sclera

*Your Answer* _____

_____

# Correct Answers

### A–27

**(D)**  Sensory or afferent neurons send signals toward the central nervous system (CNS). Associative, or internuncial, neurons are within the CNS. Motor or efferent neurons, with axons outside and directed away from the CNS, send signals out to peripheral points.

### A–28

**(C)**  The retina contains the receptor cells that receive and register incoming light rays. The choroid is a middle layer of darkly pigmented and highly vascularized tissue. This structure provides blood to the eye and absorbs light to prevent internal reflection that may blur the image. The outer sclera (white of the eye) includes the transparent cornea. The pupil is an opening in the donut-shaped, colored iris interior to the cornea.

# Questions

---

**Q–29**

Which of the following is NOT a polymer?

(A) DNA

(B) glycogen

(C) glucose

(D) RNA

---

*Your Answer* _____

_____

---

**Q–30**

Which law explains the inhalation and exhalation of air in terms of pressure changes?

(A) Archimedes' law

(B) Dalton's law

(C) Boyle's law

(D) Mendel's law

---

*Your Answer* _____

_____

# Correct Answers

**A–29**

(C)     A polymer is a long complex molecule formed by the bonding of simpler, repetitive sub-units. DNA and RNA are polymers of nucleotides. Glycogen is a polysaccharide. Polysaccharides are polymers of simple sugars, including glucose. Glucose is a subunit, not a polymer.

**A–30**

(C)     Boyle's law states that air pressure is inversely proportional to volume. As the chest cavity increases due to the flattening of the diaphragm and rib elevation, internal pressure drops below that of the atmosphere, causing an inrush of air.

# Questions

---

**Q–31**

Highest pressure of circulating blood is found in a(n):

(A) arteriole

(B) artery

(C) capillary

(D) vein

*Your Answer* _____

_____

---

**Q–32**

Which of the following is part of a human's axial skeleton?

(A) clavicle

(B) fibula

(C) humerus

(D) rib

*Your Answer* _____

_____

# Correct Answers

## A–31

**(B)** Blood flows through the circulatory system due to a pressure gradient. The blood will flow from a region of higher pressure to one of lower pressure. Therefore, blood pressure must be greatest at the beginning of blood's circuit, namely, the aorta, or artery.

## A–32

**(D)** The rib is one of the twelve pairs of bones that form a rib cage to protect the lungs and heart. Along with the skull and vertebral column, the rib cage forms the axial skeleton. The bones of the paired appendages, the pectoral and pelvic girdles belong to the appendicular skeleton.

# Questions

---

**Q–33**

Glial cells:

(A)   conduct signals

(B)   contribute to movement

(C)   cover the skin

(D)   support neurons

*Your Answer* _____

---

**Q–34**

Select the disease caused by a protozoa:

(A)   chicken pox

(B)   common cold

(C)   malaria

(D)   measles

*Your Answer* _____

# Correct Answers

## A–33

**(D)** Glial cells bind neurons together. They offer nerve cells support, protection, and nutritional supply.

## A–34

**(C)** Malaria is caused by protozoans of the genus Plasmodium, of the class Sporozoa. The other choices represent diseases caused by viruses.

# Questions

---

**Q–35**

Which of the following has a vitamin as a building block?

(A)   apoenzyme

(B)   coenzyme

(C)   holoenzyme

(D)   protein

---

*Your Answer* _____

_____

---

**Q–36**

The filtering of inhaled debris that travels through the upper respiratory tract occurs through the action of:

(A)   cilia

(B)   goblet cells

(C)   Leidig cells

(D)   villi

---

*Your Answer* _____

_____

# Correct Answers

## A-35

**(B)** All enzymes are composed primarily of protein. The more complex enzymes have non-protein portions called cofactors; the protein portion of the enzyme is called an apoenzyme. If the cofactor is an easily separated organic molecule, it is called a coenzyme. Many coenzymes are related to vitamins. An enzyme deprived of its vitamin is thus incomplete, leading to the nonexecution of a key step in metabolism. Holoenzyme refers to the RNA polymerase, with its core enzyme and sigma subunit associated together.

## A-36

**(A)** Cilia line the upper respiratory tract, waving against air inflow to filter out unneeded debris. Villi are fingerlike extensions of the membranes of cells lining the small intestine. They increase surface area to facilitate absorption of digested nutrients. Goblet cells line the same region and secrete mucus. Leidig cells are in the male testis.

# Questions

---

**Q–37**

Substances in the blood are transported across the nephron tubules by mechanisms in the process of:

(A)   filtration

(B)   osmosis

(C)   reabsorption

(D)   secretion

*Your Answer* _____

_____

---

**Q–38**

A person receives the results of a hematocrit during a series of blood tests. A hematocrit is the:

(A)   abundance of white blood cells in blood

(B)   concentration of sugar in the blood

(C)   level of circulating antibodies

(D)   percentage of blood cellular material by volume

*Your Answer* _____

_____

# Correct Answers

## A–37

**(D)**    Filtration first moves blood plasma substances from the glomerulus (capillary) into the cuplike Bowman's capsule at the nephron's origin. After monitoring these solute concentrations (e.g., glucose, sodium, etc.), reabsorption returns them to the blood from the nephron tubule at high percentage rates. Secretion is a third step, moving materials from the blood (peritubular capillaries) to the distal convoluted tubule for exit and elimination.

## A–38

**(D)**    Hematocrit is the percentage of blood cells in blood by volume. For males this value is normally $47 \pm 5$; for females, it is $42 \pm 5$. Thirty-two percent is abnormally low, indicating anemia — a diminished capacity of the blood to carry oxygen.

# Questions

The relatively large size of the mammalian brain, allowing for greater learning, association, and memory, is due to the enlargement of the

(A)   cerebellum

(B)   hypothalamus

(C)   cerebrum

(D)   midbrain

*Your Answer* _____

_____

*Drugs may be classified in one of three ways: by chemical group (e.g., alkaloids); pharmacologically (i.e., by the way they work in the body); and according to their therapeutic uses. (Encyclopedia Britannica, 2005.)*

# Correct Answers

(C)      The brains of all vertebrates are divided into the hindbrain, midbrain, and forebrain. In lower vertebrates, such as fish, the hindbrain is the dominant portion of the brain. It consists of the medulla oblongata and pons. The former deals with vital reflexes, such as cardiac activity, and it links the spinal cord to the rest of the brain. The latter contains the respiratory center, and like the former, it is the origin of many cranial nerves. The cerebellum is also part of the hindbrain: it functions in equilibrium and proprioception (awareness of body/limb position and movement).

The midbrains of fish process visual information and their forebrains function in olfactory (smell) sensation. These sensory functions are attributed to the cerebrum in higher vertebrates.

The midbrain is relatively small in humans, and, as the origin of several cranial nerves, it controls eye movements and pupillary size.

In all vertebrates, the forebrain consists of the diencephalon and the cerebrum. The diencephalon consists of the thalamus, a relay center for sensory input en route to the cerebrum, and the hypothalamus, which regulates many activities, including circadian rhythms, body temperature, emotions, food intake, and some hormone secretion. The cerebrum is highly developed in mammals: it constitutes 7/8 of the human brain. The cerebrum functions in learning, association, and memory. Birds also show great development of the cerebrum.

# Questions

---

**Q–40**

In humans, there are many anatomical adaptations that function to increase surface area for chemical reactions and transport mechanisms. All of the following are examples EXCEPT

(A) the alveoli of the lungs

(B) the microvilli of the small intestine

(C) the villi of the small intestine

(D) the sensory hairs (cilia) in the cochlea of the inner ear

---

*Your Answer* _____

_____

*Statins are drugs like Zocor and Lipitor that block (inhibit) an enzyme the body needs to produce cholesterol, thereby lowering blood cholesterol levels. (www.webmd.com)*

# Correct Answers

## A–40

**(D)** Alveoli are tiny thin-walled air sacs within the lungs. There are widespread sheets of capillaries that cover the alveoli. The millions of alveoli in each lung increase the surface area through which gases can diffuse between air and blood.

The small intestine has many adaptions that increase its surface area for both digestion and absorption (transport of nutrients from the lumen into the blood or lymph). First, the small intestine is very long (about 12 feet); second, the inner layer, or mucosa, is folded into villi that project into the lumen. Microvilli, which are folds of the epithelial cells composing the villi, further increase the surface area. Microvilli are also referred to as the brushborder. There are brushborder enzymes that complete chemical hydrolysis of nutrient molecules. Then the small monomers formed are absorbed.

# Questions

**Q–41**

The period of human gestation is divided into three trimesters. The event that is correctly matched to its trimester of occurrence is the following:

(A) The third trimester is characterized by development and differentiation.

(B) The greatest growth in size occurs in the first trimester.

(C) The limb buds develop in the first trimester.

(D) Organ development begins in the second trimester.

*Your Answer* _____

_____

**Q–42**

Name the bone that does NOT articulate with the humerus.

(A) clavicle

(B) radius

(C) scapula

(D) ulna

*Your Answer* _____

_____

# Correct Answers

## A–41

(C)     Human embryonic development takes nine months; these months are divided into three trimesters of three months each.

In the first trimester, cleavage and implantation occur within the first week. The embryonic membranes begin to develop, followed by gastrulation (the differentiation of the three primary cell layers: ectoderm, mesoderm, and endoderm) and neurulation (formation of the neural tube). By the end of the first month, organ development has begun — these organs include the eyes, heart, limb buds, and most other organs. In the second month, morphogenesis occurs. Morphogenesis refers to the development of form or structure. In short, the first trimester is a critical period of differentiation and development, but growth is not pronounced.

The second trimester is a period of rapid growth in size and weight. The mother may become aware of kicking from the baby. Growth continues and is most prominent in the final trimester.

## A–42

(A)     The humerus, or the upper arm bone, articulates with the radius and ulna (forearm bones) at its distal end. Its other end fits into the lateral socket of the scapula, or shoulder blade. It does not articulate with the clavicle, or collarbone.

# Questions

---

**Q–43**

Smoking cigarettes over a long period harms the upper respiratory tract's

(A)  alveoli

(B)  cilia

(C)  goblet cells

(D)  villi

*Your Answer* _____

_____

---

**Q–44**

Eye receptors and their function can best be summarized as:

(A)  cones – color discrimination, rods – twilight vision

(B)  cones – twilight vision, rods – color discrimination

(C)  ganglia – color discrimination, rods – twilight vision

(D)  lens – light refraction, cornea – light refraction

*Your Answer* _____

_____

# Correct Answers

**A–43**

**(B)** Cells that line the upper respiratory tract have cilia. These cilia trap and filter foreign debris. Alveoli, which would also be harmed by smoking, are in the lower respiratory tract. Villi and goblet cells are located in the small intestine.

**A–44**

**(A)** Rods and cones are retinal cells lining the eye's inner surface. Cones are specialized for color discrimination or visual activity. Rods are utilized in dim light.

# Questions

---

**Q–45**

Among humans, a universal recipient is a person that has which blood type?

(A) A+

(B) AB+

(C) AB–

(D) O+

*Your Answer* _____

_____

---

**Q–46**

Humans, great apes, and monkeys are all members of which of the following taxonomic categories?

(A) genus

(B) family

(C) order

(D) species

*Your Answer* _____

_____

# Correct Answers

**A–45**

**(B)**  A person of blood-type AB has no anti-A and no anti-B antibodies in his blood plasma. Therefore, there will be no antibodies present that would attack foreign red blood cells that enter the bloodstream during transfusion. A person whose blood has a positive Rh-factor also has no antibodies that attack Rh antigens present on red blood cells. Therefore, a person of blood-type AB+ would have no trouble in receiving any type of blood during a transfusion.

**A–46**

**(C)**  All are members of the order of Primates.

# Questions

---

**Q–47**

Following menses, the initiation of the menstrual cycle follows an increase in the secretion of the hormone:

(A)  ACTH

(B)  FSH

(C)  LH

(D)  GnRH

*Your Answer* _____

_____

---

**Q–48**

The two criteria used most often in taxonomic classifications are:

(A)  color and height

(B)  evolution and lifespan

(C)  lifespan and morphology

(D)  morphology and phylogeny

*Your Answer* _____

_____

# Correct Answers

## A–47

**(B)** The concentration of follicle-stimulating hormone, FSH, increases following menses. Thus, the menstrual cycle continues. It is secreted by the pituitary gland and serves to increase follicle growth around a selected sex cell in the ovary.

ACTH = adrenocorticotrophic hormone
LH = luteinizing hormone
GnRH = gonadotrophin-releasing hormone

## A–48

**(D)** Morphology refers to body structure and form while phylogeny represents evolutionary history. The two are related. For example, a chimpanzee is the most humanlike animal because of the recent common evolutionary ancestor of chimp and human, revealed by the fossil record.

# Questions

**Q–49**

Cells that sense sound are found in the ear's:

(A)  cochlea

(B)  pinna

(C)  semicircular canals

(D)  vestibule

*Your Answer* _____

_____

**Q–50**

Blood normally circulates through vessels in which sequence?

(A)   artery – arteriole – capillary – venule – vein

(B)   arteriole – artery – capillary – vein – venule

(C)   capillary – arteriole – artery – vein – venule

(D)   vein – capillary – venule – artery – arteriole

*Your Answer* _____

_____

# Correct Answers

**A–49**

(A)     This is a snail shell-shaped structure in the inner ear. The semicircular canals (dynamic equilibrium) and vestibule (static equilibrium) are there to control body balance. The pinna, outer ear cartilage flap, transmit sound waves from the outer ear through the middle ear and on to the inner ear.

**A–50**

(A)     Arteries take blood away from the heart, dividing into smaller, more numerous arterioles. They divide to become numerous, microscopic capillaries for exchange with cells. They collect into venules, which merge to form larger veins. Venules and veins return blood to the heart.

# Questions

---

**Q–51**

Which of the following statements is true?

(A) In prophase, the sister chromatids separate.

(B) In telophase, the nuclear membrane begins to form.

(C) In metaphase, the sister chromatids begin condensation.

(D) In anaphase, the chromosomes move to the spindle equator.

---

*Your Answer* _____

_____

*Cholesterol is an important fatlike substance (lipid) that is made in the liver and is necessary for the body to function. (www. webmd.com)*

# Correct Answers

## A–51

**(B)**     Mitosis is the phase of the cell cycle during which one cell divides into two. Strictly speaking, mitosis refers to division of the nucleus. Cytokinesis, or cytoplasmic division, follows immediately. There are four consecutive stages of mitosis: prophase, metaphase, anaphase, and telophase.

In prophase, the chromosomes become visible as the sister chromatids condense into rod-like bodies. The nuclear membrane disintegrates and the nucleolus disappears. Microtubule spindles begin their formation.

In metaphase, the spindle attaches to the centromeres (central constricted region of each chromatid). Chromosomes are guided by spindle microtubules to the spindle equator, the central plane of the cell.

In anaphase, the sister chromatids of each pair separate and move from the equator to opposite poles of the cell. This movement is perpetuated by the depolymerization of the microtubule apparatus.

Telophase is simply a reversal of prophase: the nuclear membrane and nucleolus begin formation, and the chromosomes decondense into thread-like forms. Cytokinesis follows or occurs simultaneously and the bilobed cell with two nuclei will split into two individual cells.

# Questions

**Q–52**

A subject with Type A blood

(A) has A antibodies in his plasma.

(B) has B antigens on his red blood cells.

(C) can successfully receive blood from a type O person.

(D) can successfully receive blood from a type AB person.

*Your Answer* _____

_____

*Low-density lipoprotein (LDL) is called "bad cholesterol." (www.webmd.com)*

# Correct Answers

## A-52

**(C)** The ABO blood system is based on the presence of antigens on the red blood cells and antibodies in the plasma. A type A person has A antigens on his red blood cells and anti-B antibodies in his plasma. He cannot have anti-A antibodies in his plasma as they would cause his red blood cells to agglutinate (clump). A type B person has B antigens and anti-A antibodies. A type AB person has both A and B antigens, and therefore has no antibodies, while a type O person has no antigens and therefore has both anti-A and anti-B antibodies.

Concerning blood transfusions, a risk exists when a recipient's plasma antibodies agglutinate the donor's cell antigens. There is no risk associated with the recipient's cell antigens being agglutinated by the donor's plasma antibodies, because those antibodies are diluted by the recipient's plasma.

A type A subject can only receive blood from another type A person or from a type O person, since the anti-B antibodies in the type A's subject plasma will not have anything to agglutinate. If the type A person were to receive blood from a type AB subject, his anti-B antibodies would agglutinate the B antigens from the donor's blood.

Another important group of blood antigens is the Rh factor. Someone with the Rh factor is designated Rh+. Those without the Rh factor are designated Rh−. Unlike the ABO blood groups, no antibodies are normally present, unless the blood has been exposed to the Rh antigen. There can be no prediction of the Rh blood type for the type A subject in question, as the two groups are independent.

# Questions

**Q–53**

Synapsis

(A) occurs during the second meiotic division.

(B) refers to the pairing between homologous chromosomes.

(C) is synonymous with chiasmata.

(D) refers to the tetrad of chromatids.

*Your Answer* _____

_____

High-density lipoprotein (HDL) is called "good cholesterol," and can help remove excess cholesterol from blood vessels. (www.webmd.com)

# Correct Answers

## A–53

**(B)** In the first meiotic prophase, many events occur that provide the basis for variation even between offspring of the same parents.

First, the homologous chromosomes pair up in a process called synapsis. Since each homologous chromosome has already replicated, it exists as two sister chromatids joined together by a centromere. The paired chromosomes now exist as a tetrad of chromatids. Now crossing-over, the exchange of segments between homologous non-sister chromatids, can occur. The site of cross-over is called a chiasma (*pl.* chiasmata). Since the chromosomes and later the chromatids will ultimately segregate randomly and independently, and since they contain recombined chromosome segments and hence, recombined genetic traits, the foundation for variation is laid down.

# Questions

**Q–54**

The cell organelles that are most similar to pro-karyotes are

(A) the mitochondria and chloroplasts.

(B) the rough and smooth endoplasmic reticula.

(C) the rough endoplasmic reticula and ribosomes.

(D) the rough endoplasmic reticula and Golgi apparatuses.

*Your Answer* _____

_____

*According to the National Association of Chain Drug Stores, the number of filled prescriptions increased from 1.9 million in 1992 to over 3.1 million in 2002 — about a 60% increase over 10 years. (www.aacp.org)*

# Correct Answers

**(A)** A mitochondrion is a cellular organelle that utilizes oxygen to produce ATP. It has its own DNA, which replicates autonomously from the nuclear DNA. It is suspected, based on the size, structure, and biochemistry of mitochondria, that they were once prokaryotic cells similar to bacteria that formed a symbiotic relationship with a eukaryotic host. Due to evolution, the mitochondrion has lost its independence.

A similar story holds true for chloroplasts, which also have their own DNA, similar to that of bacteria. A chloroplast, with its capacity for photosynthesis, could have originally been an independent prokaryote, now dependent on the cell in which it lives.

The endoplasmic reticula (both rough and smooth), ribosomes, Golgi apparatus, and lysosomes do not contain their own DNA. Their functions are ultimately dictated by the nucleus. The ribosomes synthesize proteins. If the ribosomes are attached to the endoplasmic reticulum, making it rough endoplasmic reticulum, the proteins will enter the reticular lumen and be transported through the cell and reach the Golgi apparatus for modification and continued distribution. The smooth endoplasmic reticulum functions primarily in lipid synthesis.

# Questions

---

**Q–55**

A phenotype refers to

(A) the genetic makeup of an individual.

(B) the expression of dominant traits.

(C) the expression of recessive traits.

(D) the manifest expression of the genotype.

*Your Answer* _____

_____

---

**Q–56**

Heating a test tube culture full of bacteria and killing them all is

(A) a density-dependent factor.

(B) an intrinsic factor.

(C) a result of exponential growth.

(D) None of the above.

*Your Answer* _____

_____

# Correct Answers

## A–55

**(D)** The genotype is the actual genetic constitution of the individual, but the phenotype is the expression of those genes. For instance, the genotypes that code for eye color are BB (homozygous dominant), Bb (heterozygous) and bb (homozygous recessive). There are thus three genotypes. But there are only two phenotypes: Bb and BB both code for brown eye color, as the allele for brown eyes (B) is dominant to that for blue eyes (b). Blue eyes are only possible with the genotype bb. (Note that green eyes are considered as blue, genotypically and phenotypically). Thus a blue-eyed person knows his genotype immediately, but a brown-eyed person needs to look at his lineage to possibly figure out his genotype.

Phenotype includes all physical characteristics of an organism that are the results of genotype. A characteristic need not be seen by an observer to be included in an organism's phenotype; e.g., one's blood type is part of one's phenotype.

## A–56

**(D)** In itself, the heat killing of the bacterial culture is unrelated to factors that regulate populations such as choices (A), (B), and (C). The decimation of this microbial population occurred when a critical environmental variable, in this case temperature, exceeded the range of tolerance that is characteristic of the species.

# Questions

---

**Q–57**

All of the following are terms that describe viruses EXCEPT:

(A)  free-living

(B)  host-dependent

(C)  noncellular

(D)  protein and nucleic acid makeup

*Your Answer* _____

_____

---

**Q–58**

Meiosis takes place in which of the following organs?

(A)  ovary

(B)  skeletal muscle of embryo

(C)  spleen

(D)  liver

*Your Answer* _____

_____

# Correct Answers

**A–57**

(A)    Viruses are incredibly small (nanometers). They lack normal cellular structures and thus need a host organism to grow and reproduce. They consist of protein coats surrounding nucleic acid cores.

**A–58**

(A)    Of all the organs mentioned, only the ovary is part of the reproductive system. Thus, meiosis would be expected to occur in some of the structures associated with the reproductive system. Choice (B) is part of the skeletal system while choices (C) and (D) are part of other body systems.

# Questions

**Q–59**

What is the relationship, if any, between color blindness and hemophilia?

(A) Both are restricted to chromosomes coming from the father.

(B) Both are restricted to chromosomes coming from the mother.

(C) Both are sex-linked conditions.

(D) Both are caused by dominant genes.

*Your Answer* _____

_____

**Q–60**

Mutations are caused by

(A) base changes in DNA.

(B) base changes in RNA.

(C) changes in the sugars of DNA.

(D) changes in the phosphates of RNA.

*Your Answer* _____

_____

# Correct Answers

**A–59**

**(C)** Both are examples of sex-linked conditions carried by recessive genes on X-chromosomes.

**A–60**

**(A)** Mutations can be caused by changes in the nitrogenous bases of DNA. One change can be the replacement of one base pair for another within a segment of DNA. Other changes can be the insertion of extra base pairs, or the deletion of one or more base pairs. A change in RNA nucleotide sequence may result in faulty translation of a gene, but RNA is constantly degraded and synthesized; as long as DNA remains unchanged, RNA will almost always be correctly synthesized.

# Questions

---

**Q–61**

What change in the normal structure of hemoglobin results in sickle-cell anemia?

(A) There is a change in the sequence of the amino acids.

(B) There is a substitution of one amino acid for another.

(C) There is a change in the number of nucleotides.

(D) The peptide bonds are broken in the sickle-cell hemoglobin molecule.

*Your Answer* _____

_____

---

**Q–62**

Fermentation

(A) results in the formation of lactic acid.

(B) does not require oxygen.

(C) does require oxygen.

(D) produces large amounts of energy.

*Your Answer* _____

_____

# Correct Answers

## A–61

**(B)** The entire structural difference between a normal and a sickle-cell hemoglobin molecule consists of the substitution of the amino acid valine for the amino acid glutamic acid. This substitution occurs in the sixth position of each of the two B-chains in hemoglobin.

## A–62

**(B)** Fermentation is the production of ethanol from glucose as done by yeast cells. In glycolysis, one glucose molecule is converted to two molecules of pyruvic acid and also provides enough energy for the synthesis of two molecules of ATP and two molecules of NADPH. The pyruvic acid, still containing much potential energy, can next enter either the anaerobic pathway or the aerobic pathway. In one type of anaerobic pathway, pyruvic acid is converted to ethanol by the action of yeast cells on sugar.

# Questions

---

**Q–63**

Which of the following tissues is NOT related to connective tissue?

(A) collagen

(B) bone

(C) cartilage

(D) lymph

---

*Your Answer* _____

---

**Q–64**

A respiratory system does not necessarily need

(A) an exchange surface with an adequate area.

(B) a means to transport gases to internal areas.

(C) a means of protecting exchange surfaces.

(D) a location deep inside an organism.

---

*Your Answer* _____

---

# Correct Answers

## A–63

**(D)**    Connective tissue provides support for body parts and binds structures together. Options B and C are examples of connective tissue. Collagen (Option A) is a protein found in skin and bone, and is secreted by the cells of connective tissue. Collagen provides a rigid matrix in which connective tissue cells exist.

## A–64

**(D)**    Options (A) through (C) refer to characteristics of the respiratory system of both unicellular and multicellular organisms. In single-celled or simple organisms such as algae and flatworms, oxygen diffuses directly through cell membranes. Thus, location deep inside an organism is not a requirement of a respiratory system.

# Questions

---

**Q–65**

T-cells are generally NOT involved in fighting

(A)   cancer cells.

(B)   transplanted foreign tissue.

(C)   viral infections.

(D)   bacterial infections.

---

*Your Answer* _____

_____

---

**Q–66**

Which statement about respiration is INCOR-RECT?

(A)   Humans use positive-pressure breathing.

(B)   When exhaling, the position of the dia-phragm and ribs in humans is: ribs lowered, diaphragm raised.

(C)   Abdominal breathing in humans does not de-pend on active transport of air.

(D)   Frogs use positive-pressure breathing.

---

*Your Answer* _____

_____

# Correct Answers

**A–65**

**(D)** The primary targets of B-cells are bacterial infections. All other options are the targets of T-cells.

**A–66**

**(A)** Humans (mammals) and birds use negative pressure breathing whereby air is drawn into the lungs. This process involves the raising of the rib cage and the downward movement of the diaphragm during inhalation. The volume of the chest cavity is increased, reducing the internal air pressure, resulting in air being drawn into the lungs to equalize the pressure. In contrast, positive-pressure breathing occurs when air is **forced** into the lungs. For example, a frog closes its nostrils and raises the floor of its mouth, thus reducing the volume of the mouth cavity and forcing air into the lungs. Active transport of air does not occur in humans.

# Questions

---

**Q–67**

In capillary exchange

(A) proteins in the blood and tissue help to determine osmotic pressure.

(B) osmotic pressure moves water outside the capillaries only.

(C) blood pressure is greater than osmotic pressure at the venous end of the capillaries.

(D) blood pressure is less than osmotic pressure at the arterial end of the capillaries.

*Your Answer* _____

---

**Q–68**

A strand of DNA is a _____ and can generate a new _____ strand of DNA.

(A) copy, identical

(B) parent, identical

(C) duplicate, duplicate

(D) template, complementary

*Your Answer* _____

# Correct Answers

### A–67

(A)      At the arterial end of the capillaries, the blood pressure is higher than the pressure of the tissue fluid outside the capillaries. This differential causes fluid to leave the capillaries and go into the tissue. At the same time the concentration of proteins in the tissue fluid is less than the concentration of proteins in the blood because the large protein molecules cannot easily diffuse through the capillary walls. Thus, water tends to move into the capillaries by osmosis to equalize the osmotic pressure; this occurs at the venous end. Approximately 99% of the water that exits capillaries at the arterial ends due to the net force of blood pressure, re-enters the capillaries at their venous ends due to the net force of osmotic pressure.

### A–68

(D)      During self-replication, the DNA unwinds at the weak hydrogen bonds that join the complementary base pairs. Free nucleotides in the environment become attached to the open bases of the parent strands if the proper catalyzing enzymes are present. The attachments follow the principle of complementary base pairing so that the strand produced is complementary, not identical, to the intact parent strand. The original strand acts as a "template" for the generation of a complementary strand.

# Questions

Q–69

Viruses have

(A) the ability to replicate their genetic material.

(B) the ability to make their own energy.

(C) their own metabolic machinery.

(D) their own enzymes.

*Your Answer* _____

_____

Q–70

Which condition is necessary for diffusion to occur?

(A) A living cell

(B) A permeable membrane

(C) A differentially permeable membrane

(D) A difference in concentration

*Your Answer* _____

_____

# Correct Answers

## A–69

**(A)** Viruses are parasites in that they cannot multiply outside their host cell. They use the energy sources (option (B)), metabolic machinery (option (C)), and enzymes (option (D)) of the host cell. Viruses do have the ability to replicate their genetic material DNA or RNA. They do so by inserting a copy of their genetic material and using the resources of the host cell to replicate the material and to form their own protein coats. The virus particle then escapes from the host cell and is ready to infect another host cell.

## A–70

**(D)** Diffusion occurs when there is a difference in the concentrations of substances and the goal is to have the particles distributed uniformly throughout. Diffusion can occur with or without a membrane (choices (B) and (C)). Lab experiments showing diffusion can be done with inanimate objects.

# Questions

---

**Q–71**

Proteins are formed by combining

(A) lipids.

(B) monosaccharide and disaccharides.

(C) nucleic acids.

(D) amino acids.

*Your Answer* —————————————————

—————————————————————————

---

**Q–72**

An enzyme is a large organic molecule with a surface geometry that is composed of

(A) amino acids.

(B) monosaccharides.

(C) glycerol and fatty acids.

(D) polysaccharides.

*Your Answer* —————————————————

—————————————————————————

# Correct Answers

**A–71**

**(D)** Proteins are composed of carbon, oxygen, hydrogen, nitrogen, and sometimes sulfur. These elements combine to form amino acids. Each amino acid has a carboxyl group (-COOH) and an amino group (-NH$_2$), which are attached to a carbon atom. In addition, side groups (called radicals) are also attached to the carbon atom. There are 20 different kinds of amino acids each with a different side group.

**A–72**

**(A)** An enzyme is a type of protein that catalyzes biological reactions. The surface geometry plays an important part in its specificity for substance molecules.

# Questions

**Q-73**

Enzymes

(A) are highly sensitive to pH charges.

(B) are highly specific to the reactions they catalyze.

(C) work best at optimum temperatures.

(D) all of the above.

*Your Answer* _____

_____

**Q-74**

Which is a characteristic of a hormone?

(A) They are produced in the tissue that they affect.

(B) Small quantities can produce effects.

(C) They work interdependently with other hormones.

(D) Both (B) and (C).

*Your Answer* _____

_____

# Correct Answers

**A–73**

**(D)** Enzymes require specific conditions of temperature, pH, and substrate under which they operate at maximum efficiency. In humans, enzymes work best at an optimum temperature of 98.6ºF, 37ºC, but at various pH values, dependent on the enzyme, the substrate, and the location of reaction.

**A–74**

**(D)** Choice (A) is incorrect. Hormones of animals are produced in certain tissues but are transported to and affect other tissues. They can exert specific influences using very small quantities.

# Questions

**Q–75**

The formation of eggs and sperm is called

(A)  gametogenesis.

(B)  gastrulation.

(C)  ovulation.

(D)  fertilization.

*Your Answer* _____

_____

**Q–76**

The heart, bones, and blood develop primarily from the:

(A)  endoderm

(B)  ectoderm

(C)  mesoderm

(D)  morula

*Your Answer* _____

_____

# Correct Answers

## A–75

(A)     The sperm and the egg form within the parental reproductive system. The sperm grows a tail that will help it move to the egg cell, and the egg cytoplasm gains nutrient.

## A–76

(C)     The endoderm (choice (A)) gives rise to the inner lining of the digestive and respiratory tract, as well as the liver and pancreas. The ectoderm (choice (B)) gives rise to the epidermis and nervous system. The morula is an early zygotic stage of division.

# Questions

**Q–77**

All living organisms are classified as eukaryotes (true nucleus) or prokaryotes (before the nucleus). An example of a prokaryote is

(A) the AIDS virus.

(B) *E. coli.*

(C) *Homo Sapiens.*

(D) an oak tree.

*Your Answer* _____

_____

*According to the U.S. Census Bureau, 1 in 5 Americans will be classified as elderly by 2030. Pharmacists play a key role in helping elderly patients navigate complicated drug medication requirements and explore ways to minimize their financial burden. (www. aacp.org)*

# Correct Answers

**(B)** Cells are classified as eukaryotic or pro-karyotic. The former are characterized by a membrane-bound nucleus, while the latter do not have an organized nucleus. All living things are grouped into one of the five kingdoms. Only kingdom Monera consists of prokaryotic organisms. Kingdom Monera includes blue-green algae and bacteria. E. coli (Escherichia coli) is a bacterium.

The other four kingdoms include only eukaryotic organisms. Kingdom Animalia, the animals, include the human being, or Homo sapiens. An oak tree falls into the kingdom Plantae.

The AIDS (Acquired Immune Deficiency Syndrome) virus is not classified here because viruses are not truly living organisms; they depend on a living host (plant, animal, bacterium) for their metabolic and reproductive mechanisms.

# Questions

---

**Q–78**

All of the following statements about the cell membrane are true EXCEPT

(A)  It functions as a selective barrier between the intracellular fluid and the extracellular fluid.

(B)  The phospholipids within are amphipathic — that is, they each contain polar and nonpolar regions.

(C)  The major lipid within it is cholesterol.

(D)  The fluid-mosaic model describes the fluidity and mobility of the membrane.

---

*Your Answer* _____

_____

*The misuse of over the counter drugs causes 178,000 hospitalizations a year. (www.UHFtips.org)*

# Correct Answers

(C)    The cell membrane, or plasma membrane, is composed primarily of phospholipids and proteins. The phospholipids form a lipid bilayer with their fatty acid chains oriented toward the center and the phosphate heads oriented toward the extracellular and intracellular fluids. Since the fatty acid tail, a long hydrocarbon chain, is nonpolar, and the charged phosphate head is polar, the phospholipid is said to be amphipathic.

The fluid mosaic model of the plasma membrane is a reminder that the membrane is very dynamic. The proteins form a mosaic upon a fluid phospholipid background; thus, the membrane has been likened to "icebergs (proteins) floating on a sea (of lipid)."

The primary function of the plasma membrane is to separate the intracellular and extracellular fluids, forming a selective barrier between the two and maintaining quite a different composition in the two fluid compartments.

Cholesterol, though present in cell membranes, is a steroid. It is not a major component of the cell membrane.

# Questions

**Q–79**

The gene for sickle cell anemia is different from the normal hemoglobin gene, because

(A)  it contains ribose.

(B)  it is missing.

(C)  it has a base substitution.

(D)  it is made of RNA instead of DNA.

*Your Answer* _____

_____

**Q–80**

Which of the following is concerned mainly with cellular respiration?

(A)  Cell membrane

(B)  Golgi apparatus

(C)  Ribosomes

(D)  Mitochondria

*Your Answer* _____

_____

# Correct Answers

## A–79

(C)    To answer this question you must know how alleles (forms of the same gene) generally differ. First of all, a gene is made of DNA rather than RNA, and, therefore, would not contain uracil or ribose. A different form of a gene might mean that the gene is missing or that there is a base substitution. Since a different form of hemoglobin is found when the defective gene is present, the gene must be present but in altered form.

## A–80

(D)    The mitochondria contain mainly respiratory enzymes and coenzymes, which are responsible for carrying out respiration. They are the chief "factories" of cellular respiration.

**Q–81**

The chromosomal mutation by which a chromosome fragment attaches to a nonhomologous chromosome is termed a(n)

(A) deletion.

(B) translocation

(C) duplication.

(D) inversion.

*Your Answer* _____

_____

**Q–82**

When a virus infects a bacterium, the material that enters the bacterium from the virus is

(A) sulfur.

(B) nucleic acid.

(C) a mutagen.

(D) protein.

*Your Answer* _____

_____

# Correct Answers

## A–81

**(B)** Translocation is the attachment of a chromosome fragment to a nonhomologous chromosome. Duplication is the attachment of the fragment to the homologous chromosome's counterpart, thus repeating gene types already there. Inversion is the reattachment of the fragment to the original chromosome, but in a reversed orientation, resulting in a reversed gene order. In a deletion, the chromosome fragment does not reattach.

## A–82

**(B)** Nucleic acid contains the genetic information. When a virus infects a bacterium, it infuses its own nucleic acid into the bacterium, and the bacterium, using the genetic code of the virus, begins to produce hundreds of more viruses.

---

**Q–83**

Which of the following conditions is due to the effects of a dominant allele?

(A)  Color blindness

(B)  Hemophilia

(C)  Sickle-cell anemia

(D)  Polydactyly

*Your Answer* _____

_____

---

**Q–84**

A cell's nucleolus is found in its

(A)  cytoplasm.

(B)  endoplasmic reticulum.

(C)  mitochondrion.

(D)  nucleus.

*Your Answer* _____

_____

# Correct Answers

## A–83

**(D)** Polydactyly, a condition in which the afflicted has six fingers, is due to the effects of a dominant gene. Both hemophilia and color blindness are sex-linked traits. The genes are on the X-chromosome and are recessive. While color blindness is more a condition than a disease, hemophilia is a dangerous disease in which the blood clotting mechanism is faulty. The alleles for albinism and sickle-cell anemia are both recessive and are both located on autosomes (chromosomes other than the sex chromosomes). Sickle-cell anemia is a type of anemia in which the distorted hemoglobin disrupts the shape of the red blood cell and hence limits its oxygen carrying capacity. Unlike other recessive diseases, in this case, a heterozygote (one with both the normal dominant and abnormal recessive allele) may show symptoms of sickle-cell anemia under conditions of low oxygen tension, occuring during severe exercise or at great altitudes.

## A–84

**(D)** The nucleolus is a dark-staining spherical body inside the cell's nucleus. It is not associated with an organelle nor is it in the cytoplasm.

# Questions

**Q–85**

In the human excretory system blood components such as glucose and amino acids are returned to the blood from the filtrate by

(A)   facilitated diffusion.

(B)   pinocytosis.

(C)   simple diffusion.

(D)   osmosis.

*Your Answer* _____

_____

*For 2005, the FDA has approved more than 459 new drugs. (USA Today Weekend. November 6, 2005.)*

# Correct Answers

## A–85

**(A)** In the human excretory system blood components such as glucose and amino acids are returned to the blood from the filtrate by facilitated diffusion.

 *Very good employment opportunities are expected for pharmacists in 2006. Pharmacists are becoming more involved in making decisions regarding drug therapy and in counseling patients. (U.S. Department of Labor, Bureau of Labor Statistics)*

# Questions

---

**Q–86**

If an individual inherits two identical alleles of a gene, he is said to be

(A)  homozygous for that trait.

(B)  heterozygous for that trait.

(C)  dominant for that trait.

(D)  recessive for that trait.

---

*Your Answer* _____

_____

*Are there any benefits to purchasing approved drugs online?  Yes. Legitimate pharmacy sites on the Internet provide consumers with a convenient, private, way to obtain needed medications, sometimes at more affordable prices....Finally, the increasing use of computer technology to transmit prescriptions from doctors to pharmacies is likely to reduce prescription errors. (U.S. Food and Drug Administration – www.fda.gov)*

# Correct Answers

(A)      Genes are the units of heredity, located on chromosomes. Genes occur in various forms, or alleles, the combinations of which code for the specific expression of traits. Each individual inherits one allele of each gene from his mother and one from his father. If an individual inherits two identical alleles of a gene, he is said to be homozygous for that trait: he is a homozygote. If the alleles are different, the individual is heterozygous for the trait; he is a heterozygote. The genotype is the individual's genetic constitution, whereas the phenotype refers to the expression of the genotype.

There are many different types of genetic inheritance patterns. The simplest is that of dominant and recessive inheritance. This is best exemplified by the inheritance of eye color in man. Let B represent the dominant allele for brown eyes and b represent the recessive allele for blue eyes. If an individual has the genotype BB, he is homozygous dominant and hence has the phenotype of brown eyes. An individual with the genotype bb is homozygous recessive and has the phenotype of blue eyes. A heterozygote, Bb, has brown eyes because B is dominant to b. Note that there are two genotypes (BB and Bb) that represent the phenotype brown eyes.

# Questions

**Q-87**

The structures responsible for movement are

(A) cilia.

(B) ribosomes.

(C) chromosomes.

(D) Golgi apparatus.

*Your Answer* _____

_____

**Q-88**

The hormone that stimulates release of milk and contraction of smooth muscle during childbirth is

(A) testosterone.

(B) glucagon.

(C) oxytocin.

(D) prolactin.

*Your Answer* _____

_____

# Correct Answers

**A–87**

**(A)**  Protein synthesis occurs on ribosomes; genes are found on chromosomes; and secretory products are packaged by the Golgi apparatus. Cilia are responsible for movement, because of the arrangement and interaction of microtubules within them.

**A–88**

**(C)**  Oxytocin, which is produced by the hypothalamus and released from the posterior pituitary gland, stimulates milk ejection from the breasts and uterine muscle contraction both during and after childbirth.

# Questions

**Q–89**

After storage in the epididymis, migrating sperm cells next encounter the

(A) vas deferens.

(B) prostate.

(C) testis.

(D) urethra.

*Your Answer* _____

_____

**Q–90**

Which characteristic differentiates RNA from DNA? RNA

(A) contains the base uracil.

(B) has a phosphate group.

(C) has five bases.

(D) is double-stranded.

*Your Answer* _____

_____

# Correct Answers

**A–89**

(A)     Sperm travel through the following structures in the following order: testis, epididymis, vas deferens, prostate gland, and the urethra. The urethra passes sperm on to and through the penis.

**A–90**

(A)     Both nucleic acids have adenine, cytosine, or guanine as three of their four possible nucleotide bases. However, their fourth bases differ – DNA contains thymine, and RNA contains uracil. Both have nucleotide phosphate groups. The other statements about RNA are untrue.

# Questions

---

**Q–91**

When distinguishing between DNA and RNA, DNA uniquely contains

(A) guanine.

(B) ribose.

(C) phosphorus (phosphates).

(D) thymine.

---

*Your Answer* _____

_____

---

**Q–92**

Which of the following is not normally filtered out of the blood in the kidney?

(A) Protein

(B) Glucose

(C) Sodium chloride

(D) Water

---

*Your Answer* _____

_____

# Correct Answers

## A–91

**(D)** DNA is a double stranded nucleic acid, with a sugar (deoxyribose) and phosphate backbone. RNA is single stranded with a sugar (ribose) and phosphate backbone. Both nucleic acids contain the bases adenine, guanine, and cytosine. In addition, DNA contains the base thymine, while RNA contains uracil.

## A–92

**(A)** For this question an understanding of the functioning of the kidney is important. Some of the components of the blood that enter the glomerulus are filtered out into the nephron. These components are smaller in size and include glucose, sodium chloride, and water. Protein is too large to pass through the glomerulus into the nephron tubule under normal circumstances.

# Questions

**Q–93**

Excess tissue fluid is returned to the blood by the

(A)  respiratory system.

(B)  lymphatic system.

(C)  digestive system.

(D)  circulatory system.

*Your Answer* _____

_____

**Q–94**

Separation of homologous chromosomes occurs during what phase of mitosis?

(A)  Interphase

(B)  Anaphase

(C)  Prophase

(D)  Telophase

*Your Answer* _____

_____

# Correct Answers

## A–93

**(B)** The respiratory system provides for gas exchanges, intake of oxygen, and release of carbon dioxide. The digestive system breaks down food molecules into their components for absorption by the cells of the body. The circulatory system transports food, oxygen, and waste products throughout the body. As the blood circulates through the body, some of the plasma seeps out and bathes the cells of the body, providing for exchanges of materials with these cells. Tissue fluid that is not returned to the capillaries is picked up by the lymphatic vessels that run parallel to the circulatory system. These vessels drain into veins in the circulatory system.

## A–94

**(B)** Separation of homologous chromosomes occurs during anaphase. During interphase, the cell performs metabolic activities and DNA synthesis. Condensation of chromosomes, separation of the centrioles, and dissolution of the nuclear membrane are some of the major events of prophase. During telophase, the chromosomes begin to decondense, the nucleolus reappears, and cytokinesis occurs.

# Questions

**Q–95**

Viruses have

(A)  the ability to replicate their genetic material.

(B)  the ability to make their own energy.

(C)  their own metabolic machinery.

(D)  their own enzymes.

*Your Answer* _____

_____

**Q–96**

An enzyme is all of the following EXCEPT

(A)  a catalyst.

(B)  made by living organisms.

(C)  used up during a chemical reaction.

(D)  a protein.

*Your Answer* _____

_____

# Correct Answers

## A–95

**(A)** Viruses are parasites in that they cannot multiply outside their host cell. They use the energy sources (option (B)), metabolic machinery (option (C)), and enzymes (option (D)) of the host cell. Viruses do have the ability to replicate their genetic material (DNA or RNA). They do so by inserting a copy of their genetic material and using the resources of the host cell to replicate the material and to form their own protein coats. The virus particle then escapes from the host cell and is ready to infect another host cell.

## A–96

**(C)** Enzymes are specialized proteins made by living organisms that serve to speed up chemical reactions in the body. Thus, they serve as biological catalysts. Enzymes are not used up during the reaction, but can react over and over again with new molecules of substrate.

**Q–97**

Which of the following cannot be digested by humans?

(A)  Sucrose

(B)  Cellulose

(C)  Starch

(D)  Fructose

*Your Answer* _____

_____

**Q–98**

Which of the following has a vitamin as a building block?

(A)  Apoenzyme

(B)  Coenzyme

(C)  Holoenzyme

(D)  Protein

*Your Answer* _____

_____

# Correct Answers

## A–97

**(B)** Cellulose is a linear polymer of glucose subunits joined by 1–4 linkages. Humans lack the enzyme cellulase that can break the 1–4 linkages. Therefore, they are unable to digest cellulose.

## A–98

**(B)** All enzymes are composed primarily of protein. The more complex enzymes can have non-protein portions called cofactors; the protein portion of the enzyme is called an apoenzyme. If the cofactor is an easily separated organic molecule, it is called a coenzyme. Many coenzymes are related to vitamins. An enzyme deprived of its vitamin is thus incomplete, leading to the nonexecution of a key step in metabolism.

# Questions

**Q–99**

Which of the following derived characteristics in animals allows the internal organs of animals to move independently of the outer body wall?

(A)  True tissue

(B)  Bilateral symmetry

(C)  Vascular tissues

(D)  Coelom

*Your Answer* _____

_____

*Investing in pharmacies is hot in 2006: Would-be buyers of independent pharmacies far outnumber owners ready to sell. (www. drugtopics.com)*

# Correct Answers

## A-99

**(D)**    The coelom is a fluid-filled cavity that is lined by mesoderm and lies between the digestive tract and the outer body wall. It is found in mollusks, annelids, arthropods, echinoderms, and chordates. True tissues and bilateral symmetry are important derived characteristics in animal phylogeny but they are not cavities. Vascular tissues are found in plants. The archenteron is an embryonic cavity.

# Questions

---

**Q–100**

Fructose is an example of a(n)

(A)  monosaccharide.

(B)  disaccharide.

(C)  polysaccharide.

(D)  saccharin.

---

*Your Answer* _____

_____

*In the U.S. for 2004, there was $221 billion in retail prescription drug sales. (www.nacds.org)*

# Correct Answers

## A-100

**(A)**    The organic nutrients that contribute calories to the diet are carbohydrates, lipids, and proteins. Carbohydrates have the empirical formula $C_nH_{2n}O_n$. Saccharum is Latin for sugar; hence, the simple sugars are called monosaccharides. These include glucose, fructose, and galactose, all six-carbon sugars. Disaccharides are the chemical bonding of two monosaccharides. Glucose and fructose yield sucrose (table sugar); glucose and galactose yield lactose (milk sugar); and two glucoses combine to form maltose. Polysaccharides are molecules composed of many monosaccharides; they are long polymers. The three major polysaccharides are all polymers of glucose. Plants store glucose in the form of starch, which is edible. Animals store glucose as glycogen in the liver and muscle. Another polysaccharide in plants is cellulose — it is a component of plant cell walls and thus serves a structural role. However, unlike starch, cellulose found in wood and vegetable fibers is not digestible by humans due to lack of the enzyme that hydrolyzes it.

Saccharin is an artificial sweetener that was banned by the FDA (Food and Drug Administration) due to its possible carcinogenic (cancer-causing) properties.

# Section IV
# Chemistry

**DIRECTIONS:** Each of the questions or incomplete statements in this section is followed by four suggested answers or completions. Select the one that is best in each case.

# Questions

**Q-1**

The element with atomic number 32 (see page 602) describes

(A)   a metal.

(B)   a nonmetal.

(C)   a metalloid.

(D)   a halogen.

*Your Answer* _____

_____

**Q-2**

The electronic configuration of $N_2$ is best represented as

(A)   : N : N :

(B)   : N : : N

(C)   : N : : N :

(D)   : N : : : N :

*Your Answer* _____

_____

# Correct Answers

## A–1

**(C)**  Referring to the periodic table we see that element 32 is germanium. Germanium is a metalloid as are boron, silicon, arsenic, antimony, tellurium, polonium, and astatine. Chemically, metalloids exhibit both positive and negative oxidation states and combine with metals and nonmetals. They are characterized by approximately half-filled outer electron shells and electronegativity values between those of the metals and the nonmetals.

## A–2

**(D)**  The prime consideration in representing the bonding of a polyatomic element or compound is that each atom bonded should have a complete valence shell (eight electrons except hydrogen and helium which have two). Since nitrogen is in Group VA it has five valence electrons illustrated as

$$: \overset{\displaystyle .}{N} \cdot$$

Diatomic nitrogen must have the structure

$$: N : : : N : (\text{or} : N \equiv N :)$$

to completely fill the valence shells of both atoms.

# Questions

---

**Q–3**

All of the following are chemical changes except

(A)  dissolving NaCl in water.

(B)  burning a piece of wood.

(C)  ozone absorbing ultraviolet light.

(D)  dissolving Na metal in water.

*Your Answer* _____

_____

---

**Q–4**

The greatest reduction of kinetic activity of water molecules occurs when water is

(A)  cooled as a solid.

(B)  cooled as a liquid.

(C)  converted from a liquid to a gas.

(D)  converted from a gas to a liquid.

*Your Answer* _____

_____

# Correct Answers

## A–3

**(A)** Dissolving sodium chloride in water is an example of a physical change. A physical change alters the physical properties of a substance while maintaining its composition. If the water solution of NaCl were to be evaporated we would once again have solid sodium chloride. Chemical changes involve altering the composition and structure of a substance and are always associated with changes in energy. Wood and oxygen are changed to $CO_2$, $H_2O$ and nitrogen oxides while ozone is changed to diatomic oxygen and sodium and water are changed to sodium hydroxide and hydrogen gas.

## A–4

**(D)** Molecules in the gaseous state have the greatest kinetic activity. The difference in energy between the liquid and gas phases is greater than the difference in energy between the solid and liquid phases. This may be readily seen by the energy changes occurring in water; the heat of fusion of water is 80 calories/gram, while the heat of vaporization is 540 calories/gram.

# Questions

---

**Q–5**

The extremely high melting point of diamond (carbon) may be explained by large numbers of

(A) covalent bonds.

(B) ionic bonds.

(C) hydrogen bonds.

(D) van der Waals forces.

---

*Your Answer* _____

_____

---

**Q–6**

The oxidation number of sulfur in $NaHSO_4$ is

(A)   0.

(B)   +2.

(C)   –2.

(D)   +6.

---

*Your Answer* _____

_____

# Correct Answers

## A–5

**(A)** Diamond, composed solely of carbon, cannot have ionic bonds or hydrogen bonds. van der Waals attraction between the nucleus of one atom and the electrons of an adjacent atom are relatively weak compared to the covalent bonding network ($sp^3$ hybrid) between the carbon atoms in diamond. On the other hand, graphite (another allotropic form of carbon) is $sp^2$ hybrid and not strongly bonded as compared to diamond.

## A–6

**(D)** The oxidation state of sulfur in sodium bisulfate may be determined by recalling that the oxidation states of sodium, hydrogen, and oxygen are usually +1, +1, and –2, respectively. Since the sum of the oxidation states for the atoms of a neutral compound are zero we have:

oxidation state of S + 1 + 1 + 4(–2) = 0

∴ oxidation state of S = +6

So, the oxidation number of sulfur in $NaHSO_4$ is +6.

# Questions

**Q-7**

The salt produced by the reaction of perchloric acid with barium hydroxide is

(A) $BaClO_3$

(B) $BaClO_4$

(C) $Ba(OH)_2$

(D) $Ba(ClO_4)_2$

Your Answer _____

**Q-8**

The transition metals are characterized by

(A) completely filled d subshells.

(B) completely filled f subshells.

(C) partially filled d subshells.

(D) Both (A) and (C) are correct.

Your Answer _____

# Correct Answers

## A–7

**(D)** This is an example of a neutralization reaction in which an acid and a base react to produce water and a salt. It must be known that barium has an oxidation number of +2 and that perchloric acid is $HClO_4$.

$$2HClO_4 + Ba(OH)_2 \rightarrow 2H_2O + Ba(ClO_4)_2$$

## A–8

**(D)** The transition metals may have either completely filled or partially filled, but not empty, subshells (3d, 4d, and 5d). Lanthanides and actinides are characterized by the electrons in the 4f and 5f subshells, respectively.

# Questions

**Q–9**

An equilibrium reaction may be forced to completion by

(A) adding a catalyst.

(B) increasing the pressure.

(C) increasing the temperature.

(D) removing the products from the reaction mixture as they are formed.

*Your Answer* _____

_____

*Slightly more than half (55%) of full-time chain pharmacists are male. (www.nacds.org)*

# Correct Answers

**(D)** Le Chatelier's Principle may be used to predict equilibrium reactions: If a stress is placed on a system in equilibrium, the equilibrium shifts so as to counteract that stress. Hence, increasing the reactant concentration favors formation of the products while decreasing the reactant concentration favors formation of the reactants. The same holds true for altering the product concentrations. Increasing the temperature favors the reaction that absorbs heat while decreasing the temperature favors the reaction that releases heat. Increasing the pressure favors the reaction that decreases the volume of a closed system while decreasing the pressure favors the reaction resulting in an increased volume (moles of gaseous product produced are the only things counted since liquids and solids occupy a relatively small volume in comparison). However, temperature and pressure dependencies cannot be inferred from this question. The addition of a catalyst alters the reaction rate but not the position of equilibrium. The only way completion can be obtained is to remove the products as they are formed. Now the state of the reaction becomes nonequilibrium, but it tries to come in equilibrium state once again. This leads to formation of more products, which in turn leads to completion of the given reaction.

# Questions

Q–10

Which of the following salts will result in a basic solution when dissolved in water?

(A)  $Ba(NO_3)_2$

(B)  $Na_2S$

(C)  $Al_2(SO_4)_3$

(D)  $Pb_3(PO_4)_2$

*Your Answer* _____

*Successful completion of the academic and clinical requirements of a graduate degree from an accredited program, passage of a state board examination, and a period internship under the guidance of a licensed pharmacist are all required in order to obtain a license to practice pharmacy.*

# Correct Answers

**A–10**

**(B)** The salts of strong bases and weak acids hydrolyze to form a basic solution, while the salts of weak bases and strong acids hydrolyze to form an acidic solution.

$$Ba(NO_3)_2 + 2H_2O \rightarrow 2HNO_3 + Ba(OH)_2$$

A neutral solution is produced since both nitric acid and barium hydroxide are completely dissociated and each is present in the same concentration (barium hydroxide has 2 hydroxy groups)

$$Na_2S + 2H_2O \rightarrow H_2S + 2NaOH$$

A basic solution is produced since hydrosulfuric acid is a weak acid and sodium hydroxide is a strong base.

$$Al_2(SO_4)_3 + 6H_2O \rightarrow 3H_2SO_4 + 2Al(OH)_3$$

An acidic solution is produced since aluminum hydroxide is insoluble and sulfuric acid is a strong acid.

$$Pb_3(PO_4)_2 + 6H_2O \rightarrow 2H_3PO_4 + 3Pb(OH)_2$$

An acidic solution is produced since phosphoric acid is a weak acid and lead (II) hydroxide is insoluble.

$$NaCl + H_2O \rightarrow HCl + NaOH$$

A neutral solution is produced since hydrochloric acid is a strong acid and sodium hydroxide is a strong base.

# Questions

**Q–11**

The radioactive decay of plutonium –238 (Pu) produces an alpha particle and a new atom. That new atom is

(A) $^{234}_{92}$Pu.

(B) $^{234}_{92}$Cm.

(C) $^{234}_{92}$U.

(D) $^{242}_{96}$Cm.

*Your Answer* _____

_____

*"There are a few guarantees in life, but I have one for you: If you develop the right habits you will be a successful pharmacist. And what are the "right" habits? There are three that I will discuss briefly: 1. The habit of empathy. 2. The habit of translating complexity into simplicity. 3. The habit of recognizing and acting on the obvious." (Adapted from: Zellmer, W.A. The Habits of Successful Pharmacists – www. careerpharm.com)*

# Correct Answers

## A–11

(C)    Plutonium-238 has a mass of 238 and an atomic number of 94. The atomic mass tells us the number of protons and neutrons in the nucleus, while the atomic number tells us the number of protons. An alpha particle ($^4_2\alpha$) is a helium nucleus composed of 2 neutrons and 2 protons (atomic mass of 4). Hence, upon emission of an alpha particle, the atomic number decreases by 2 and the atomic mass decreases by 4. This gives us $^{234}_{92}X$. Examining the periodic table we find that element 92 is uranium. Thus, our new atom is $^{234}_{92}U$. $^{234}_{92}Pu$ and $^{234}_{92}Cm$ are impossible since the atomic number of plutonium is 94 and that of curium is 96. $^{242}_{96}Pu$ and $^{242}_{96}Cm$ are impossible since these nuclei could only be produced by fusion of $^{238}_{94}Pu$ with an alpha particle. In addition, $^{242}_{96}Pu$ is incorrectly named.

$\therefore$ The reaction (decay) is $_{94}Pu^{238} \rightarrow {}_{92}U^{234} + 2^{\alpha 4}$

# Questions

---

**Q–12**

What is the approximate melting point of 0.2 liters of water containing 6.20g of ethylene glycol $(C_2H_6O_2)$?

(A) −1.86°C

(B) −0.93°C

(C) 0°C

(D) 0.93°C

---

*Your Answer* _____

_____

*The first professional pharmacies are said to have been in Baghdad in the 13th century. (www.who2.com)*

# Correct Answers

## A–12

**(B)**  First, we determine the number of moles present in solution taking the molecular weight of ethylene glycol to be 62g. Thus,

$$6.20g \times \frac{1\ mole}{62g} = 0.1\ mole\ of\ ethylene\ glycol$$

We must also know the molality—the ratio of moles of solute to kilograms of solvent. The number of kilograms of solvent is

$$0.2l \times \frac{1\ kg}{1l} = 0.2\ kg$$

since the density of water is 1g/ml. The molality of the solution is

$$\frac{0.1\ mole}{0.2\ kg} = 0.5\ molal.$$

For $H_2O$, the molal freezing point depression constant is 1.86°C/molal. Thus, the freezing point depression is

$$0.5\ molal \times \frac{1.86°C}{molal} = 0.93°C$$

Thus, the melting point would be
$$0°C - 0.93°C = -0.93°C$$

# Questions

---

**Q–13**

What is the molecular formula of a compound composed of 25.9% nitrogen and 74.1% oxygen?

(A)  NO

(B)  $NO_2$

(C)  $N_2O$

(D)  $N_2O_5$

*Your Answer* _____

_____

---

**Q–14**

How many moles of sulfate ion are in 200 ml of a $2M$ sodium sulfate solution?

(A)  0.2 mole

(B)  0.4 mole

(C)  0.6 mole

(D)  0.8 mole

*Your Answer* _____

_____

# Correct Answers

## A–13

**(D)** A 100g sample of this gas contains 25.9g of nitrogen and 74.1g of oxygen. Dividing each of these weights by their respective atomic weights gives us the molar ratio of N to O for the gas. This gives

$$N_{\frac{25.9}{14}} O_{\frac{74.1}{16}} = N_{1.85} O_{4.63}$$

Dividing both subscripts by the smallest subscript gives

$$N_{\frac{1.85}{1.85}} O_{\frac{4.63}{1.85}} = N_1 O_{2.5}$$

Doubling both subscripts so as to have whole numbers gives us $N_2 O_5$.

## A–14

**(B)** A $1M$ sodium sulfate ($Na_2SO_4$) solution contains one mole of sulfate ion per liter of solution. Thus $0.2l$ of a $1M$ solution contains 0.2 mole of sulfate ion. $0.2l$ of a $2M$ solution would then contain 0.4 mole of sulfate ion.

# Questions

---

**Q–15**

What volume of water is required to produce 5 liters of oxygen by the process below?

$$H_2O_{(g)} \rightarrow H_{2(g)} + O_{2(g)}$$

(A)  3 liters

(B)  5 liters

(C)  10 liters

(D)  14 liters

*Your Answer* _____

---

**Q–16**

The structure of the third member of the alkyne series is

(A)  $H - C \equiv C - H$

(B)  $H - C \equiv C - CH_3$

(C)  $H - C \equiv C - CH_2 - CH_3$

(D)  $H - C \equiv C - C \equiv C - H$

*Your Answer* _____

# Correct Answers

## A–15

(C)    Balancing the reaction equation gives
$$2H_2O \rightarrow 2H_2 + O_2$$
As may be seen from the equation, two units of water react to produce one unit of oxygen. Thus $10L$ of water are required to produce $5L$ of oxygen.

## A–16

(C)    The first member of the alkyne series is acetylene (or ethyne), whose structure is
$$HC \equiv CH$$
The second is propyne:    $HC \equiv C - CH_3$
The third is butyne:    $HC \equiv C - CH_2 - CH_3$
Note that there are no analogous compounds in the alkene or alkyne series for the first member of the alkane series (methane $- CH_4$).

# Questions

---

**Q–17**

Sodium chloride (NaCl) would be most soluble in

(A)   ether.

(B)   benzene.

(C)   water.

(D)   carbon tetrachloride.

*Your Answer* _____

---

**Q–18**

Hydrolysis of sodium acetate yields

(A)   a strong acid and a strong base.

(B)   a weak acid and a weak base.

(C)   a strong acid and a weak base.

(D)   a weak acid and a strong base.

*Your Answer* _____

# Correct Answers

**A–17**

**(C)**    Polar solutes such as sodium chloride are more soluble in polar solvents than in non-polar solvents and non-polar solutes are more soluble in non-polar solvents (like dissolves like). Water is the only polar solvent given.

**A–18**

**(D)**    The hydrolysis reaction for sodium acetate proceeds as follows:

$$CH_3\overset{\displaystyle O}{\overset{\|}{C}}ONa + H_2O \rightarrow CH_3\overset{\displaystyle O}{\overset{\|}{C}}OH + NaOH$$

The products of the reaction are a weak acid (acetic acid) and a strong base (sodium hydroxide).

# Questions

**Q-19**

How many moles of electrons must be removed from 0.5 mole of $Fe^{2+}$ to produce $Fe^{3+}$?

(A)  0.5

(B)  1.0

(C)  1.5

(D)  2.0

*Your Answer* _____

**Q-20**

What is the pH of a $0.01M$ NaOH solution?

(A)  4

(B)  7

(C)  10

(D)  12

*Your Answer* _____

# Correct Answers

## A–19

**(A)** Iron loses 1 mole of electrons when one mole of $Fe^{2+}$ reacts to produce $Fe^{3+}$. The removal of 0.5 mole of electrons is required to oxidize iron from the +2 to the +3 state.

## A–20

**(D)** The pH of a solution is defined as

$$pH = -log[H^+]$$

We are not given the $[H^+]$ however. There are two ways of solving this problem. The first relies on the fact that:

$$K_w = [H^+][OH^-] = 1 \times 10^{-14}$$

Rearranging gives

$$[H^+] = \frac{K_w}{[OH^-]} = \frac{1 \times 10^{-14}}{1 \times 10^{-2}} = 1 \times 10^{-12}$$

and $\quad pH = -log\ 1 \times 10^{-12} = 12$

Alternatively, we define $pOH$ as

$$pOH = -log[OH^-]$$

which gives

$$pOH = -log\ 1 \times 10^{-2} = 2.$$

Recalling that $pH + pOH = 14$ we have upon rearrangement:

$$pH = 14 - pOH = 12$$

# Questions

---

**Q–21**

Twenty liters of NO gas react with excess oxygen. How many liters of $NO_2$ gas are produced if the NO gas reacts completely?

(A)  5 liters

(B)  10 liters

(C)  20 liters

(D)  40 liters

*Your Answer* _____

---

---

**Q–22**

What is the molar concentration of $I^-$ in 1 liter of a saturated water solution of $PbI_2$ if the $K_{sp}$ of lead iodide is $1.4 \times 10^{-8}$?

(A)  $3.0 \times 10^{-3}$

(B)  $1.2 \times 10^{-4}$

(C)  $5.9 \times 10^{-5}$

(D)  $2.4 \times 10^{-3}$

*Your Answer* _____

---

# Correct Answers

## A–21

**(C)** The reaction in question is
$$NO + \frac{1}{2}O_2 \rightarrow NO_2$$
or using the given coefficients
$$20\ NO + 10\ O_2 \rightarrow 20\ NO_2$$
Note that the unit of the coefficients used is liters, not moles. This does not affect the calculation since moles and liters are directly related in the case of gases (1 mole of a gas occupies 22.4 liters of STP).

## A–22

**(A)** The solubility product of lead (II) iodide is given by
$$K_{sp} = [Pb^{2+}]\ [I^-]^2$$
where $[Pb^{2+}]$ and $[I^-]$ are the concentrations of lead ion and iodide in solution, respectively. We know that $K_{sp} = 1.4 \times 10^{-8}$ and that the concentration of iodide in solution is twice that of the lead ion from the dissociation:
$$PbI_2 \rightarrow Pb^{2+} + 2I^-$$
Setting $[Pb^{2+}] = x$, we know that $[I^-] = 2x$. Thus,
$$K_{sp} = [Pb^{2+}]\ [I^-]^2 = (x)\ (2x)2 = 1.4 \times 10^{-8}.$$
Solving for $x$ gives
$$4x^3 = 1.4 \times 10^{-8}$$
and $x = 1.5 \times 10^{-3}$
Recalling that $[I^-] = 2x$ we have
$$[I^-] = 2(1.5 \times 10^{-3}) = 3 \times 10^{-3}$$

# Questions

A 0.5 molal solution could be prepared by dissolving 20g of NaOH in

(A)  0.5 liter of water.

(B)  1 liter of water.

(C)  0.5 kg of water.

(D)  1 kg of water.

*Your Answer* _____

_____

*Famous people who spent time behind the pharmacy counter: Dante, Isaac Newton, O. Henry, Henrik Ibsen, Hubert H. Humphrey, Benedict Arnold. (www.who2.com)*

# Correct Answers

## A–23

**(D)** The molality of a solution ($m$) is defined as the number of moles of solute dissolved in one kilogram of solvent. The number of moles of NaOH to be used is determined to be:

$$20g \text{ of NaOH} \times \frac{1 \text{ mole of NaOH}}{40g \text{ of NaOH}}$$

$$= 0.5 \text{ moles of NaOH}$$

Thus:

$$0.5m = \frac{0.5 \text{ mole of NaOH}}{x \text{ kilograms of water}}$$

Rearranging:

$$x = \frac{0.5}{0.5} = 1 \text{ kg of water}$$

# Questions

---

**Q–24**

The equilibrium expression, $K_e = [CO_2]$ represents the reaction

(A) $C_{(s)} + O_{2(g)} \rightleftharpoons CO_{2(g)}$

(B) $CO_{(g)} + \frac{1}{2}O_{2(g)} \rightleftharpoons CO_{2(g)}$

(C) $CaCO_{3(s)} \rightleftharpoons CaO_{(s)} + CO_{2(g)}$

(D) $CO_{2(g)} \rightleftharpoons C_{(s)} + O_{2(g)}$

---

*Your Answer* _____

_____

*Aspirin went on sale as the first pharmaceutical drug in 1899, after Felix Hoffman, a German chemist at the drug company Bayer, successfully modified Salicylic Acid, a compound found in willow bark to produce Aspirin. (www.corsinet.com)*

# Correct Answers

## A–24

(C)    The equilibrium constant is defined as the product of the concentrations of the gaseous products raised to the power of their coefficients, divided by the product of the gaseous reactant concentrations raised to the power of their coefficients. Only gaseous reactants and products are included in $K_e$ since the concentrations of liquids and solids participating in the reaction are assumed to be large (as compared to those of the gases) and relatively constant. The expressions of the equilibrium constants for the reactions given are:

(A)    $K_e = \dfrac{[CO_2]}{[O_2]}$

(B)    $K_e = \dfrac{[CO_2]}{[CO][O_2]^{1/2}}$

(C)    $K_e = [CO_2]$

(D)    $K_e = \dfrac{[O_2]}{[CO_2]}$

# Questions

The following reaction coordinates cannot be associated with

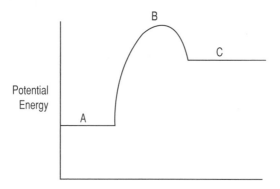

Reaction Coordinate

(A)   an endothermic reaction from A to C.

(B)   an exothermic reaction from A to C.

(C)   the activation energy for the reaction.

(D)   the energy for the intermediate.

*Your Answer* _____

_____

*1900: Bayer Aspirin was the first drug ever to be marketed in tablet form. (www.corsinet.com)*

# Correct Answers

## A–25

**(B)** Heat was absorbed by the system during the reaction as indicated by the products having a greater potential energy than the reactants. A reaction in which heat is absorbed in order to produce the products is said to be endothermic.

*The United States Pharmacopeia (USP) is the official public standards-setting authority for all prescription and over-the-counter medicines, dietary supplements, and other healthcare products manufactured and sold in the United States. (www.usp.org)*

# Questions

**Q–26**

The primary products of hydrocarbon combustion are

(A) water and carbon.

(B) water and carbon monoxide.

(C) water and carbon dioxide.

(D) hydrogen and carbon monoxide.

*Your Answer* _____

**Q–27**

How many moles of $CO_2$ are represented by $1.8 \times 10^{24}$ atoms?

(A) 1

(B) 2

(C) 3

(D) 4

*Your Answer* _____

# Correct Answers

## A–26

(C)    Water and carbon dioxide are the primary products of hydrocarbon combustion. These are the only products in the case of complete combustion. For example,

$$C_2H_6 + \frac{7}{2}O_2 \rightarrow 2\ CO_2 + 3H_2O$$

## A–27

(A)    By simple unit conversion:

$$1.8 \times 10^{24}\ atoms \ \times \frac{1\ mole}{6.02 \times 10^{23}\ molecules}$$
$$\times \ \frac{1\ molecule}{3\ atoms} = 1\ mole$$

since each $CO_2$ molecule is composed of three atoms.

# Questions

---

**Q–28**

Which of the following is responsible for the abnormally high boiling point of water?

(A) Covalent bonding

(B) Hydrogen bonding

(C) High polarity

(D) Large dielectric constant

---

*Your Answer* _____

_____

---

**Q–29**

About how many grams of sodium chloride would be dissolved in water to form a 0.5 m solution in 500 ml of solution?

(A) 7

(B) 29

(C) 14.5

(D) 58

---

*Your Answer* _____

_____

# Correct Answers

## A–28

**(B)** Hydrogen bonding between molecules increases their stability and thus increases the boiling point of water.

## A–29

**(C)** The formula weight of *NaCl* is about 58 grams, which forms a 1 m solution in 1000 ml of solution. 29 grams forms a 0.5 m solution in 1000 ml. In 500 ml, 14.5, or half this amount, is needed.

# Questions

---

**Q–30**

Which of the following is true of an electrochemical cell?

(A) The cell voltage is independent of concentration.

(B) The anode is negatively charged.

(C) The cathode is the site of reduction.

(D) Charge is carried from one electrode to the other by metal atoms passing through the solution.

*Your Answer* _____

_____

---

**Q–31**

An element of atomic number 17 has an atomic weight of 37. How many neutrons are in its nucleus?

(A) 17

(B) 18

(C) 20

(D) 37

*Your Answer* _____

_____

# Correct Answers

## A–30

**(C)** The cathode of an electrochemical cell is defined as the site of reduction and the anode is defined as the site of oxidation.

## A–31

**(C)** The atomic number gives the number of protons in the nucleus and the atomic weight gives the sum of the number of protons and neutrons. Thus, the number of neutrons is given by the difference between the atomic number and the atomic weight.

# Questions

**Q–32**

The most probable oxidation number of an element with an atomic number of 53 is

(A)  −5.

(B)  −1.

(C)  +1.

(D)  +5.

*Your Answer* _____

_____

**Q–33**

What is the concentration of [OH⁻] in a $NH_4OH$ solution if it has a pH of 11?

(A)  $10^{-1}$

(B)  $10^{-3}$

(C)  $10^{-5}$

(D)  $10^{-9}$

*Your Answer* _____

_____

# Correct Answers

## A–32

**(B)** Element 53 is iodine, a member of the halogens (Group VIIA). The halogens usually have an oxidation number of −1 although some other values sometimes (rarely) occur.

## A–33

**(B)** A solution of $pH$ 11 has $[H^+] = 1 \times 10^{-11}$ by the equation $pH = -log[H^+]$. Recalling that $K_w = [H^+][OH^-] = 10^{-14}$ we have

$$[OH^-] = \frac{K_w}{[H^+]} = \frac{10^{-14}}{[H^+]} = \frac{10^{-14}}{10^{-11}} = 10^{-3}$$

# Questions

**Q–34**

20 ml of NaOH is needed to titrate 30 ml of a 6M HCl solution. The molarity of the NaOH is

(A) 1M.

(B) 3M.

(C) 6M.

(D) 9M.

*Your Answer* _____

*More than 100 years ago, the felt hat makers of England used mercury to stabilize wool. Most of them eventually became poisoned by the fumes, as demonstrated by the Mad Hatter in Lewis Carroll's "Alice in Wonderland." (www.corsinet.com)*

# Correct Answers

**A–34**

**(D)** Using the formula $M_1V_1 = M_2V_2$ and rearranging we obtain

$$M_2 = \frac{M_1V_1}{V_2} = \frac{(6M)(30ml)}{20ml} = 9M\ NaOH$$

*The American Pharmacists Association (APhA), the national professional society of pharmacists, founded in 1852 as the American Pharmaceutical Association, is the first-established and largest professional association of pharmacists in the United States with more than 50,000 members. (www.aphanet.org)*

# Questions

This method is best suited for producing and collecting a gas which is

Litmus
Solution
of Hypo

(A)  lighter than air.

(B)  heavier than air.

(C)  soluble in water.

(D)  nonsoluble in water.

*Your Answer* _____

_____

# Correct Answers

**A–35**

**(B)** This setup is used to prepare gases such as $Cl_2$ and $HCl$, which are heavier than air.

# Questions

---

**Q–36**

How many grams of water can be produced when 8g of hydrogen reacts with 8g of oxygen?

(A)  8g

(B)  9g

(C)  18g

(D)  27g

*Your Answer* _____

---

**Q–37**

The relation $P_1V_1 = P_2V_2$ is known as

(A)  Boyle's Law.

(B)  Charles's Law.

(C)  van der Waal's Law.

(D)  the combined gas law.

*Your Answer* _____

# Correct Answers

## A–36

**(B)** The reaction in question is

$$2H_2 + O_2 \rightarrow 2H_2O$$

Converting the given quantities to moles:

$$8g \text{ of } H_2 \times \frac{1 \text{ mole of } H_2}{2g \text{ of } H_2} = 4 \text{ moles of } H_2$$

$$8g \text{ of } O_2 \times \frac{1 \text{ mole of } O_2}{32g \text{ of } O_2} = 0.25 \text{ moles of } O_2$$

Oxygen is the limiting reactant in this reaction. Multiplying all coefficients by 0.25 in order to obtain $0.25 \, O_2$ we have

$$0.5H_2 + 0.25O_2 \rightarrow 0.5H_2O$$

Converting to grams:

$$0.5 \text{ mole of } H_2O \times \frac{18g \text{ of } H_2O}{1 \text{ mole of } H_2O} = 9g \text{ of } H_2O$$

## A–37

**(A)** Boyle's Law shows that the volume of a gas varies inversely with the pressure at constant temperature.

# Questions

---

**Q–38**

Which of the following indicates a basic solution?

(A) $[H^+] > 10^{-7}$

(B) $[H^+] > 10^{-10}$

(C) pH = 5

(D) pH = 9

---

*Your Answer* _____

_____

---

**Q–39**

Amphoteric substances are best described as

(A) having the same number of protons and electrons but different numbers of neutrons.

(B) having the same composition but occurring in different molecular structures.

(C) being without definite shape.

(D) having both acid and base properties.

---

*Your Answer* _____

_____

# Correct Answers

## A–38

**(D)** A basic (alkaline) solution is indicated by a hydronium ion concentration less than $10^{-7}$ or identically, $pH > 7$ since $pH = -log[H^+]$. A solution with $[H^+] > 10^{-10}$ may be basic ($10^{-10} < [H^+] < 10^{-7}$) or acidic ($[H^+] > 10^{-7}$).

## A–39

**(D)** An amphoteric substance has both acid and base properties. Isotopes of an element have the same number of protons and electrons but different numbers of neutrons.① Isomers of a compound are indicated by the same molecular formulas but different structures.② Amorphous substances are designated as having no definite shape.③ Allotropes of a substance have the same composition but have different crystalline structures.④

① (for example, $^{12}_{6}C$ and $^{13}_{6}C$)

② (for example, 1-propanol and 2-propanol)

③ (for example, the product obtained when liquid sulfur is poured in water)

④ (for example, rhombic and monoclinic sulfur)

# Questions

---

**Q-40**

The Fahrenheit temperature corresponding to 303K is

(A)  −15°.

(B)  22°.

(C)  49°.

(D)  86°.

*Your Answer* _____

_____

---

**Q-41**

What is the density of bromine vapor at STP?

(A)  2.5g/liter

(B)  2.9g/liter

(C)  3.6g/liter

(D)  7.1g/liter

*Your Answer* _____

_____

# Correct Answers

**A–40**

(D)     Converting to the Celsius scale ($t = T - 273$) we have
$$t = 303 - 273 = 30°$$
Converting to the Fahrenheit scale:
$$°F = \frac{9}{5}(°C) + 32$$
$$°F = \frac{9}{5}(30) + 32$$
$$°F = 86$$

**A–41**

(D)     Since the volume of one mole of an ideal gas is 22.4 liters, we have
$$\frac{160g \text{ of } Br_2}{1 \text{ mole of } Br_2} \times \frac{1 \text{ mole of } Br_2}{22.4 \text{ liters}} = \frac{7.1g \text{ of } Br_2}{\text{liter}}$$

# Questions

**Q–42**

The yield of $AB_{(g)}$

$$A_{(g)} + B_{(g)} \rightleftharpoons AB_{(g)} + heat$$

would be increased by

(A) decreasing the pressure.

(B) adding additional AB to the reaction mixture.

(C) decreasing the temperature.

(D) adding a nonreactive liquid to the reaction mixture.

*Your Answer* _____

_____

*"Soldiers disease" is a term for morphine addiction. The Civil War produced over 400,000 morphine addicts. (www.corsinet. com)*

# Correct Answers

**A–42**

(C)    According to Le Chatelier's Principle, if a stress is placed on an equilibrium system, the equilibrium is shifted in the direction, which reduces the effect of that stress. This stress may be in the form of changes in pressure, temperature, concentrations, etc. By decreasing the pressure on the system, the system shifts in a direction so as to increase the pressure. For our reaction, the reverse reaction rate would increase since a larger volume (hence a greater pressure) results. This is due to the fact that two moles of gaseous product will result as opposed to one mole if the forward reaction were favored. Note that only gaseous products are accounted for when considering pressure effects. Adding $AB$ to the reaction mixture would also serve to favor the reverse reaction since the system reacts to this stress by producing more $A$ and $B$. Decreasing the temperature favors the forward reaction since heat (which will counteract the stress by increasing the temperature) is liberated in this process. The addition of a nonreactive liquid to the reaction mixture has no effect on the reaction rates (assuming pressure and temperature to remain constant). Decreasing the volume of the reaction mixture has the same effect as increasing the pressure (Boyle's Law) if the temperature is constant.

# Questions

**Q–43**

The functional group shown below represents

$$
\begin{array}{c}
O \\
\parallel \\
R - C - H
\end{array}
$$

(A)  an alcohol.

(B)  an ether.

(C)  an aldehyde.

(D)  a ketone.

*Your Answer* _____

_____

*Medicinal hard capsules—for powders and semi-solid preparations—were invented in America in 1833. They were, and are today, made of gelatin. (www.rpsgb.org.uk)*

# Correct Answers

**A–43**

**(C)**  The functional group of an alcohol is indicated by
    R – OH;
that of an ether is
    R – O – R$^1$;
an aldehyde is indicated by

$$\begin{matrix} & O \\ & \| \\ R - & C - H; \end{matrix}$$

while that of a ketone is

$$\begin{matrix} & O \\ & \| \\ R - & C - R^1 \end{matrix}$$

Derivatives of organic acids; esters, amides, and acid anhydrides for example, have the following functional groups:

carboxylic acid

$$\begin{matrix} & O \\ & \| \\ R - & C - OH \end{matrix}$$

ester

$$\begin{matrix} & O \\ & \| \\ R - & C - O - R^1 \end{matrix}$$

amide

$$\begin{matrix} & O \\ & \| \\ R - & C - NH_2 \end{matrix}$$

acid anhydride

$$\begin{matrix} & O & & O \\ & \| & & \| \\ R - & C - O - & C - R^1 \end{matrix}$$

# Questions

**Q–44**

What is the molarity of a 10 ml solution in which 3.7g of KCl are dissolved?

(A)  0.05$M$

(B)  0.1$M$

(C)  1$M$

(D)  5$M$

*Your Answer* _____

_____

**Q–45**

Isomers differ in

(A)   the number of neutrons in their nuclei.

(B)   their atomic compositions.

(C)   their molecular weights.

(D)   their molecular structures.

*Your Answer* _____

_____

# Correct Answers

**A–44**

**(D)** Converting to moles:

$$3.7g \text{ of } KCl \times \frac{1 \text{ mole of } KCl}{74g \text{ of } KCl} = 0.05 \text{ mole of } KCl$$

Converting to liters of solution:

$$10 \text{ ml} \times \frac{1 \text{ liter}}{1,000 \text{ ml}} = 0.01 \text{ liter of solution}$$

Molarity is defined as the number of moles of solute dissolved in one liter of solution. Thus,

$$M = \frac{0.05 \text{ mole of } KCl}{0.01 \text{ liter of solution}}$$

**A–45**

**(D)** Isomers differ only in their molecular structures. Isotopes vary in the number of neutrons in the nucleus and thus have different weights.

# Questions

---

**Q–46**

Which of the following indicates the functional group of an ether?

(A) $R - OH$

(B) $R - O - R^1$

(C)
$$R - \overset{\overset{\displaystyle O}{\|}}{C} - H$$

(D)
$$R - \overset{\overset{\displaystyle O}{\|}}{C} - R^1$$

---

*Your Answer* _____

---

**Q–47**

The equilibrium expression, $K = [Ag^+][Cl^-]$ describes the reaction

(A) $AgCl \rightarrow Ag^+ + Cl^-$

(B) $Ag^+ + Cl^- \rightarrow AgCl$

(C) $Ag^+ + Cl^- \rightarrow Ag + Cl$

(D) $Ag + Cl \rightarrow Ag^+ + Cl^-$

---

*Your Answer* _____

# Correct Answers

**A–46**

**(B)**

| | |
|---|---|
| R — OH | alcohol |
| R — O — R$^1$ | ether |

$$R - \overset{\overset{\textstyle O}{\|}}{C} - H \qquad \text{aldehyde}$$

$$R - \overset{\overset{\textstyle O}{\|}}{C} - R^1 \qquad \text{ketone}$$

$$R - \overset{\overset{\textstyle O}{\|}}{C} - OH \qquad \text{carboxylic acid}$$

---

**A–47**

**(A)**   The equilibrium constant is given by the product of the concentrations of the products divided by the product of the reactant concentrations. Recall that the concentrations of solid products or reactants and water are omitted since they are assumed to be constant. This gives:

$$K = [Ag^+][Cl^-] \text{ for } AgCl \rightarrow Ag^+ + Cl^-$$

$$K = \frac{1}{[AG^+][Cl^-]} \text{ for } Ag^+ + Cl^- \rightarrow Ag$$

Atomic chlorine does not exist in nature, so the reactions proposed for it are irrelevant.

# Questions

---

**Q–48**

Which of the following shifts the equilibrium of the following reaction to the right?

$$A_{(g)} + B_{(g)} + C_{(g)} \rightleftharpoons A_{(g)} + BC_{(g)}$$

(A) Addition of more A

(B) Removal of B

(C) Increasing the pressure

(D) Decreasing the temperature

*Your Answer* _____

---

**Q–49**

Which of the following is a nonelectrolyte in water?

(A) Sodium nitrate

(B) Sulfuric acid

(C) Sodium bicarbonate

(D) Carbon tetrachloride

*Your Answer* _____

# Correct Answers

## A–48

**(C)** Addition of more *A* does not affect the equilibrium because *A* appears both as a reactant and a product. Removal of *B* causes the equilibrium to shift to the left. Increasing the pressure causes the system to move to the right in order to reduce the number of moles of gas present. Changes in temperature will not affect the equilibrium since there is no heat released to or absorbed from the environment during the reaction. The previous explanations are all based on Le Chatelier's Principle: a system when subjected to a stress will shift in a direction so as to minimize that stress.

## A–49

**(D)** A nonelectrolyte is characterized by not dissociating in water solution. Of the choices given, only carbon tetrachloride satisfies this requirement.

# Questions

Which molecule among the following has the lowest molecular weight?

(A)
$$
\begin{array}{ccc}
H & H & H \\
| & | & | \\
H-C-C-C-H \\
| & | & | \\
H & H & H
\end{array}
$$

(B)
$$
\begin{array}{c}
H \\
| \\
H-C\equiv C-C-H \\
| \\
H
\end{array}
$$

(C)
$$
\begin{array}{cc}
H & H \\
\backslash & | \\
C=C-C-H \\
/ & | \\
H & H
\end{array}
$$

(D)  $H-C\equiv C-C\equiv C-H$

*Your Answer* _____

_____

# Correct Answers

**A–50**

**(C)**     It has only three carbon atoms and six hydrogen atoms.

C: $3 \times 12 = 36$

H: $6 \times 1 = 6$

$36 + 6 = 42$, which is the molecular weight.

# Questions

---

**Q-51**

What is the solubility of AgCl in water if $K_{sp} = 1.6 \times 10^{-10}$?

(A)   $1.6 \times 10^{-10}$

(B)   $3.2 \times 10^{-10}$

(C)   $1.3 \times 10^{-5}$

(D)   $1.6 \times 10^{-5}$

---

*Your Answer* _____

_____

*The Scottish Scientist Sir Alexander Fleming discovered the antibiotic penicillin accidentally in 1928. He was culturing bacteria and he went on holiday. In his haste to go away he left the Petri dish lid ajar and when he returned a mold had killed the bacteria in the same dish. It took 10 years for scientists to extract the penicillin from the bacteria. (www.fashion-era.com)*

# Correct Answers

## A–51

**(C)** The solubility product of $AgCl$ is
$$K_{sp} = [Ag^+][Cl^-] = 1.6 \times 10^{-10}$$
Letting $x = [Ag^+]$ and since $[Ag^+] = [Cl^-]$, we have
$$x^2 = 1.6 \times 10^{-10}$$
and $x = 1.3 \times 10^{-5}$

Since $[Ag^+] = [Cl^-] = [AgCl]$, the solubility of silver chloride is $1.3 \times 10^{-5}$ mole/liter.

# Questions

Which of the following structures represents 1, 1-dibromoethane?

```
            Br    H
            |     |
(A)   Br — C  —  C — H
            |     |
            H     H
```

```
            Br    Br
            |     |
(B)   H — C  —  C — H
            |     |
            H     H
```

(C)   $CH_3 - CH_2 - Br - CH_2 - CH_3$

(D)   $Br - C \equiv C - BR$

*Your Answer* _____

_____

# Correct Answers

## A–52

**(A)** Dibromoethane is ethane, $CH_3CH_3$, with two hydrogen atoms replaced by bromine. The numbers "1,1" indicate that both bromine atoms are on the first carbon.

Thus

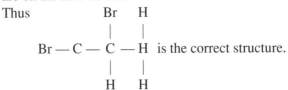

is the correct structure.

**Questions 53 – 54 refer to the following:**

$A_{(aq)} + 2B_{(aq)} \rightarrow C_{(aq)}$

The rate law for the reaction above is:

$$rate = K\,[B]^2$$

---

**Q–53**

What is the order of the reaction with respect to B?

(A)  0

(B)  1

(C)  2

(D)  3

---

*Your Answer* _____

---

**Q–54**

What will happen to the rate of the reaction if the amount of A in the solution is doubled?

(A)   The rate will double

(B)   The rate will halve

(C)   The rate will be four times bigger

(D)   No effect

---

*Your Answer* _____

# Correct Answers

**A–53**

**(C)**   The rate law includes the concentration of $B$ raised to the second power, thus it is second order in $B$. The rate law includes no factor dependent on $A$ and so it is zero order in $A$. The rate law is second order overall.

**A–54**

**(D)**   Since $A$ is not a factor in the rate law, changes in the concentration of $A$ have no effect on the rate of reaction.

# Questions

---

**Q–55**

Which of the following structures has the IUPAC name propyl butanoate?

(A)  $CH_3CH_2CH_2OCH_2CH_2CH_2CH_3$

(B)  $CH_3CH_2\overset{\overset{\displaystyle O}{\|}}{C}OCH_2CH_2CH_2CH_3$

(C)  $CH_3CH_2CH_2CH_2\overset{\overset{\displaystyle O}{\|}}{C}OCH_2CH_2CH_3$

(D)  $CH_3CH_2CH_2\overset{\overset{\displaystyle O}{\|}}{C}OCH_2CH_2CH_3$

---

*Your Answer* _____

---

**Q–56**

Enzymes, which are organic catalysts, always partly consist of:

(A)  carbohydrates

(B)  lipids

(C)  nucleic acids

(D)  proteins

---

*Your Answer* _____

# Correct Answers

## A–55

**(D)** The first word of the ester name is the name of the group attached to oxygen (propyl in our case). The second word is the name of the parent carboxylic acid with the suffix -ic replaced by -ate (butanoate in our case). Thus, we are looking for an ester with a propyl group attached to the oxygen of butanoic acid. This structure is

$$\underset{\text{CH}_3\text{CH}_2\text{CH}_2\overset{\displaystyle O}{\overset{\displaystyle \|}{\text{C}}}\text{OCH}_2\text{CH}_2\text{CH}_3}{}$$

$\text{CH}_3\text{CH}_2\text{CH}_2\text{OCH}_2\text{CH}_2\text{CH}_2\text{CH}_3$ has the assigned name butyl propyl ether

$$\underset{\text{CH}_3\text{CH}_2\overset{\displaystyle O}{\overset{\displaystyle \|}{\text{C}}}\text{OCH}_2\text{CH}_2\text{CH}_2\text{CH}_3}{}$$ has the assigned name butyl propanoate

$$\underset{\text{CH}_3\text{CH}_2\text{CH}_2\text{CH}_2\overset{\displaystyle O}{\overset{\displaystyle \|}{\text{C}}}\text{OCH}_2\text{CH}_2\text{CH}_3}{}$$ has the assigned name propyl pentanoate

## A–56

**(D)** Enzymes are proteins that act as catalysts for biochemical reactions.

# Questions

---

**Q–57**

Complete ionization of an aluminum hydroxide particle yields:

(A) $Al^+$, $OH^-$

(B) $Al^+$, $2OH^-$

(C) $Al^+$, $3OH^-$

(D) $2Al^+$, $3OH^-$

---

*Your Answer* _____

---

**Q–58**

An example of a dipole molecule is:

(A) $CH_4$

(B) $H_2$

(C) $H_2O$

(D) $NaCl$

---

*Your Answer* _____

# Correct Answers

**A–57**

**(C)** Aluminum hydroxide's formula is $Al(OH)_3$. Thus, one aluminum ion and three hydroxyl ions are yielded by dissociation.

**A–58**

**(C)** A dipole is an electrically asymmetrical molecule due to the unequal sharing of electron pairs between the spheres of bonding atoms. The two shared electron pairs of water spend more time in the command of oxygen's sphere than hydrogen's with its lower attracting power. Sodium chloride is not molecular but ionic. Methane ($CH_4$), hydrogen gas and oxygen gas share electron pairs equally and are thus nonpolar molecules.

# Questions

Question 59 refers to the valence electron dot formulas in the figure below. The letters merely identify the different atoms. They do not stand for actual known elements.

Valence Electron Dot Formulas

$$\overset{\cdot}{A} \qquad\qquad \overset{\cdot\cdot}{D}$$

$$\cdot \overset{\cdot}{\underset{\cdot}{X}} \cdot \qquad\qquad : \overset{\cdot\cdot}{\underset{\cdot}{Y}} \cdot$$

$$: \overset{\cdot\cdot}{\underset{\cdot}{X}} :$$

---

**Q–59**

A possible compound by covalent bonding is:

(A)   $AD_2$

(B)   $AX_3$

(C)   $XZ_4$

(D)   $YZ$

---

*Your Answer* _____

_____

# Correct Answers

## A–59

**(C)** Element $X$, with four electrons to offer, can satisfy four $Z$ atoms, each in need of one electron for an outer, stable configuration of 8.

*The American Chemical Society designated the 1940's research of Selman Waksman and his Rutgers University students into the actinomycete antibiotics a National Historic Chemical Landmark on May 24, 2005. They developed most notably the first effective treatment for tuberculosis, cholera, and typhoid fever. (www.acswebcontent.acs.org)*

# Questions

---

**Q–60**

In organic chemistry, the so-called "aromatic behavior" consists of:

(A)   addition reactions

(B)   substitution reactions

(C)   oxidation reactions

(D)   reduction reactions

*Your Answer* _____

_____

---

**Q–61**

Which of the following equations can be used to calculate the emf of this voltaic cell at various concentrations?

(A)   $E = E° - \dfrac{0.05915}{n} \log Q$

(B)   $E = q{-}w$

(C)   $E = E°$ products $- E°$ reactants

(D)   $E = E° - \dfrac{0.05915}{n} \ln Q$

*Your Answer* _____

_____

# Correct Answers

## A–60

**(B)** The aromatic compounds are very stable, due to resonance, so substitution is the most likely to happen.

## A–61

**(A)** In order to calculate the emf value of a voltaic cell at various concentrations we use the Nernst equation

$$E = E° - \frac{0.05915}{n} \log Q$$

where $E$ = the emf for the reaction at the new concentration

$E°$ = the standard electrode potential

$n$ = the number of moles of electrons involved in the half reactions

$Q$ = the reaction quotient

# Questions

---

**Q–62**

The abbreviated electronic configuration of an element of atomic number 42 can be:

(A) $[Kr]5s^14d^5$

(B) $[Kr]5s^24d^4$

(C) $[Kr]4d^6$

(D) $[Kr]5s^25p^4$

---

*Your Answer* _____

_____

**Questions 63 – 64 refer to the statement below:**

A voltaic cell consists of a combination of a standard silver electrode and another silver electrode in which the concentration of silver ions is $10^{-3}R\neg$ $E^0_{Ag+/Ag}$ = 0.80V.

---

**Q–63**

The cell standard potential $E^0_{cell}$ is

(A) 0.00V

(B) +0.80V

(C) –0.80V

(D) +1.6V

---

*Your Answer* _____

_____

# Correct Answers

## A–62

**(A)** The abbreviated electronic configuration of an element of atomic number 42 is $[Kr]\, 5s^1 4d^5$, where $[Kr]$ stands for the electronic arrangement of Krypton, element 36, indicating the filling of all sublevels through $4p^6$. The remaining 6 electrons go into $5s$ and $4d$ orbitals. The $5s^1 4d^5$ configuration is preferred over the $5s^2 4d^4$ configuration because of the stability of the half-filled $4d$ sublevel.

## A–63

**(A)** The cell in these problems is called the concentration cell.

Let the half-cell equations be:

anode: $Ag \rightarrow Ag^+_{dilute} + e^-$ $\qquad \Sigma^\circ = -0.8V$

cathode: $Ag^+_{std} + e \rightarrow Ag$ $\qquad \Sigma^\circ = +0.8V$

overall: $Ag^+_{std} + Ag \rightarrow Ag^+_{dilute} + Ag$, $\Sigma^\circ = 0.00V$

$E^\circ_{cell} = 0.00V$

# Questions

---

**Q–64**

Which of the following is true?

(A)  The standard electrode is the cathode.

(B)  The standard electrode is the anode.

(C)  There will be no electron transfer.

(D)  This cell will work like a perpetual source of energy.

---

*Your Answer* _____

_____

*Medications are an integral part of space flight, used to treat space motion sickness, headache, sleeplessness, backache, and nasal congestion. With extended-duration space habitation, pharmacologic countermeasures will be used in part to respond to issues of nutritional status, musculoskeletal integrity, and immune response. (www.wylelabs.com)*

# Correct Answers

## A–64

(A)     To find out if the reaction will take place as written, we use a Nernst equation to evaluate the cell potential.

$$E_{cell} = E^\circ_{cell} \quad \frac{-0.059^{\log}}{n} \quad \left\{ \frac{[Ag^+_{dilute}]}{[AG^+_{std}]} \right\}$$

$n = 1$ in this example

Therefore, $E_{cell} = -0.059 \log \dfrac{10^{-3}}{1.0}$

$$= -0.059 \times (-3)$$

$$E_{cell} = 0.177$$

Since $E_{cell}$ is positive, the reaction will proceed as written; if $E_{cell}$ had been negative, then it would imply that we had written the equation in the wrong direction. From the half-cell reactions, we conclude that the standard electrode is the cathode, so the only correct statement is (A). (D) is false, since the cell will stop functioning after the concentration of $Ag^+$ ions around the electrodes evens out.

# Questions

---

**Q–65**

What type of formula of ethane is depicted below?

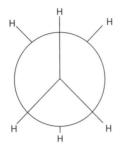

(A)  Fisher projection formula

(B)  Newman projection formula

(C)  Lewis projection formula

(D)  Kekulé projection formula

*Your Answer* _____

---

**Q–66**

According to Hund's rule, how many unpaired electrons does the ground state of iron have?

(A)  6

(B)  5

(C)  4

(D)  2

*Your Answer* _____

# Correct Answers

## A–65

**(B)** Three dimensional shapes of molecules are important to the chemist and biochemist. The Newman projection is a way of showing molecular conformations of alkanes. Conformations are the arrangements of atoms depending on the angle of rotation of one carbon with respect to another adjacent carbon. A Newman projection is obtained by looking at the molecule along the bond on which rotation occurs. The carbon in front is indicated by a point and at the back by a circle, the 3 remaining valences are placed 120° to each other (but remember that the bond angles about each of the carbon atoms are 109.5° and not 120° as the Newman projection formula might suggest). For example, for $CH_3 - CH_3$.

## A–66

**(C)** The ground state configuration of iron is $[Ar]\, 4s^2 3d^6$. There are five d orbitals and with minimum pairing Fe has **4** unpaired electrons.

# Questions

---

**Q–67**

Which of the following compounds have only non-polar bonds?

(A) $KO_2$

(B) NaF

(C) HF

(D) $I_2$

---

*Your Answer* _____

_____

---

**Q–68**

Lithium (AW = 6.941) exists as two naturally occurring isotopes, Li and Li, with relative atomic masses of 6.015 and 7.016. Find the percent abundances of the two isotopes.

(A) 23.1, 46.2

(B) 74.30, 25.70

(C) 90, 10

(D) 92.51, 7.49

---

*Your Answer* _____

_____

# Correct Answers

## A–67

**(D)** The polarity of a bond can be estimated by the difference in electro-negativity ($\Delta EN$) between the 2 atoms in the bond. The compounds in $A$ to $D$ are ionic (large $\Delta EN$). $\Delta EN$ for $I_2$ is, of course, zero.

## A–68

**(D)** Let $x$ = fraction of $^{6}_{3}Li$ and $1-x$ = fraction of $^{7}_{3}Li$. $6.015x + 7.016 (1-x) = 6.941$. $x = .0749$ or $7.49\%$; $1-x = .9251$ or $92.51\%$.

# Questions

---

**Q–69**

The student treats some fresh solution of the salt with $BaCl_2$. A precipitate forms. Which anions could have been present?

(A) $SO_4^{2-}$, $PO_4^{3-}$

(B) $Br^-$, $Cl^-$, $I^-$

(C) $CH_3COO^-$ only

(D) $Br^-$ only

*Your Answer* _____

_____

---

**Q–70**

Calculate the molecular weight of an unknown gas X if the ratio of its effusion rate to that of He is .378 (MW of He = 4.00)

(A) 9.47

(B) 42.3

(C) 10.6

(D) 28.0

*Your Answer* _____

_____

# Correct Answers

## A–69

**(A)**  $Ba^{2+}$ will form insoluble salts with sulfate and phosphate.

## A–70

**(D)**  Effusion rates of gases are related as $r_A/r_B = (MW_B/MW_A)^{1/2}$.

$$\frac{r_x}{r_{He}} = .378$$

$$.378 = \left(\frac{4.00}{MW_A}\right)^{\frac{1}{2}}$$

$$MW_A = 28.0$$

# Questions

---

**Q–71**

How many molecules are there in 22 g of $CO_2$? The molecular weight of $CO_2$ is 44.

(A)  3

(B)  $6.02 \times 10^{23}$

(C)  44

(D)  $3.01 \times 10^{23}$

---

*Your Answer* _____

_____

---

**Q–72**

What is the hydrogen ion concentration of a buffer solution that is .05M in acetic acid and .1M in sodium acetate. (The $K_i$ for acetic acid is $1.8 \times 10^{-5}$.)

(A)  $9.0 \times 10^{-6}$

(B)  $1.8 \times 10^{-5}$

(C)  $1.0 \times 10^{-14}$

(D)  $1.8 \times 10^{-6}$

---

*Your Answer* _____

_____

# Correct Answers

**A–71**

**(D)** The number of molecules in one mole is given by Avogadro's number which is: 1 mole of molecules contains $6.02 \times 10^{23}$ molecules. Since the amount of $CO_2$ given is 22g it is first necessary to find the number of moles of $CO_2$ in 22g. This is calculated from:

$$moles = \frac{g}{MW} = \frac{22g}{44g/mol} = 0.5 \ moles \ of \ CO_2$$

It is now necessary to calculate the number of molecules in .5 moles of $CO_2$. This is obtained using Avogadro's number.

$$\frac{1 \ mole}{0.5 \ moles} = \frac{6.02g \times 10^{23} molecules}{x \ molecules}$$

$$x = 3.01 \times 10^{23} \text{ molecules}$$

**A–72**

**(A)** Acetic acid ionizes,

$$HC_2H_3O_2 \leftrightarrow H^+ + C_2H_3O_2^-$$

and sodium acetate completely dissociates,

$$NaC_2H_3O_2 \rightarrow Na^+ + C_2H_3O_2^-$$

The solution is a buffer solution since it is composed of a weak acid and a salt of the weak acid. The hydrogen ion concentration of such a buffer can be calculated from the expression:

$$H^+ = \frac{[acid]}{salt} \times K_i$$

$$[H^+] = \frac{.05}{.1} \times 1.8 \times 10^{-5}$$
$$= .90 \times 10^{-5} \text{ or } 9.0 \times 10^{-6}$$

# Questions

Which one of the following drawings represents the region of space an electron with a quantum number of l = 1 would be found?

(A)  A

(B)  B

(C)  C

(D)  D

(A)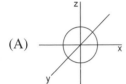

(B)

(C)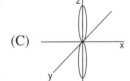

(D)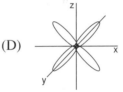

*Your Answer* _____

_____

# Correct Answers

(C)    The value of the azimuthal quantum number, $l$, may have values 0, $l$, 2 up to a maximum of $n - 1$, where $n$ is the principle quantum number. The $l$ value tells the subshell or orbital that the electron is in.

When $l = 0$   the electron is in an $s$ orbital

$l = 1$   the electron is in a $p$ orbital

$l = 2$   the electron is in a $d$ orbital

The only $p$ orbital that is shown is in diagram (C), which represents the $p_z$ orbital since the lobes are going through the z axis.

Answer    A    is an $s$ orbital

B    is the $d_{x2-y2}$ orbital

D    i the $d_{xy}$ orbital

The correct answer is (C).

---

**Q-74**

In the van der Waal's equation:

$$\left(P + \frac{n^2a}{V^2}\right)(V - nb) = nrt$$

The constant a is best described as a correction factor due to:

(A) temperature

(B) intermolecular attractions of real gases

(C) the molecular weights of gases

(D) the volume of the actual gas molecules

*Your Answer* _____

_____

---

**Q-75**

Neutral atoms of F (fluorine) have the same number of electrons as

(A) $N^+$

(B) $Ne^-$

(C) $Na^-$

(D) $Mg^{3+}$

*Your Answer* _____

_____

# Correct Answers

**A–74**

**(B)** The Ideal gas law equation, $PV = nRT$ derived from kinetic and molecular theory neglects two important factors in regard to real gases. First, it neglects the actual volume of gas molecules, and secondly, it does not take into account the intermolecular forces that real gases exhibit.

The factor $b$ in the van der Waal equation is a correction for the actual volume of the gas molecules and the factor a is a correction of the pressure due to the intermolecular attractions that occur in real gases.

**A–75**

**(D)** Neutral fluorine atoms have 9 electrons as determined by their atomic number. Magnesium atoms have 12 electrons so $Mg^{3+}$ has 9 electrons. Nitrogen has 7 electrons so $N^+$ has 6 electrons (the same as carbon). Neon has 10 electrons so $Ne^-$ has 11 electrons (the same as sodium). Sodium has 11 electrons so $Na^-$ has 12 electrons (the same as magnesium).

**Q–76**

The molecular weight of a gas is 16. At STP, 4.48 liters of this gas weighs

(A)  2.3g.

(B)  2.7g.

(C)  3.2g.

(D)  4.1g.

*Your Answer* _____

**Q–77**

How many moles of electrons are required to reduce 103.6g of lead from $Pb^{2+}$ to the metal?

(A)  0.5 mole

(B)  1 mole

(C)  2 moles

(D)  4 moles

*Your Answer* _____

# Correct Answers

## A–76

**(C)** A molecular weight of 16g tells us that a volume of 22.4 liters (molar volume) of that gas weighs 16g. To determine the weight of a 4.48l sample we multiply

$$4.48l \times \frac{16g}{22.4l} = 3.2g$$

## A–77

**(B)** The atomic weight of lead is 207.2g/mole from the periodic table. The number of moles present in 103.6g of lead is given by

$$103.6g \times \frac{1\ mole}{207.2g} = 0.5\ mole$$

Since lead is in the +2 oxidation state, two moles of electrons are required for every mole of lead to reduce it to the metals. However, only one mole of electrons is required to reduce 0.5 mole of $Pb^{2+}$ to $Pb^0$.

# Questions

---

**Q-78**

What is the molecular weight of $HClO_4$?

(A) 52.5

(B) 73.5

(C) 96.5

(D) 100.5

*Your Answer* _____

---

**Q-79**

The systematic (IUPAC) name of this structure is

```
      H    H    H    OH    H    H
      |    |    |    |     |    |
 H — C — C — C — C  — C — C — H
      |    |    |    |     |    |
      H    H    H    H     H    H
```

(A) hexanol.

(B) 3-hydroxyhexane.

(C) 3-hexanol.

(D) 4-hexanol.

*Your Answer* _____

# Correct Answers

## A-78

**(D)**   The molecular weight of a compound is the sum of its constituents' atomic weights. Elements or groups followed by a subscript have their atomic weight multiplied by that subscript. Thus, the molecular weight of perchloric acid ($HClO_4$) is

atomic weight of $H$ + atomic weight of $Cl$ + 4 × atomic weight of $O$

or $1 + 35.5 + 4(16) = 100.5$

## A-79

**(C)**   Alcohols are named by replacing the -e of the corresponding hydrocarbon name by the suffix -ol. The position of the hydroxy substituent is numbered from the shorter end of the chain. Thus, the structure is named 3-hexanol. It is a hexanol because the parent hydrocarbon has six carbons and the prefix 3- (not 4-) is used to indicate the location of the hydroxy group on the third carbon.

# Questions

---

**Q–80**

Which of the elements in Group IA of the periodic table has the greatest metallic character?

(A) Li

(B) Na

(C) K

(D) Fr

---

*Your Answer* _____

_____

---

**Q–81**

Which of the following serves as a catalyst in the reaction

$$CH_2 = CH_2 + H_2 + Pt \rightarrow CH_3CH_3 + Pt$$

(A) C

(B) $CH_2 = CH_2$

(C) $H_2$

(D) Pt

---

*Your Answer* _____

_____

# Correct Answers

**A–80**

**(D)**    The metals are found on the left side of the periodic table, with metallic character increasing as one goes down a group. All the choices given are in Group IA, so the one farthest down in the group has the greatest metallic character. This is francium (Fr).

**A–81**

**(D)**    One characteristic of a catalyst is that it remains unchanged by the reaction process. It may now be seen that the platinum, Pt, is the catalyst for this reaction.

# Questions

**Q–82**

The expected electron configuration of propanal is:

(A)
```
     H  H  H
     ·· ·· ·· ··
H : C : C : C : O :
     ·· ··    ··
     H  H
```

(B)
```
     H     H  H
     ··    ·· ·· ··
H : C : : C : C : O :
              ·· ··
              H
```

(C)
```
     H           H
     ··          ··
H : C : : C : : C : O
```

(D)
```
     H  H  H
     ·· ·· ··
H : C : C : C : : O :
     ·· ··    ··
     H  H
```

*Your Answer* _____

_____

*The FDA Approved Animal Drug Products, (Green Book), is published by the Drug Information Laboratory; paper copies are available by subscription. (www.fda.gov)*

# Correct Answers

(**D**)    From the name propanal, we find that we must describe an aldehyde (from the -al suffix) composed of a 3-carbon skeleton (from the prop-prefix) with no multiple bonds (from the -ane root). Remembering that an aldehyde is characterized by the functional group

$$\begin{matrix} & O \\ & \| \\ -\,&C-H \end{matrix}$$

we obtain

$$CH_3 - CH_2 - \overset{\overset{\textstyle O}{\|}}{C} - H$$

as a result. This is equivalent to the electron configuration in (D), since each bond (1) represents two electrons.

# Questions

---

**Q–83**

The attractive force between the protons of one molecule and the electrons of another molecule is strongest

(A)   in the solid phase.

(B)   in the liquid phase.

(C)   in the gas phase.

(D)   during sublimation.

---

*Your Answer* _____

_____

---

**Q–84**

The oxidation state of manganese in $KMnO_4$ is

(A)   +1.

(B)   +2.

(C)   +3.

(D)   +7.

---

*Your Answer* _____

_____

# Correct Answers

## A–83

**(A)** The attractive force between the protons of one atom and the electrons of another is inversely proportional to the distance between the atoms, i.e., (F a 1/d) where $F$ = force and $d$ = distance between two atoms. This shows that the attraction is strongest at small distances (as in solids) and weakest at large distances (as in gases).

## A–84

**(D)** The oxidation states of the atoms of a neutral compound must add up to equal zero. For $KMnO_4$, the oxidation state of $K$ must be $+1$ since it is in Group $IA$ and the oxidation state of $O$ must be $-2$ since it is in Group $VIA$. Thus we have:

$$1 + Mn + 4(-2) = 0 \text{ and } Mn = +7$$

# Questions

---

**Q–85**

An increase in pressure will change the equilibrium constant by

(A) shifting to the side where a smaller volume results.

(B) shifting to the side where a larger volume results.

(C) favoring the exothermic reaction.

(D) None of the above.

*Your Answer* _____

---

**Q–86**

The most active metal of the alkali metals is

(A) Li.

(B) Mg.

(C) K.

(D) Cs.

*Your Answer* _____

# Correct Answers

### A–85

**(D)**      The equilibrium constant is independent of pressure and volume but dependent on temperature.

### A–86

**(D)**      Activity increases as one moves down a group of the periodic table since the outermost electrons are further away from the nucleus and not held as tightly as those of the smaller atoms. Also, metallic character is greatest at the far left of the periodic table.

# Questions

---

**Q–87**

A gas has a volume of 10 liters at 50°C and 200mm Hg pressure. What correction factor is needed to give a volume at STP?

(A) $\frac{0}{50} \times \frac{200}{760}$

(B) $\frac{0}{50} \times \frac{760}{200}$

(C) $\frac{273}{323} \times \frac{200}{760}$

(D) $\frac{273}{323} \times \frac{760}{200}$

*Your Answer* _____

---

**Q–88**

How much reactant remains if 92g of $HNO_3$ is reacted with 24g of LiOH assuming the reaction to be complete?

(A) 46g of $HNO_3$

(B) 29g of $HNO_3$

(C) 12g of $HNO_3$

(D) 2g of LiOH

*Your Answer* _____

# Correct Answers

## A–87

**(C)** This problem is solved by applying the combined as law:

$$\frac{P_1 V_1}{T_1} = \frac{P_2 V_2}{T_2}$$

Rearranging gives:

$$V_2 = V_1 \times \frac{T_2}{T_1} \times \frac{P_1}{P_2}$$

Substituting given values:

$$V_2 = 10 \times \frac{273}{323} \times \frac{200}{760}$$

This gives the correction factor:

$$\frac{273}{323} \times \frac{200}{760}$$

## A–88

**(B)** The molecular weight of $HNO_3$ is 63 grams/mole and that of $LiOH$ is 24 grams/mole. $HNO_3$ and $LiOH$ react in a 1:1 ratio by mole as seen by

$$HNO_3 + LiOH \rightarrow H_2O + LiNO_3$$

There is an excess of $HNO_3$, since only one mole of it can react with the one mole of $LiOH$ available. Thus, there is an excess of 92 – 63 or 29 grams of nitric acid.

# Questions

---

**Q–89**

What is the density of a diatomic gas whose gram-molecular weight is 80g?

(A)  1.9g/liter

(B)  2.8g/liter

(C)  3.6g/liter

(D)  4.3g/liter

*Your Answer* _____

---

**Q–90**

The name of the compound $HClO_2$ is

(A)  hydrochloric acid.

(B)  hypochlorous acid.

(C)  chlorous acid.

(D)  chloric acid.

*Your Answer* _____

# Correct Answers

## A–89

**(C)** Recalling that density equals

$$\rho = \frac{m}{V}$$

gives $\rho = \frac{80 g/mole}{22.4 l/mole} = 3.6 g/liter$

## A–90

**(C)** The structure $HClO_2$ is chlorous acid. Binary acids, such as $HCl$, are given the prefix hydro- in front of the stem of the nonmetallic element and the ending -ic. Ternary acids (composed of three elements—usually hydrogen, a nonmetal, and oxygen) usually have a variable oxygen content so the most common member of the series has the ending -ic. The acid with one less oxygen than the -ic acid has the ending -ous. The acid with one less oxygen than the -ous acid has the prefix hypo- and the ending -ous. The acid containing one more oxygen than the -ic acid has the prefix per- and the ending -ic. For example,

| | |
|---|---|
| HCl | hydrochloric acid |
| HClO | hypochlorous acid |
| $HClO_2$ | chlorous acid |
| $HClO_3$ | chloric acid |
| $HClO_4$ | perchloric acid |

# Questions

---

**Q–91**

Which statement is true for a liquid/gas mixture in equilibrium?

(A) The equilibrium constant is dependent on temperature.

(B) The amount of the gas present at equilibrium is independent of pressure.

(C) All interchange between the liquid and gas phases has ceased.

(D) All of the above.

---

*Your Answer* _____

_____

---

**Q–92**

Calculate the concentration of HI present in an equilibrium mixture produced by the reaction

$$H_{2(g)} + I_{2(g)} \rightleftharpoons 2HI_{(g)} \text{ if } K_e = 3.3 \yen 10^{-1}$$

and the concentrations of $H_2$ and $I_2$ are $0.1M$ and $0.3M$, respectively, at equilibrium.

(A) $0.01M$

(B) $0.03M$

(C) $0.05M$

(D) $0.1M$

---

*Your Answer* _____

_____

# Correct Answers

## A-91

**(A)** The equilibrium constant is dependent only on temperature but the amount of each substance present at equilibrium is dependent on pressure, volume, and temperature. There is still an interchange between the phases, but the same number of molecules leave and enter both phases so the equilibrium concentrations and equilibrium constant are the same for a given pressure, volume, and temperature.

## A-92

**(D)** The equilibrium constant expression for the reaction is:

$$K_e = \frac{[HI]^2}{[H_2][I_2]}$$

Substituting given values, we obtain:

$$3.3 \times 10^{-1} = \frac{[HI]^2}{(0.1)(0.3)}$$

Rearranging:

$$[HI]^2 = (3.3 \times 10^{-1})(0.1)(0.3) = 9.9 \times 10^{-3}$$

and    $[HI] = 0.1\ M$

# Questions

---

**Q–93**

The production of alkanes from alkenes is accomplished by

(A) burning in the presence of water.

(B) distillation.

(C) methylation.

(D) catalytic hydrogenation.

*Your Answer* _____

_____

---

**Q–94**

$sp^2$ hybridization will be found for carbon in

(A) $CH_4$.

(B) $C_2H_4$.

(C) $C_2H_2$.

(D) $CH_3OH$.

*Your Answer* _____

_____

# Correct Answers

**A–93**

**(D)**    Hydrogenation using a metal catalyst is a common method of producing alkanes from alkenes.

$$C_2H_4 + H_2 \xrightarrow{Pt} C_2H_6$$

---

**A–94**

**(B)**    A simple method for determining hybridization in carbon compounds is by determining how many atoms are attached to the carbon atom. If two atoms are attached, the hybridization is sp, if three, $sp^2$, and if four, $sp^3$. Thus,

$H — C \equiv C — H$    has sp hybridization

$$\begin{array}{cc} H & H \\ \diagdown & \diagup \\ & C = C \\ \diagup & \diagdown \\ H & H \end{array}$$    has $sp^2$ hybridization

$$\begin{array}{cc} H & H \\ | & | \\ H — C & — C — H \\ | & | \\ H & H \end{array}$$    has $sp^3$ hybridization

# Questions

---

**Q–95**

How many grams of Cu could be produced from $CuSO_4$ by 0.5 faradays of charge?

(A)  15.9

(B)  31.75

(C)  63.5

(D)  127.0

---

*Your Answer* _____

_____

---

**Q–96**

Reacting $CO_2(g)$ with water results in the production of

(A)  methane and oxygen.

(B)  carbonous acid.

(C)  carbonic acid.

(D)  carbon and oxygen.

---

*Your Answer* _____

_____

# Correct Answers

## A–95

(A)     A faraday is the amount of electricity that allows the reaction of one mole of electrons. Each $Cu^{2+}$ ion requires two electrons to be reduced to elemental copper.

$$0.5F \times \frac{\text{one mole } Cu^{2+}\text{ reduced to Cu}}{2F}$$

$$= 0.25 \text{ mole of } Cu^{2+} \text{ reduced to Cu}$$

Since the atomic weight of copper is 63.5g/mole, we have

$$0.25 \text{ mole} \times \frac{63.5g}{1 \text{ mole}} = 15.9\text{g of Cu.}$$

## A–96

(C)     $CO_2$ is an acid anhydride since an acid is produced upon reaction with water

$$CO_{2(g)} + H_2O \rightarrow H_2CO_3 \text{ (carbonic acid)}$$

**Q-97**

What is Kb for a 0.1$M$ solution of $NH_4OH$ if $[OH^-]$ = $1.3 \times 10^{-3}$?

(A)  $7.6 \times 10^{-1}$

(B)  $1.1 \times 10^{-2}$

(C)  $4.2 \times 10^{-3}$

(D)  $1.7 \times 10^{-5}$

*Your Answer* _____

_____

**Q-98**

How many grams of $HNO_3$ are required to produce a one liter aqueous solution of pH 2?

(A)  0.063

(B)  0.63

(C)  6.3

(D)  1.26

*Your Answer* _____

_____

# Correct Answers

## A–97

**(D)** $K_b$, the base dissociation constant, is defined as

$$K_b = \frac{[X^+][OH^-]}{[XOH]}$$

Since $[OH^-] = 1.3 \times 10^{-3}$ we know that $= 1.3 \times 10^{-3}$ and that the original concentration of $NH_4OH$ is 0.1M. Substituting values we obtain

$$K_b = \frac{(1.3 \times 10^{-3})(1.3 \times 10^{-3})}{(0.1 - 1.3 \times 10^{-3})} = \frac{1.69 \times 10^{-6}}{0.0987}$$

$$K_b = 1.7 \times 10^{-5}$$

## A–98

**(B)** The pH of a solution is defined as
$$pH = -\log[H^+]$$
Solving for $[H^+]$, we obtain
$$[H^+] = 10^{-pH} = 10^{-2}$$
Nitric acid is assumed to dissociate completely in solution since it is a strong acid. In addition, nitric acid has only one proton so the concentration of hydronium ions is equal to the initial concentration of $HNO_3$. We are working with one liter of solution so the concentration is identical to the number of moles by

$$M = \frac{number\ of\ moles\ of\ solute}{liters\ of\ solution}$$

Thus, we require $10^{-2}$ mole of $HNO_3$. Converting to grams:
$$10.2\ mole\ of\ HNO_3 \times \frac{63g\ of\ HNO_3}{1\ mole\ of\ HNO_3} = 0.63g$$
of $HNO_3$

# Questions

---

**Q–99**

A one liter solution of $2M$ NaOH can be prepared with

(A) 20g of NaOH.

(B) 40g of NaOH.

(C) 60g of NaOH.

(D) 80g of NaOH.

*Your Answer* _____

_____

---

**Q–100**

What is/are the product gas/gases if $NH_4Cl$ and $Ca(OH)_2$ are used as reactants?

(A) $N_2$

(B) $NH_3$

(C) $H_2O$

(D) $NH_3 + H_2O$

*Your Answer* _____

_____

# Correct Answers

---

**A–99**

**(D)** Molarity is defined as the number of moles of solute divided by the number of liters of solution. Thus,

$$M = \frac{moles\ of\ solute}{liters\ of\ solution}$$

Rearranging,

moles of solute = $(M)$ (liters of solution)

$$= (2)\,(1)$$
$$= 2$$

Converting to grams:

$$2\ moles\ of\ NaOH \times \frac{40g\ of\ NaOH}{1\ mole\ of\ NaOH} = 80g\ of\ NaOH$$

---

**A–100**

**(D)** The reaction is

$$2NH_4Cl_{(s)} + Ca(OH)_{2(s)} \rightarrow CaCl_2 + 2H_2O_{(g)} + 2NH_{3(g)}$$

# Questions

---

**Q–101**

Which of the following is incorrect?

(A)  1 liter = 1,000 $cm^3$

(B)  1 meter = 100 cm

(C)  1 milliliter = 1 $cm^3$

(D)  1 liter = 1 $meter^3$

*Your Answer* _____

_____

---

**Q–102**

The number of electrons in sulfur atom associated with the primary quantum number n:

(A)  )2  )8  )6

(B)  )2  )10  )4

(C)  )2  )2  )6  )2  )4

(D)  )2  )2  )2  )6  )4

*Your Answer* _____

_____

# Correct Answers

## A–101

**(D)**    The correct expression would be

$$1 \text{ liter} = 1{,}000 \ cm^3 \times \left( \frac{1m}{100 \ cm} \right)^3$$

$$1 \text{ liter} = 1{,}000 \ cm^3 \times \frac{1m^3}{1 \times 10^6 \ cm^3}$$

$$1 \text{ liter} = 1 \times 10^{-3} \ m^3$$

## A–102

**(A)**    The electronic configuration of sulfur is $1s^2 \ 2s^2 \ 2p^6 \ 3s^2 \ 3p4$ as given by the periodic table. Thus, we have 2 electrons in the first energy level, 8 in the second, and 6 in the third. This configuration is represented as )2 )8 )6.

# Questions

---

**Q–103**

The oxidizing agent in the reaction

$Pb + HgSO_4 \rightarrow PbSO_4 + Hg$ is

(A) Pb.

(B) $PbSO_4$.

(C) $Hg^{+2}$.

(D) $Hg^0$.

*Your Answer* _____

---

**Q–104**

The relation between the absolute temperature and volume of a gas at constant pressure is given by

(A) Boyle's Law.

(B) Charles's Law.

(C) the combined gas law.

(D) the ideal gas law.

*Your Answer* _____

# Correct Answers

## A–103

**(C)** The oxidizing agent in the reaction is the reagent that gains electron oxidizing another element or compound in a redox reaction.

$$Pb^0 + Hg^{+2}SO_4^{-2} \rightarrow Pb^{+2}SO_4^{-2} + Hg^0$$

We see that $Hg^{+2}$ served as an oxidizing agent by oxidizing $Pb$, while also becoming reduced.

## A–104

**(B)** Charles's Law states that the volume of a gas varies directly with the absolute temperature at constant pressure.

# Questions

---

**Q–105**

Which of the following would produce a highly conductive aqueous solution at equal concentrations?

(A) Cyclohexane

(B) Hydrochloric acid

(C) Benzene

(D) Acetic acid

*Your Answer* _____

---

**Q–106**

Which of the following should be reacted with sodium hydroxide to produce sodium chlorite?

(A) HCl

(B) HClO

(C) $HClO_2$

(D) $HClO_3$

*Your Answer* _____

# Correct Answers

## A–105

**(B)** The conductivity of a solution is directly related to the number of ions in solution. Hydrochloric acid, being a strong acid, dissociates completely while acetic acid, a weak acid, is only slightly dissociated. Cyclohexane and benzene may be said to be undissociated in solution.

## A–106

**(C)** The nomenclature of salts is based upon the names of the acids used to produce them. This system is based upon the following rules: -ic acids form -ate salts, -ous acids form -ite salts, and hydro- -ic acids form -ide salts. Thus, in reacting with sodium hydroxide, $HCl$, hydrochloric acid, produces sodium chloride; $HClO$, hypochlorous acid, produces sodium hypochlorite; $HClO_2$, chlorous acid, produces sodium chlorite; and $HClO_3$, chloric acid, produces sodium chlorate.

# Questions

All of the following are spontaneous reactions except

$$Co^{+2} + 2e- \rightarrow Co \qquad E° = -0.28V$$
$$Sn^{+2} + 2e- \rightarrow Sn \qquad E° = -0.14V$$
$$Zn^{+2} + 2e- \rightarrow Zn \qquad E° = -0.76V$$
$$Fe^{+2} + 2e- \rightarrow Fe \qquad E° = -0.44V$$
$$Mg^{+2} + 2e- \rightarrow Mg \qquad E° = -2.37V$$
$$F_2 + 2e- \rightarrow 2F^- \qquad E° = +2.87V$$
$$Cn^{+2} + 2e- \rightarrow Mn \qquad E° = -1.18V$$
$$2(Li^{+1} + e- \rightarrow Li) \qquad E° = -3.00V$$
$$2 (Ag^{+1} + e- \rightarrow Ag) \qquad E° = +0.80V$$

(A) $Co^{2+} + Zn \rightarrow Zn^{2+} + Co$

(B) $Mg^{2+} + Mn \rightarrow Mn^{2+} + Mg$

(C) $2Ag^+ + H_2 \rightarrow 2H^+ + 2Ag$

(D) $Sn^{2+} + Fe \rightarrow Fe^{2+} + Sn$

*Your Answer* _____

_____

# Correct Answers

## A–107

**(B)** Using the standard electrode potentials and recalling that a positive value indicates that the reaction is spontaneous while a negative value shows that the reverse reaction is spontaneous:

$$Co^{2+} + 2e^- \rightarrow Co \qquad E° = -0.28V$$

$$\underline{Zn \rightarrow Zn^{2+} + 2e^- \qquad E° = +0.76V}$$

$$Co^{2+} + Zn \rightarrow Zn^{2+} + Co \qquad E° = +0.48V$$

$$Mg^{2+} + 2e^- \rightarrow Mg \qquad E° = -2.37V$$

$$\underline{Mn \rightarrow Mn^{2+} + 2e^- \qquad E° = +1.18V}$$

$$Mg^{2+} + Mn \rightarrow Mn^{2+} + Mg \qquad E° = -1.19V$$

$$2(Ag^+ + e^- \rightarrow Ag) \qquad E° = +0.80V$$

$$\underline{H_2 \rightarrow 2H^+ + 2e^- \qquad E° = 0.00V}$$

$$2Ag^+ + H_2 \rightarrow 2H^+ + 2Ag \qquad E° = +0.80V$$

$$Sn^{2+} + 2e^- \rightarrow Sn \qquad E° = -0.14V$$

$$\underline{Fe \rightarrow Fe^{2+} + 2e^- \qquad E° = +0.44V}$$

$$Sn^{2+} + Fe \rightarrow Fe^{2+} + Sn \qquad E° = +0.30V$$

$$F_2 + 2e^- \rightarrow 2F^- \qquad E° = +2.87V$$

$$\underline{2(Li \rightarrow Li^+ + e^-) \qquad E° = +3.00V}$$

$$F_2 + 2Li \rightarrow 2Li^+ + 2F^- \qquad E° = +5.87V$$

# Questions

---

**Q–108**

What is $X$ in the reaction $X + {}^{1}_{1}H \rightarrow {}^{12}_{6}C + {}^{4}_{2}He$?

(A) ${}^{15}_{7}O$

(B) ${}^{15}_{7}N$

(C) ${}^{17}_{9}F$

(D) ${}^{17}_{9}O$

*Your Answer* _____

_____

---

**Q–109**

An example of an acid salt is

(A) $NaCl$

(B) $Na_2SO_4$

(C) $NaHCO_3$

(D) $Mg(HSO_4)_2$

*Your Answer* _____

_____

# Correct Answers

## A–108

**(B)** The total composition of the products must equal that of the reactants. Summing the number of protons and the atomic masses of the products we have $6 + 2 = 8$ protons and an atomic mass of $12 + 4 = 16$. Subtracting $_1^1H$, we have $_7^{15}X$. The atomic number 7 corresponds to nitrogen, so we have $_7^{15}N$.

## A–109

**(D)** An acid salt yields an acidic solution upon hydrolysis.

$$NaCl + H_2O \rightarrow HCl + NaOH$$

The solution produced by $NaCl$ is neutral since $HCl$ is a strong acid and $NaOH$ is a strong base.

$$Na_2SO_4 + 2H_2O \rightarrow H_2SO_4 + 2NaOH$$

This is also a neutral solution since $H_2SO_4$ is a strong acid.

$$NaHCO_3 + H_2O \rightarrow H_2CO_3 + NaOH$$

A basic solution is produced by hydrolysis of $NaHCO_3$ since $H_2CO_3$ is a weak acid. Therefore $NaHCO_3$ is a basic salt.

$$Mg(HSO_4)_2 + 2H_2O \rightarrow H_2SO_4 + Mg(OH)_2$$

$Mg(HSO_4)_2$ is an acid salt since hydrolysis produces a strong acid and a weak base.

# Questions

---

**Q–110**

How many moles of ions are present in a saturated one liter solution of $BaSO_4$ ($K_{sp} = 1.1 \times 10^{-10}$)?

(A)  $1 \times 10^{-10}$

(B)  $2 \times 10^{-10}$

(C)  $4 \times 10^{-10}$

(D)  $2 \times 10^{-5}$

---

*Your Answer* _____

_____

*A barrier isolator is new technology for hospital pharmacy departments. The barrier isolator is used when preparing intravenous medications to ensure a completely sterile environment. (www.uspharmd.com)*

# Correct Answers

**A–110**

**(D)**    The solubility product of $BaSO_4$ is given by

$$K_{sp} = [Ba^{2+}] [SO_4^{2-}] = 1.1 \times 10^{-10}$$

where $[Ba^{2+}]$ and $[SO_4^{2-}]$ are the concentrations of $Ba^{2+}$ and $SO_4^{2-}$ in solution, respectively. It is necessary, stoichiometrically, that $[Ba^{2+}] = [SO_4^{2-}]$ so if we let $x = [Ba^{2+}] = [SO_4^{2-}]$, we have

$$K_{sp} = x^2 = 1.1 \times 10^{-10}$$

and  $x = \sqrt{1.1 \times 10^{-10}} = 1 \times 10^{-5}$

The total number of ions present in a saturated one liter solution is given by the sum of the concentrations of the individual species present. Note that this is true only if the solution is of one liter volume. Since the molarity is the number of moles per liter of total solution, then for one liter of total solution, the total number of ions is given by:

$[Ba^{2+}] + [SO_4^{2-}] = 1 \times 10^{-5} + 1 \times 10^{-5} = 2 \times 10^{-5}$

# Questions

---

**Q–111**

What is the boiling point of an aqueous solution containing 117g of NaCl in 1,000g of $H_2O$?

$$Kb \ (H_2O) = 0.52° \ C\text{-kg/mol}$$

(A)  98.96°C

(B)  99.48°C

(C)  100.52°C

(D)  102.08°C

---

*Your Answer* _____

_____

---

**Q–112**

The sum of the coefficients of the reaction

___ $C_6H_6$ + ___ $O_2$ → ___ $CO_2$ + ___ $H_2O$

when it is balanced is

(A)  7.

(B)  14.

(C)  28.

(D)  35.

---

*Your Answer* _____

_____

# Correct Answers

## A-111

**(D)**     Converting to moles:

$$117g \text{ of } NaCl \times \frac{1 \, mole \text{ of } NaCl}{58.5 \text{ g of } NaCl} = 2 \text{ moles of } NaCl$$

The molality of a solution is defined as the number of moles of dissolved solute per 1,000g of solvent. Therefore the molality of the solution is $2m$ in $NaCl$. However, since $NaCl$ dissociates completely to $Na^+$ and $Cl^-$, the molality of the solution is $4m$ in particles. It has been found that a $1m$ aqueous solution freezes at $-1.86°C$ and boils at $100.52°C$, a change of $-1.86C°$ and $+0.52C°$, respectively. Thus, the boiling point increase for a $4m$ solution (since boiling point elevation is a colligative property) is

$$4m \times \frac{0.52C°}{1m} = 2.08C°$$

Therefore, the boiling point of the solution is
$$100°C + 2.08C° = 102.08°C$$

## A-112

**(D)**     The balanced reaction is

$$C_6H_6 + \frac{15}{2}O_2 \rightarrow 6CO_2 + 3H_2O$$

Since the carbon in $CO_2$ can only be obtained from benzene, which has 6 carbons, we know that the coefficient of $CO_2$ will be 6. In a similar fashion, the coefficient of $H_2O$ will be 3 since benzene has 6 hydrogens. There are 12 oxygens in $6CO_2$ and 3 oxygens in $3H_2O$ so the coefficient of $O_2$ is $^{15}/_2$. Multiplying by 2 to remove the fraction, we obtain
$$2C_6H_6 + 15O_2 \rightarrow 12CO_2 + 6H_2O$$

# Questions

---

**Q–113**

How many orbitals can one find in a p subshell?

(A)  2

(B)  3

(C)  6

(D)  7

---

*Your Answer* _____

_____

---

**Q–114**

Which of the following is a chemical property?

(A)  Melting point

(B)  Density

(C)  Viscosity

(D)  Burning

---

*Your Answer* _____

_____

# Correct Answers

## A–113

**(B)** The number of orbitals in a subshell is described by the quantum number $m_l$ in the following manner:

| subshell | $l$ | $m_l = 2l + 1$ |
|----------|-----|----------------|
| s | 0 | 1 |
| p | 1 | 3 |
| d | 2 | 5 |
| f | 3 | 7 |

## A–114

**(D)** A chemical property is one that refers to the way in which a substance is able to change into other substances—its reactivity. Burning is the process of uncontrolled oxidation. Choices A through C are physical properties—those that do not involve a change in the chemical identity of the substance.

# Questions

---

**Q–115**

What is the pOH of a solution with $[H^+] = 1 \times 10^{-3}$?

(A)  –3

(B)  1

(C)  3

(D)  11

*Your Answer* _____

_____

---

**Q–116**

A student titrates 100 ml of acid with $5M$ NaOH. Phenolphthalein indicator changes color after 50 ml of NaOH have been added. What is the molarity of the monoprotic acid?

(A)  $0.1M$

(B)  $1M$

(C)  $1.5M$

(D)  $2.5M$

*Your Answer* _____

_____

# Correct Answers

**A–115**

**(D)** Using the definition of *pH*, we find that
$$pH = -log[H^+] = 3$$
Since $pH + pOH = 14$, we have $pOH = 11$.

**A–116**

**(D)** Since $M_1V_1 = M_2V_2$, we have

$$M_2 = \frac{M_1V_1}{V_2} = \frac{(5)(50)}{100} = 2.5$$

# Questions

---

**Q–117**

The normal electronic configuration of chlorine gas is

(A)  $\overset{..}{C}l : \overset{..}{C}l$
      $\overset{..}{\phantom{}}\phantom{l}\overset{..}{\phantom{}}$

(B)  $: \overset{..}{C}l : \overset{..}{C}l :$
      $\overset{..}{\phantom{}}\phantom{l}\overset{..}{\phantom{}}$

(C)  $\overset{..}{C}l : : \overset{..}{C}l$
      $\overset{..}{\phantom{}}\phantom{l}\overset{..}{\phantom{}}$

(D)  $: Cl : : Cl :$

---

*Your Answer* _____

_____

---

**Q–118**

Molecules of sodium chloride

(A)  display ionic bonding.

(B)  display polar covalent bonding.

(C)  are polar.

(D)  do not exist.

---

*Your Answer* _____

_____

# Correct Answers

## A–117

**(B)**    The most stable electronic configuration of a molecule is that in which each atom has a complete octet of electrons surrounding it. Chlorine, being in Group VIIA has seven electrons in its valence shell. Therefore, $Cl_2$ has 14 electrons. This leads to the structure

$$:\overset{..}{Cl}:\overset{..}{\underset{..}{Cl}}:$$

## A–118

**(D)**    Molecules of sodium chloride do not exist individually. Rather sodium and chloride ions occupy points in a crystal lattice structure.

**Q–119**

An element, A, forms a sulfide with the formula AX. Which of the following formulas is correct?

(A)  ABr

(B)  $AO_2$

(C)  $AH_2$

(D)  $A_2O_3$

*Your Answer* _____

_____

**Q–120**

Which is the empirical formula of a compound consisting of 70% iron and 30% oxygen?

(A)  FeO

(B)  $FeO_2$

(C)  $Fe_2O$

(D)  $Fe_2O_3$

*Your Answer* _____

_____

# Correct Answers

## A–119

**(C)**     Sulfur has a common oxidation state of −2. Therefore, A must have an oxidation state of +2. The bromide of A would be $ABr_2$ since bromine has an oxidation state of −1. The oxide of A would have the same formula as the sulfide. The hydrogens in a hydride have an oxidation state of −1 so the hydride of A would have the formula $AH_2$.

## A–120

**(D)**     A 100g sample of this compound would contain 70g of iron and 30g of oxygen. Converting these weights to moles

$$70g \text{ of } Fe \times \frac{1 \text{ mole of } Fe}{56 \text{ g of } O} = 1.25 \text{ moles of } Fe$$

$$30g \text{ of } O \times \frac{1 \text{ mole of } O}{16 \text{ g of } O} = 1.9 \text{ moles of } O$$

This gives an empirical formula of $Fe_{1.25}O_{1.9}$. We convert to whole numbers by dividing each subscript by the smallest subscript:

$$Fe_{\frac{1.25}{1.25}} O_{\frac{1.9}{1.25}} = FeO_{1.5}$$

Multiplying each subscript by 2 to obtain integer values, we obtain $Fe_2O_3$.

# Questions

---

**Q–121**

What is the IUPAC name for the structure below?

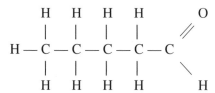

(A) Butanal

(B) Pentanal

(C) Butanol

(D) Pentanol

---

*Your Answer* _____

---

**Q–122**

What is the electronic configuration of sulfur?

(A) $1s^2\,2s^2\,2p^8\,3s^2\,3p^2$

(B) $1s^2\,2s^2\,2p^6\,3s^2\,3p^4$

(C) $1s^2\,2s^2\,3s^2\,2p^8\,3p^2$

(D) $1s^2\,2s^2\,2p^8\,3s^2\,3p^8$

---

*Your Answer* _____

# Correct Answers

**A–121**

**(B)** The carbon skeleton of this molecule contains five carbons so we name it with the prefix pentan-. The molecule contains the functional group of an aldehyde, which gives us the suffix -al. Thus, the structure is named pentanal. The correct structures associated with the other choices are

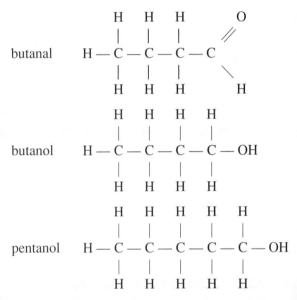

**A–122**

**(B)** Consulting the periodic table, we find that sulfur (atomic number 16) has the electronic configuration

$$1s^2\, 2s^2\, 2p^6\, 3s^2\, 3p^4$$

# Questions

What correction factor must be applied to the volume of a gas if it is heated from 10°C to 200°C and the pressure is changed from 1 atmosphere to 0.1 atmosphere?

(A) $\frac{760}{76} \times \frac{473}{283}$

(B) $\frac{760}{76} \times \frac{283}{473}$

(C) $\frac{76}{760} \times \frac{283}{473}$

(D) $\frac{76}{760} \times \frac{200}{10}$

*Your Answer* _____

# Correct Answers

**A–123**

**(A)** Rearranging the combined gas law

$$\frac{P_1 V_1}{T_1} = \frac{P_2 V_2}{T_2}$$

to give

$$V_2 = V_1 \times \frac{P_1}{P_2} = \frac{T_2}{T_1}$$

allows us to substitute

$$V_2 = V_1 \times \frac{760}{76} \times \frac{473}{283}$$

using 1 atm = 760 torr and $T = t + 273$.

# Questions

---

**Q–124**

The equilibrium constant for the reaction

$CO_{2(g)} + O_{2(g)} \rightarrow CO_{2(g)}$ (not balanced)
may be expressed as

(A) $K = \dfrac{[CO_2]}{[CO][O_2]}$

(B) $K = \dfrac{[CO][O_2]}{[CO_2]}$

(C) $K = [CO]_2 [O_2] [CO_2]_2$

(D) $K = \dfrac{[CO_2]^2}{[CO]^2 [O_2]}$

*Your Answer* _____

---

**Q–125**

A sample of hydrogen gas is in a closed container, at 1.0 atmosphere pressure and 27°C. If the sample is heated to 127°C, the pressure will be approximately which of the following?

(A) 4.0 atm

(B) 1.3 atm

(C) .75 atm

(D) .67 atm

*Your Answer* _____

# Correct Answers

## A–124

**(D)**     The equilibrium expression of a reaction is specified as the concentrations of the products divided by the concentrations of the reactants, each being raised to the power of the corresponding stoichiometric coefficient. For the general reaction

$$aA + bB \rightarrow cC + dD$$

the equilibrium expression is

$$K = \frac{[C]^c [D]^d}{[A]^a [B]^b}$$

The concentrations of pure liquids and solids are omitted from the equilibrium expression since their concentrations change negligibly during the reaction. For the reaction in question, we have

$$K = \frac{[CO]^2}{[CO]^2 [O_2]}$$

since the balanced reaction is

$$2CO + O_2 \rightarrow 2CO_2$$

## A–125

**(B)**     We can use the ideal gas law, $PV=nRT$. Since $V$ and $n$ are constant, an increase in $T$ will cause a proportional increase in $P$. Remember that we must use the absolute (Kelvin) temperature scale. The temperature increases from $300°K$ to $400°K$, thus the pressure will also increase by a third from 1.0 atm to 1.3 atm. We might express this in the equation below:

$$\frac{T_1}{T_2} = \frac{P_1}{P_2}$$

# Questions

---

**Q–126**

Hydrolysis of sodium acetate yields

(A)  a strong acid and a strong base.

(B)  a weak acid and a weak base.

(C)  a strong acid and a weak base.

(D)  a weak acid and a strong base.

*Your Answer* _____

---

**Q–127**

Which of the following has the smallest mass?

(A)  a hydrogen nucleus

(B)  an alpha particle

(C)  a neutron

(D)  a beta particle

*Your Answer* _____

# Correct Answers

## A–126

**(D)**  The hydrolysis reaction for sodium acetate proceeds as follows:

$$CH_3\overset{\displaystyle O}{\overset{\displaystyle \|}{C}}ONa + H_2O \rightarrow CH_3\overset{\displaystyle O}{\overset{\displaystyle \|}{C}}OH + NaOH$$

The products of the reaction are a weak acid (acetic acid) and a strong base (sodium hydroxide).

## A–127

**(D)**  A beta particle is a fast electron of mass $9.11 \times 10^{-28}g$ while a proton and a neutron both have a mass of $1.67 \times 10^{-24}g$. A hydrogen nucleus is a proton, and an alpha particle is a helium nucleus (two protons and two neutrons). Thus the electron (beta particle) has the smallest mass of the choices given.

# Questions

---

**Q–128**

For the reaction $PCl_5 \rightarrow PCl_3 + Cl_2$, the rate of the reaction is proportional by mole amounts to:

(A) $Cl_2 \times PCl_3$

(B) $PCl_5$

(C) $\dfrac{Cl_2 \times PCl_3}{PCl_5}$

(D) $\dfrac{PCl_5}{Cl_2 \times PCl_3}$

---

*Your Answer* _____

_____

---

**Q–129**

$H_2 + S \leftrightarrow H_2S + energy$

In this reversible reaction, select the factor that will shift the equilibrium to the right:

(A) adding heat

(B) adding $H_2S$

(C) blocking hydrogen gas reaction

(D) removing hydrogen sulfide gas

---

*Your Answer* _____

_____

# Correct Answers

**A–128**

**(B)** For the general reaction
$$A \to B + C$$
The rate is written as
$$\text{rate} \propto [A]^n$$
where $n$ is the experimentally determined order of the reaction. The only answer that conforms with the rate as written above is (B), i.e., rate $[PCl_5]$. In this case, $n = 1$.

**A–129**

**(D)** The left to right reaction is exothermic, therefore, adding heat drives the reaction equilibrium to the left. From the equilibrium constant

$$K_{eq} = \frac{[H_2S]}{[H_2][S]}$$

it is clear that an increase in the concentration of $H_2S$ increases the value of this ratio, i.e., the equilibrium is disturbed. To return to the equilibrium constant value, $H_2S$ decomposes, so that the reaction is shifted to the left. Blocking $H_2$ removes reactant, inhibiting formation to the right side. Removing $S$ has the same effect. Removing $H_2S$, however, lowers the value of the equilibrium constant. To restore it, more $H_2S$ is produced, i.e., the reaction shifts to the right. The above analysis is the application of Le Chatelier's principle.

# Questions

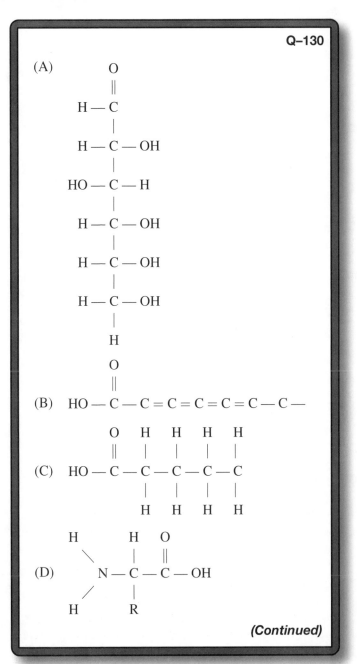

Q–130

(A)

```
        O
        ||
    H — C
        |
    H — C — OH
        |
 HO — C — H
        |
    H — C — OH
        |
    H — C — OH
        |
    H — C — OH
        |
        H
```

(B)

```
        O
        ||
 HO — C — C = C = C = C = C — C —
```

(C)

```
        O   H   H   H   H
        ||  |   |   |   |
 HO — C — C — C — C — C
        |   |   |   |
        H   H   H   H
```

(D)

```
    H           H   O
     \          |   ||
       N — C — C — OH
     /          |
    H           R
```

*(Continued)*

557

# Questions

**Q–130 *(Continued)***

The following refers to the diagrams. The outline for a molecular sub-unit for a saturated fat molecule is depicted at:

(A)  A

(B)  B

(C)  C

(D)  D

*Your Answer* _____

_____

# Correct Answers

## A–130

(C)  Illustration A shows the molecular formula of glucose. (D) shows an amino acid's formula. Both (B) and (C) are outlines of fatty acids. (B), however, is not saturated with hydrogen atoms, covalently bonded to its carbon chain. This is because of the double C–to–C bonds, limiting availability for hydrogen covalent bonding. Carbon's valence is four. The carbon atoms in illustration (C) are single bonded, leaving more bonding sites for hydrogen atoms. It is relatively saturated with these atoms. Fatty acids are the molecular sub-units of fat molecules.

# Questions

---

**Q–131**

Select the correct rule about solubility of substances:

(A)  All ammonium salts are insoluble.

(B)  All nitrates are insoluble.

(C)  All silver salts, except $AgNO_3$ are insoluble.

(D)  All sodium salts are insoluble.

*Your Answer* _____

---

**Q–132**

A Fahrenheit temperature is converted to a corresponding Centigrade (Celsius) value by the equation: $C = \frac{5}{9}(F-32)$. A recorded Fahrenheit value is 82 degrees. Its value on the Kelvin temperature scale is approximately:

(A)  355.0 K

(B)  27.7 K

(C)  83.7 K

(D)  300.7 K

*Your Answer* _____

# Correct Answers

## A-131

**(C)** The other statements are the opposite of what is correct due to substances' ability to ionize (soluble) or not ionize (insoluble) among the molecules of the solvent water. Silver salts form insoluble precipitates except for the ionizing silver nitrate, $AgNO_3$.

## A-132

**(D)** By computation with the formula, 82 degrees F becomes 27.7 degrees C. Centigrade to Kelvin conversion requires adding the constant 273: $K = C + 273$.

# Questions

Question 133 refers to the valence electron dot formulas in the figure below. The letters merely identify the different atoms. They do not stand for actual known elements.

Valence Electron Dot Formulas

A                           D

· X ·                      : Y ·

: X :

---

**Q-133**

The most active metal is:

(A)  A

(B)  D

(C)  X

(D)  Y

*Your Answer* _____

---

# Correct Answers

## A–133

**(A)** Metals have four or fewer outer shell electrons, which they tend to lose. The most active have only one loosely held valence electron, which is easily lost.

# Questions

---

**Q–134**

Light nuclei combine to yield somewhat heavier, stable nuclei with energy release. This is a definition of

(A)  atomic fission.

(B)  atomic fusion.

(C)  binding energy.

(D)  chain reaction.

---

*Your Answer* _____

_____

*You may think herbal supplements are safe because they're labeled "natural." But many herbal supplements contain active ingredients that can harm you if taken with certain prescription or over-the-counter (OTC) drugs. (www.mayoclinic.com)*

# Correct Answers

**A–134**

**(B)** This is a straightforward definition of atomic fusion as opposed to a splitting or fission.

# Questions

**Q–135**

Which of the expressions below represents the correct rate law of the reaction?

$$2A + B \rightarrow C$$

| Experiment | A | B | initial rate (mole/l sec) |
|---|---|---|---|
| 1 | 1 | 1 | 1.2 |
| 2 | 2 | 1 | 4.8 |
| 3 | 1 | 2 | 2.4 |
| 4 | 3 | 1 | 10.8 |
| 5 | 1 | 3 | 3.6 |

(A)   rate = K[A] [B]   (C)   rate = K[A]

(B)   rate = K[A]$^2$ [B]   (D)   rate = K[B]

*Your Answer* _____

_____

# Correct Answers

**(B)** Solution:

Let the rate be expressed as follows:

$$\text{rate} = K[A]^n[B]^m$$

To find n, examine the data and find the ratios of rates for reactions where [B] was kept constant as:

$$\frac{rate_2}{rate_1} = \frac{K[2A]^n[B]^m}{K[A]^n[B]^m} = \frac{4.8}{1.2} = 4$$

Simplifying we have

$$2^n = 4 = 2^2$$
$$\rightarrow \qquad n = 2$$

or $\quad \dfrac{rate_4}{rate_1} = \dfrac{K[3A]^n[B]^m}{K[A]^n[B]^m} = \dfrac{10.8}{1.2} = 9$

$$\rightarrow \qquad 3^n = 9 = 3^2$$

Similarly for m consider reactions where [A] = constant.

$$\frac{rate_3}{rate_1} = \frac{K[A]^n[2B]^m}{K[A]^n[B]^m} = \frac{2.4}{1.2} = 2$$

or $\qquad 2^m = 2 = 2^1$
$$\rightarrow \qquad m = 1$$

or $\quad \dfrac{rate_5}{rate_1} = \dfrac{K[A]^n[3B]^m}{K[A]^n[B]^m} = \dfrac{3.6}{1.2} = 3$

$$3^m = 3$$
$$m = 1 \qquad rate = K[A]^2[B].$$

# Questions

**Q–136**

Allotropes are best described as

(A) having the same composition but occurring in different molecular structures.

(B) having both acid and base properties.

(C) elements with more than one molecular or crystalline form and with different physical and chemical properties.

(D) having the same number of protons and electrons, but a different number of neutrons.

*Your Answer* _____

_____

*Pharmacy Terms:* **Formulary**: *A preferred list of drug products that typically limits the number of drugs available within a therapeutic class for purposes of drug purchasing, dispensing and/or reimbursement. (www.hrsa.gov)*

# Correct Answers

## A-136

**(C)** Allotropes are elements with more than one form due to molecular structure differences, as in $O_2$ and $O_3$ (see figure below), or as a result of differences in the arrangement of atoms or molecules, as with diamond and graphite, which are allotropic forms of carbon.

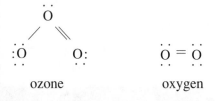

ozone                    oxygen

# Questions

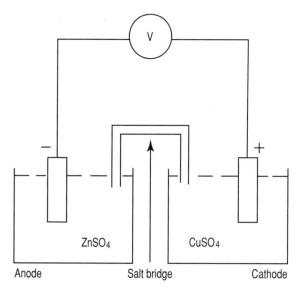

Anode       Salt bridge       Cathode

**Given two solutions, $ZnSO_4(1M)$ and $CuSO_4(1M)$, answer question 137 based on this diagram.**

---

**Q–137**

What reaction, if any, takes place at the cathode?

(A)   $Cu^{2+} + 2e^- fi\ Cu$

(B)   $Zn^{2+} + 2e^- fi\ Zn$

(C)   $Cu\ fi\ Cu^{2+} + 2e^-$

(D)   $Zn\ fi\ Zn^{2+} + 2e^-$

---

*Your Answer* _____

# Correct Answers

**A–137**

**(A)** Oxidation takes place at the anode while reduction takes place at the cathode. Alternatives (C) and (D) are wrong since they both describe oxidative processes. Upon reviewing the cell solution, choice (A) is the correct answer.

*The National Community Pharmacists Association, founded in 1898 as the National Association of Retail Druggists (NARD), represents the pharmacist owners, managers, and employees of nearly 25,000 independent community pharmacies across the United States. (www.ncpanet.org)*

**Q–138**

For the molecules listed above, the resultant dipole moments are oriented as (from left to right)

(A)  O, →, ←

(B)  ↑, O, ↓

(C)  ↑, O, ↑

(D)  ↓, O, ↑

*Your Answer* _____

_____

*Formed in 1976 by the American Pharmacists Association, the Board of Pharmaceutical Specialties offers pharmacists certification in five areas of specialty: nuclear, nutrition support, oncology, pharmacotherapy and psychiatry. (www.healthcare.monster.com)*

# Correct Answers

**A–138**

**(B)** The dipole moment of a bond is directed from the partial positive charge to the partial negative charge or from the less electronegative to the more electronegative atom in the bond.

Example: $H - Cl$

$\xrightarrow{\quad \propto+ \quad \propto- \quad}$ direction of dipole moment.

If the molecule contains more than one bond moment, then the resultant dipole moment is the vector sum of all the bond moments.

Thus for $H_2O$ we have:

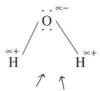

bond moments:
resultant dipole moment is oriented according to the resultant i.e.:

For $CO_2$ we have: $\overset{\propto-}{O} = \overset{\propto+}{C} = \overset{\propto-}{O}$

bond moments $\quad \leftarrow \qquad \rightarrow$

The vector sum is zero, therefore the resultant dipole moment is 0.

For $SO_2$

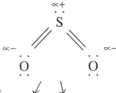

bond moments $\qquad \swarrow \quad \downarrow$

resultant is vector sum is oriented as $\downarrow$ so the combination of resultant dipole moments is $\uparrow$, O, $\downarrow$

# Questions

**Q-139**

A protein can be described as

(A)  an addition polymer.

(B)  an addition copolymer.

(C)  a condensation polymer.

(D)  a polyester.

*Your Answer* _____

_____

*2006 FEB 24 – (NewsRx.com) – A Greystone Associates study shows that advances in materials processing – technologies that include micromachining, nanoprocessing and structured film forming – are creating new devices and new opportunities for minimally invasive drug delivery. (www.pharmacychoice.com)*

# Correct Answers

(C)     A protein is the polymer of amino acids. Amino acids have the general formula

$$\begin{array}{ccc} & H & O \\ & | & \| \\ H_2N - & C - & C - OH \\ & | & \\ & R_1 & \end{array}$$

There are two functional groups $-NH_2$ (amino group) and

$$\begin{array}{c} O \\ \| \\ - C - OH \end{array} - \text{carboxylic group.}$$

In proteins, the amino acids are linked in a long chain.

$$\begin{array}{ccc} & H & O \\ & | & \| \\ \ldots + H_2N - & C - & C - OH \quad + \\ & | & \\ & R_n & \end{array}$$

$$\begin{array}{cccc} & H & H & O \\ & | & | & /\!/ \\ H - N - & C - & C - OH + \quad \ldots - H_2O \\ & | & & \rightarrow \\ & R_{n+1} & & \end{array}$$

$$\begin{array}{cccccc} & H & O & & H & O \\ & | & \| & & | & \| \\ \ldots - N - & C - & C - N - & C - & C - & \ldots \\ & | & | & | & | \\ & H & R_n & H & R_2 \end{array}$$

**(Continued)**

# Correct Answers

**A–139 (Continued)**

Since water is eliminated in the reaction it is a condensation polymerization.
The bond formed between amino acids

is called a peptide bond. So the protein can be described as a polypeptide or a condensation polymer.

# Questions

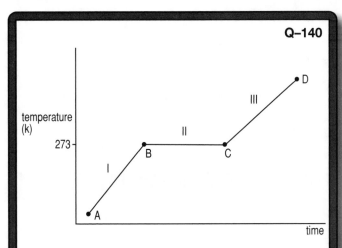

The above sketch represents a warming curve for water at 1 atm pressure. Select the one **incorrect** statement. (Note: $C_I$ = heat capacity of water in region I, $\Delta T$ = change in temperature between points specified, $\Delta H_f$ = heat of fusion)

(A)   Water is a solid in region I of the curve.

(B)   Water exists in a solid/liquid equilibrium in region II.

(C)   The energy absorbed by a sample of mass N in the temperature range A to C is $(C_I)(\Delta T_{A,B})(N) + (\Delta H_f)(\Delta T_{B,C})(N)$.

(D)   The energy absorbed by a sample in the range B to C is $\Delta H_f N$.

*Your Answer* _____

_____

# Correct Answers

**A–140**

(C)    The second part of the equation is incorrect. The energy gained in region II equals $\Delta H_f N$. There is no temperature change during the melting process. All the energy gained is involved in the change from solid to liquid structure—an entropy gain.

# Questions

---

**Q–141**

A professor needs to make a buffer solution for a class demonstration. He mixes together equal volumes of various solutions. Identify the combination of solutions that would **not** produce a buffer solution.

(A)  1 M $CH_3COOH$, 1 M HCl, .2 M $NaCH_3COO$

(B)  1 M $CH_3COOH$, 1 M $NaCH_3COO$

(C)  1 M $CH_3COOH$, .5 M NaOH

(D)  1 M $CH_3COOH$, 1 M HCl, 1 M NaOH, 1 M $NaCH_3COO$

*Your Answer* _____

---

**Q–142**

The species $O_2^-$

(A)  has 2 unpaired electrons

(B)  has 1 unpaired electron

(C)  has 0 unpaired electrons

(D)  has a bond order of 2

*Your Answer* _____

# Correct Answers

## A–141

**(A)**     A buffer solution contains a weak acid (or base) and the salt of its conjugate base (or acid). Solutions $B$-$D$, when mixed, yield $CH_3COOH$ and $NaCH_3COO$. Solution A yields $CH_3COOH$, $HCl$, and $NaCl$. There is no $NaCH_3COO$ remaining, hence we do not have a buffer.

## A–142

**(B)**     The $MO$ (molecular orbital) bonding schemes for simple diatomic species must be used to answer this question. For $O_2^-$ the $MO$ scheme is $(\sigma 1s)^2(\sigma^*1s)^2(\sigma 2s)^2(\sigma^*2s)^2(\sigma 2p)(\pi 2p)^4(\pi^*2p)^3$. $O_2^-$ has 3 net bonding electrons and a $BO$ (bond order) of $11/2$. It also has 1 unpaired electron (2 electrons in one of the $\pi^*$ orbitals and the 1 unpaired electron in the other $\pi^*$ orbital).

# Questions

Identify the incorrect Lewis structure(s).

(A) $CH_4$

```
        H
        |
   H — C — H
        |
        H
```

(B) $NH_3O$

```
        H                              H
        |        ..                    |        ..
   H — N —  O:         ↔        H — N —  O
        |        ..                    |       ..
        H                              H
```

(C) $C_2H_3N$

```
        H
        |
   H — C — C ≡ N:
        |
        H
```

(D) $NH_4^+$

```
             ⌐     H     ⌐ +
             |     |     |
             | H — N — H |
             |     |     |
             ⌊     H     ⌋
```

*Your Answer* _____

_____

# Correct Answers

**(B)**   One of the resonance forms of (B) places 10 electrons around the $N-$ a violation of the octet rule for a second row element. A far better structure is

$$H - N - O - H$$
with $H$ above $N$

# Questions

---

**Q–144**

What is the hydronium ion concentration, $H_3O^+$ of a solution that has a hydroxide concentration of $1.4 \times 10^{-4}$ M?

(A) $7.2 \times 10^{-11}$

(B) $1.4 \times 10^{-10}$

(C) $1.0 \times 10^{-14}$

(D) $7.0 \times 10^{-7}$

*Your Answer* _____

---

**Q–145**

If oxygen is collected over water at 25°C and at a pressure of 760 torr, the pressure due to just the oxygen is: (the vapor pressure of $H_2O$ at 25°C is 19.0 torr)

(A) 779 torr

(B) 760 torr

(C) 19 torr

(D) 741 torr

*Your Answer* _____

# Correct Answers

## A–144

**(A)** The hydronium ion concentration can be calculated from the ion – product constant for water, $K_w$

$$K_w = [H_3O^+] [OH^-] = 1 \times 10^{-14}$$

Due to the auto ionization of water, both the $OH^-$ and the $H_3O^+$ ions exist in acid or basic solutions. However, the product of the $OH^-$ ion concentration and the $H_3O^+$ ion concentration will always be equal to $1 \times 10^{-14}$, therefore substituting the $OH^-$ concentration into the $K_w$ expression we can calculate the $H_3O^+$ ion concentration.

$$K_w = [H_3O^+] [OH^-] = 1 \times 10^{-14}$$

$$H_3O^+ = \frac{1 \times 10^{-14}}{1.4 \times 10^{-4}} = 7.2 \times 10^{-11}$$

## A–145

**(D)** According to Dalton's Law of partial pressures, the total pressure is equal to the sum of the partial pressures …

$$P_T = Pa + Pb + Pc + …$$

In this case there are two gases present in the container, the oxygen and the water vapor. Since the vapor pressure of water is 19 torr at 25°C, the partial pressure of the water vapor is 19 torr, and the total pressure in the container is 760 torr. From Dalton's Law we can calculate the pressure due to just the oxygen.

$$P_{total} = PO_2 + P_{H\,O\,vapor}$$
$$760\ torr = PO_2 + 19\ torr$$
$$PO_2 = 760\ torr - 19\ torr$$

# Questions

How many times faster will hydrogen effuse from the same effusion apparatus than nitrogen at the same temperature?

(A)  14.0

(B)  .3

(C)  5.3

(D)  3.8

*Your Answer* _____

_____

*August 2004: New York Attorney General Eliot Spitzer announced the results of a statewide survey of prescription drug prices showing that prices for the same medication can vary significantly among local pharmacies and can differ widely across the state. (www.oag.state.ny.us)*

# Correct Answers

## A–146

**(D)** Graham's law of effusion states that the rates of effusion of gases are inversely proportional to the square roots of their molecular weights or densities.

$$\text{rate of effusion} \propto \frac{1}{\sqrt{MW}}$$

or, rate of effusion $\times \sqrt{MW} = t_0$ a constant

Hence, when 2 gases effuse from the same apparatus at the same conditions:

$$\frac{rate_A}{rate_B} = \frac{\sqrt{MW_B}}{\sqrt{MW_A}}$$

Substituting the molecular weight for $N_2$ and $H_2$:

$$\frac{\text{rate } H_2}{\text{rate } N_2} = \frac{\sqrt{28}}{\sqrt{2}} = \frac{5.29}{1.41} = 3.8$$

# Questions

**Q–147**

2.4 liter of $HNO_3$ solution reacts with 63 ml of 1.9N $Ba(OH)_2$ to produce a neutral solution. What is the molarity (M) of the original $HNO_3$ solution?

(A) $\dfrac{63\,(1.9)}{1000\,(2.4)}\,M$

(B) $\dfrac{63\,(1.9)}{1000}\,M$

(C) $\dfrac{2\,(63)\,(1.9)}{1000}\,M$

(D) $\dfrac{(63)\,(1.9)}{1000\,(2)\,(2.4)}\,M$

*Your Answer* _____

_____

*The Washington State Board of Pharmacy says the most common prescription errors are the wrong dose, the wrong drug, and mislabeled medicine. (www.komotv.com)*

# Correct Answers

## A-147

(A) Molarity is by definition the number of moles of solute divided by the liters of solution. $HNO_3$ reacts with $OH^-$ on a one-to-one molar basis. The moles of $OH^-$ are equal to

$$63 \text{ ml} \times \frac{1 \text{ liter}}{1000 \text{ ml}} \times \frac{1.9 \text{ moles}}{1 \text{ liter}} = 0.12 \text{ moles}$$

The original $HNO_3$ solution had to contain 0.12 moles of $HNO_3$ in 2.4 liters of solution. Thus, its molarity is

$$\frac{0.12 \text{ moles H}^+}{2.4 \text{ liters}} = 0.05 \text{M}$$

# Blank Cards for
# Your Own Questions

# Correct Answers

# Blank Cards for
# Your Own Questions

# Correct Answers

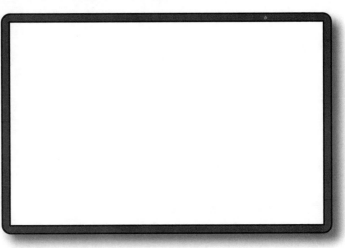

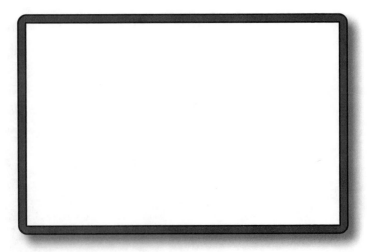

# Blank Cards for
# Your Own Questions

# Correct Answers

# Blank Cards for
# Your Own Questions

# Correct Answers

# Blank Cards for
# Your Own Questions

# Correct Answers

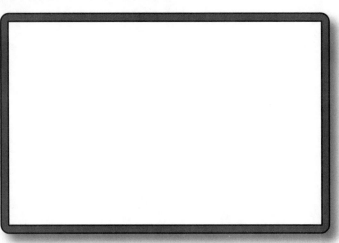

# THE PERIODIC TABLE

**KEY**

Atomic Number → 22
Symbol → Ti
Atomic Weight → 47.88

( •) indicates most stable or best known isotope

Group Classification

METALS — NONMETALS

TRANSITIONAL METALS

Alkali Metals · Alkaline Earth Metals · Halogens · Noble Gases

| 1 IA IA | 2 IIA IIA | 3 IIIA IIIB | 4 IVA IVB | 5 VA VB | 6 VIA VIB | 7 VIIA VIIB | 8 VIIIA VIII | 9 VIIIA VIII | 10 VIIIA VIII | 11 IB IB | 12 IIB IIB | 13 IIIB IIIA | 14 IVB IVA | 15 VB VA | 16 VIB VIA | 17 VIIB VIIA | 18 VIII 0 |
|---|---|---|---|---|---|---|---|---|---|---|---|---|---|---|---|---|---|
| 1 H 1.008 | | | | | | | | | | | | | | | | | 2 He 4.003 |
| 3 Li 6.941 | 4 Be 9.012 | | | | | | | | | | | 5 B 10.811 | 6 C 12.011 | 7 N 14.007 | 8 O 15.999 | 9 F 18.998 | 10 Ne 20.180 |
| 11 Na 22.990 | 12 Mg 24.305 | | | | | | | | | | | 13 Al 26.982 | 14 Si 28.086 | 15 P 30.974 | 16 S 32.066 | 17 Cl 35.453 | 18 Ar 39.948 |
| 19 K 39.098 | 20 Ca 40.078 | 21 Sc 44.956 | 22 Ti 47.88 | 23 V 50.942 | 24 Cr 51.996 | 25 Mn 54.938 | 26 Fe 55.847 | 27 Co 58.933 | 28 Ni 58.693 | 29 Cu 63.546 | 30 Zn 65.39 | 31 Ga 69.723 | 32 Ge 72.61 | 33 As 74.922 | 34 Se 78.96 | 35 Br 79.904 | 36 Kr 83.8 |
| 37 Rb 85.468 | 38 Sr 87.62 | 39 Y 88.906 | 40 Zr 91.224 | 41 Nb 92.906 | 42 Mo 95.94 | 43 Tc (97.907) | 44 Ru 101.07 | 45 Rh 102.906 | 46 Pd 106.4 | 47 Ag 107.868 | 48 Cd 112.411 | 49 In 114.818 | 50 Sn 118.710 | 51 Sb 121.757 | 52 Te 127.60 | 53 I 126.905 | 54 Xe 131.29 |
| 55 Cs 132.905 | 56 Ba 137.327 | 57 La 138.906 | 72 Hf 178.49 | 73 Ta 180.948 | 74 W 183.84 | 75 Re 186.207 | 76 Os 190.23 | 77 Ir 192.22 | 78 Pt 195.08 | 79 Au 196.967 | 80 Hg 200.59 | 81 Tl 204.383 | 82 Pb 207.2 | 83 Bi 208.980 | 84 Po (208.982) | 85 At (209.982) | 86 Rn (222.018) |
| 87 Fr (223.020) | 88 Ra (226.025) | 89 Ac (227.028) | 104 Unq (261.11) | 105 Unp (262.114) | 106 Unh (263.118) | 107 Uns (262.12) | 108 Uno (265) | 109 Une (266) | 110 Uun (269) | 111 Uuu (272.153) | 112 Uub (277) | | | | | | |

**LANTHANIDE SERIES**

| 58 Ce 140.115 | 59 Pr 140.908 | 60 Nd 144.24 | 61 Pm (144.913) | 62 Sm 150.36 | 63 Eu 151.965 | 64 Gd 157.25 | 65 Tb 158.925 | 66 Dy 162.50 | 67 Ho 164.930 | 68 Er 167.26 | 69 Tm 168.934 | 70 Yb 173.04 | 71 Lu 174.967 |
|---|---|---|---|---|---|---|---|---|---|---|---|---|---|

**ACTINIDE SERIES**

| 90 Th 232.038 | 91 Pa 231.036 | 92 U 238.029 | 93 Np (237.048) | 94 Pu (244.064) | 95 Am (243.061) | 96 Cm (247.070) | 97 Bk (247.070) | 98 Cf (251.080) | 99 Es (252.083) | 100 Fm (257.095) | 101 Md (258.1) | 102 No (259.101) | 103 Lr (262.11) |
|---|---|---|---|---|---|---|---|---|---|---|---|---|---|